Cooking

for

Two

Also by JoAnna M. Lund

Cooking
for
Two

A HEALTHY EXCHANGES® COOKBOOK

JoAnna M. Lund

with
Barbara Alpert

A Perigee Book

THE BERKLEY PUBLISHING GROUP
Published by the Penguin Group
Penguin Group (USA) Inc.
375 Hudson Street, New York, New York 10014, USA
Penguin Group (Canada), 90 Eglinton Avenue East, Suite 700, Toronto, Ontario M4P 2Y3, Canada
(a division of Pearson Penguin Canada Inc.)
Penguin Books Ltd., 80 Strand, London WC2R 0RL, England
Penguin Group Ireland, 25 St. Stephen's Green, Dublin 2, Ireland (a division of Penguin Books Ltd.)
Penguin Group (Australia), 250 Camberwell Road, Camberwell, Victoria 3124, Australia
(a division of Pearson Australia Group Pty. Ltd.)
Penguin Books India Pvt. Ltd., 11 Community Centre, Panchsheel Park, New Delhi—110 017, India
Penguin Group (NZ), Cnr. Airborne and Rosedale Roads, Albany, Auckland 1310, New Zealand
(a division of Pearson New Zealand Ltd.)
Penguin Books (South Africa) (Pty.) Ltd., 24 Sturdee Avenue, Rosebank, Johannesburg 2196,
South Africa

Penguin Books Ltd., Registered Offices: 80 Strand, London WC2R 0RL, England

Copyright © 2006 by Healthy Exchanges, Inc.
Cover design by Ben Gibson.
Cover photo by Mark McElhiney.
Diabetic Exchanges calculated by Rose Hoenig, R.D., L.D.

Before using the recipes and advice in this book, consult your physician or health-care provider to be sure they are appropriate for you. The information in this book is not intended to take the place of any medical advice. It reflects the author's experiences, studies, research, and opinions regarding a healthy lifestyle. All material included in this publication is believed to be accurate. The publisher assumes no responsibility for any health, welfare, or subsequent damage that might be incurred from use of these materials.

For more information about Healthy Exchanges products, contact:
Healthy Exchanges, Inc.
P.O. Box 80
DeWitt, Iowa 52742-0080
(563) 659-8234
www.HealthyExchanges.com

ISBN: 0-399-53254-4

PRINTING HISTORY
Perigee trade paperback edition / May 2006

PERIGEE is a registered trademark of Penguin Group (USA) Inc.
The "P" design is a trademark belonging to Penguin Group (USA) Inc.

This book has been cataloged by the Library of Congress

PRINTED IN THE UNITED STATES OF AMERICA

10   9   8   7   6   5   4   3   2   1

Dedication

This cookbook is dedicated in loving memory to my parents, Jerome and Agnes McAndrews. They were married for over forty years; in those years Mom cooked wonderful meals that served only the two of them *and* she prepared enough to serve our entire family when we gathered together to break bread. Whatever the number of table settings, each meal was another opportunity for Mom to share both her culinary and artistic talents with others. And Daddy was there to sing her praises whether the meal consisted of everyday boiled ham and cabbage for just the two of them or Thanksgiving dinner with all the trimmings for a crowd!

Mom was as prolific with poems as I am with recipes! I found this poem she wrote about an old cookbook, and I thought it was perfect for my Healthy Exchanges Way of creating easy and healthy recipes for when there are only two at the table. May both her words and my recipes bring you years of enjoyment!

An Old Cookbook

*I came across an old cookbook, the cover was
tattered and frayed with age.
But the recipes intrigued me very much, as I
thumbed through every page.
The ingredients made me curious, for some of
the recipes sounded so rare,
Salads were called Water Lilly, Birds Nest,
Butterfly, and Alligator Pear.
From one sweet yeast dough recipe, several
breads you could readily make—
Including Pocketbooks, Swedish Tea Rings, and
Bohemian Coffee Cake.
Roseleaf Syrup for desserts was the most
unusual recipe I found.
It called for one quart water, four pounds sugar,
and fresh Rose leaves weighing a pound.
The beverages, too, were so different than what
we often serve today—
Such as Irish Moss Lemonade, Catnip Tea, and
Hot Lemon Whey.
I found many versions of the baked goods that
Mother used to make,
Like Cinnamon Rolls, Kolaches, and Old-
Fashion Johnny Cake.
Her method was a pinch of this, a dash of that,
and she didn't use a book.
She never had a failure, and was known as a
wonderful cook.
With all the gadgets and prepared foods we now
have on display,
I hope we don't lose the art of "cooking from
scratch," the good old-fashioned way!*

Agnes Carrington McAndrews

Acknowledgments

Even when there are only two at the table—it still takes time to create, test, type, calculate, and write a cookbook. For helping me do just that, I want to thank:

Cliff Lund—my husband and my favorite person to share a table with. His hearty appreciation of my good-tasting food, which happens to be healthy, is something I still cherish. And, it's been fifteen years now since I put that first Healthy Exchanges "dinner for two" in front of him!

Shirley Morrow, Rita Ahlers, Phyllis Bickford, Cheryl Hageman, Gina Griep, and Jean Martens—my employees and daily taste testers. Each day at lunchtime, we stop whatever we are doing and gather at my kitchen table to taste the recipes stirred up that morning. While it's a "free lunch," so to speak, all of my staff are expected to write down their honest opinions on the comment sheets. From those comments, many a recipe has been "tweaked" so it's "just right" for you!

Barbara Alpert—my writing partner. While our schedules are such that we more often than not "visit" via the computer, we still take time to talk about specific dishes that pique Barbara's interest. As she has a tiny galley kitchen, I take her space and time constraints into consideration when creating my recipes—and they're all the better for it!

Coleen O'Shea—my agent. I love creating recipes and cookbook concepts, and she loves helping me turn them into more than daydreams. She's been encouraging me to write my Healthy Exchanges cookbooks for more than a dozen years now—and she knows I have at least that many more years of projects dancing around in my mind!

John Duff—my publisher. Thank goodness he's willing to let me fill the bookshelf with my "common folk" healthy cookbooks. With his support and suggestions I've written over thirty cookbooks for him since 1995. And it's as much fun today as when I first began!

God—my creator. Every day I'm blessed to create another recipe or write another paragraph, I say a prayer of thankfulness. And daily, as I work on my many Healthy Exchanges projects, I recite from Psalms 118:24: "For this is the day the Lord hath made. Let us be glad and rejoice in it."

Contents

Why Cooking for Two Is Easy, Smart, and Healthy

Ever since the earliest days of Healthy Exchanges, I've gotten letters (and later, e-mail) from my readers asking about cooking for one or two instead of four or six (as most of my soups, salads, and main dishes served) as well as desserts that served fewer than eight (as my pies and cheesecakes usually do).

They wrote, "My refrigerator is too small for all those leftovers," or "You wouldn't believe how tiny my freezer is. There's room for two ice cube trays and a few boxes of frozen vegetables, and that's *it*."

Some asked for help because having eight servings of even a delicious low-sugar, low fat dessert on hand was entirely too tempting; others simply said, "There's only me, and as much as I like this particular pie, I don't want to eat eight servings of the same dessert in a row. And I haven't got room or enough plastic containers to store the remaining pieces of several of your pies!"

I understood right away what my readers wanted, and I immediately began offering a "Dinner for Two" column in my monthly food newsletter. I even created a self-published "cookbooklet" of recipes designed to serve no more than two. While I had been cooking for four or more most of my adult life, I knew that not everyone prepared meals for big families; I understood that many apartment dwellers had half-size refrigerators and mini-freezers; and I got it that many people who lived alone would find themselves overwhelmed by unused leftovers that they just couldn't devour before they spoiled.

But it took all these many years for me to finally write a full-length book with this readership in mind—and it took a while for my publisher to find a spot for it in his busy schedule for me!

Is Cooking for Two Right for You?

You might be asking yourself this question, especially if you've been cooking meals from my cookbooks for years now. Maybe you've figured out clever ways to squeeze two layers of Lock and Lock or Tupperware containers onto one refrigerator shelf; perhaps you've gotten used to eating Mexican rice for breakfast, lunch, and dinner without flinching; maybe you've chosen only to make one of my cheesecakes or pies when you've got company coming.

The thing is, should you have to make those concessions in order to eat the Healthy Exchanges Way?

I don't think so.

So let's find out if you fit into one of the categories I had in mind when I began creating all the recipes for this book.

- Are you single, living in an apartment on your own or with one roommate?

- Are you and your husband retired, with your kids grown and moved away?

- Are you a widow or widower who just isn't that interested in cooking these days?

- Are you a student with access to a kitchen but whose hours are different from others in your house?

- Are you a busy mom or dad concerned about a health issue but feel it's too difficult to change the menu of the entire household?

- Are you often on the road in your RV or spending lots of time on your boat, coping with smaller appliances and a lot less storage than at home?

If you answered yes to any of those questions, I think this book may quite frankly change your life! (Or at least the way you cook and eat . . .) And I believe it's going to be a real change for the better.

Why Cooking for Two Is Easy

I won't be asking you to go searching for fancy ingredients in order to cook great meals for just two people. (You knew that already, right?) And I won't require you to purchase foods in tiny packages that are not only expensive to buy but also not good for the environment. And while I do suggest preparing these dishes in just-right baking cups and pans, you can pick up these useful items at discount stores, kitchen stores, garage sales and online for very little money.

But easy isn't only about how you cook, and that's one of the ways this book is special. You'll quickly discover that it's never been easier to design satisfying meals and varied menus—you've got an abundance of ideas for intriguing dishes, and most of them can be prepared in a very short time. Instead of finding yourself with a bundle of planned leftovers, you're now free to experiment, innovate, and see what excites your taste buds!

Easy also means knowing that you can eat it *all* (not all at once!)—and be confident that you are eating for better health. I've done the work for you—figured the nutritional content, sized the servings, and suggested the brands that will produce results you'll love. If that's not the definition of easy, I don't know what is.

Why Cooking for Two Is Smart

One of the biggest reasons that people fail in their efforts to follow a healthy eating plan is that they get bored eating the same foods all the time. It's a common problem, one you may have experienced even before you heard of Healthy Exchanges. Lots of dieters become best friends (for a while, anyway) with a can of tuna or a container of cottage cheese. It's safe, it's reliable, it's always there—and it's a recipe for disaster when you eat it day after day!

But cooking for two means preparing a smaller number of portions, which lowers the risk that you'll eat the same entrée for several meals in a row. It also lessens the quantity of ingredients you'll have invested in (in case you don't love the finished product). And because I've stuck to my promise not to leave you with half-used cans or packages, you'll feel smart about food preparation because you won't be wasting food or leaving it to go bad.

It's smart to cook for two when you live alone, because you'll be cooking in dishes that fit your lifestyle. No giant pots or huge casserole dishes, just handy glass custard cups or petite loaf pans. Smaller pans and pots generally cook faster, which means you'll often spend less time cooking and baking; you'll also save time for next time, because you'll be chopping vegetables and saving part of what you've chopped for the next recipe you prepare. That's *really* smart.

And it's smart to cook for two if you're part of a couple. Variety is the spice of life, they say, and now that you're preparing just two servings at a time, you'll be able to vary your menu as much as you like! And just think—you'll never again have to argue about who got the larger piece of something, when both of you will be getting the same-size cup or bowl of something yummy.

What else? Well, you'll be cooking and serving many of these dishes in the same container, so there should be less dishwashing (more important to those of you who don't have an electric dishwasher!). And because you'll be stirring up smaller quantities, you'll be using your smaller bowls, which means *more* counter space— and less need to use every surface in your kitchen to hold your bowls, pots, and pans!

Why Cooking for Two Is Healthy

It goes without saying (but I'm saying it in case this is your first Healthy Exchanges cookbook!) that every one of my recipes meets my Healthy Exchanges requirements—low in sugar, low in fat, reasonably low in sodium, and made from ingredients I can find in my small Midwest town of DeWitt, Iowa, (which has only *one* small supermarket). So I can say with confidence that cooking for two is healthy—because you're eating dishes made from healthy foods.

But cooking for two is healthy in other important ways. If you live alone and eat many of your meals alone, I hope this cookbook will encourage you to invite others to share a meal with you often. All the research suggests that people with strong social connections stay healthier, physically as well as emotionally. That's not to say you should never enjoy a solitary supper or private lunch again (of course you will!)—but I want to encourage your commitment to a "socially healthy" way of life, and dining with friends can be a truly healthy habit.

Take a minute to think about some of the last six meals you've eaten. Were you sitting alone in front of the TV or munching something as you read the paper on the bus? Was a takeout container or commercially frozen entrée involved? Were you working at your desk, staring at the computer screen, while you ate a sandwich from the corner deli?

We all eat meals like that sometimes, but it's just not a healthy choice to eat all your meals that way. Now, don't think that I'm suggesting you do a complete turnaround and magically transform into a gourmet chef and superstar hostess. That's not realistic, either, and if you did it, I can bet it wouldn't last very long. But making the decision to eat at least one meal each week with office colleagues, or planning to have dinner with a neighbor one evening soon, may have a positive effect on how you nourish yourself—and that's *healthy*.

I've thought a lot about this in recent months as we've been testing the recipes for this book. My husband, Cliff, the truck drivin' man, spends most of the week on the road in his big rig. I eat lunch most days with my staff because we're always taste-testing recipes, but many nights I eat dinner on my own, in the company of my beloved dog, Duke, and my sweet cats, Jeff and Jason. I can tell you, it's been a great help to be able to open the fridge and see all these individual servings ready for me to heat and eat.

After a busy day, I don't always feel like cooking, so I've taken real comfort in knowing that I've got all these healthy options in front of me. And I believe that you will, too.

Have I convinced you to join me in my "Cooking for Two" crusade? I hope so! To coin a popular commercial phrase, you'll definitely be "doubling your pleasure" *and* your fun—in addition to doubling your refrigerator and freezer storage space by preparing fewer servings of all the dishes you love!

Jo Anna

Please note:

In many of my cookbooks, I've included my Healthy Exchanges eating plan, which explains how to use my version of the "exchange" system for planning what to eat and how much to eat for optimum health and weight loss (or maintenance). Because this is a "special-interest" cookbook, I've chosen to focus just on the recipes in this volume. If this is your first Healthy Exchanges cookbook, please check one of my other books for an explanation of the exchange system and an abundance of healthy cooking tips! Good recent choices include *The Open Road Cookbook* or *Cooking Healthy with a Man in Mind.*

A Peek Into My

Cooking for Two

Pantry

I always include a "Peek Into My Pantry" section with every cookbook I write, and this one is no exception. You'll see that most of the listed ingredients found in my other books will be found here, too. But, I've also added a few additional ingredients that are good choices when cooking a smaller number of portions. Two examples are egg substitute and dry bouillon granules. Since there are analytical reasons (as well as creative ones) for my choices, I thought I'd explain my reasons.

Why am I using egg substitute in this book when in my other books I just list it as an option? Because it's not easy cutting a raw egg in half, that's why! In many of my recipes for baked goods, I discovered that a whole egg was just too much. During recipe testing, I found that if I used 2 or 3 tablespoons of egg substitute instead, my finished baked goods came out beautifully.

Likewise, a 14-ounce can of reduced-sodium fat-free chicken or beef broth was often just too much liquid in the finished soup or main dish. But, by using a teaspoon of dry bouillon and only 1 cup or so of water, I could achieve the final results I wanted—without worrying that you'd put the unused canned broth in your refrigerator and promptly forget about it . . . that is, until it came time to clean out the fridge!

I just don't believe in wasting food, so for this collection it was easier *and* cheaper to go in a different direction. I hope you enjoy the results!

Egg substitute—*Egg Beaters*
Fat-free plain yogurt—*Dannon*
Nonfat dry milk powder—*Carnation*
Evaporated fat-free milk—*Carnation*
Fat-free milk
Fat-free cottage cheese
Fat-free cream cheese—*Philadelphia*
Fat-free half & half—*Land O Lakes*
Fat-free mayonnaise—*Kraft*
Fat-free dressings—*Kraft*
No-fat sour cream—*Land O Lakes*
"Diet" margarine—*I Can't Believe It's Not Butter! Light*
Cooking sprays
   Olive oil– and Butter-flavored—*Pam*
   Butter-flavored—for spritzing *after* cooking—*I Can't Believe It's Not Butter!*
Cooking oil—*Puritan Canola Oil*
Reduced-calorie whipped topping—*Cool Whip Lite* or *Free*
White sugar substitute—*Splenda*
Baking mix—*Bisquick Heart Smart*
Quick oats—*Quaker*
Graham cracker crumbs—*Nabisco Honey Maid*
Sugar-free pancake syrup—*Log Cabin* or *Cary's*
Parmesan cheese—*Kraft Reduced Fat Parmesan Style Grated*
Reduced-fat cheese (shredded and sliced)—*Kraft 2% Reduced Fat*
Processed cheese—*Velveeta Light*
Shredded frozen potatoes—*Mr. Dell's* or *Ore Ida*
Reduced-fat peanut butter—*Peter Pan, Skippy,* or *Jif*
Spreadable fruit spread—*Welch's* or *Smuckers*
Chicken and Beef broth—*Swanson*
Dry beef or chicken bouillon—*Wyler's Granules Instant Bouillon*
Tomato sauce—*Hunt's*
Canned soups—*Healthy Request*

Tomato juice—*Healthy Request*
Ketchup—*Heinz No Salt Added*
Pastrami and corned beef—*Carl Buddig Lean*
Luncheon meats—*Healthy Choice* or *Oscar Mayer*
Ham—*Dubuque 97% Fat Free* or *Healthy Choice*
Bacon bits—*Oscar Mayer* or *Hormel*
Kielbasa sausage & frankfurters—*Healthy Choice* or *Oscar Mayer Light*
Canned white chicken, packed in water—*Swanson*
Canned tuna, packed in water—*Starkist*
Canned salmon, packed in water—*Starkist*
95% to 97% lean ground sirloin beef or turkey breast
Crackers—*Nabisco Soda Fat Free* and *Ritz Reduced Fat*
Reduced-calorie bread (40 calories per slice)
Small hamburger buns (80 calories per bun)
Rice—instant, regular, and wild—*Minute Rice*
Instant potato flakes
Noodles, spaghetti, macaroni and rotini pasta
Salsa
Pickle relish—dill, sweet, and hotdog
Mustard—Dijon, prepared yellow, and spicy
Unsweetened apple juice—*Musselman's*
Reduced-calorie cranberry juice cocktail—*Ocean Spray*
Unsweetened orange juice—*Simply Orange*
Unsweetened applesauce—*Musselman's*
Fruit—fresh, frozen, and canned in fruit juice
Vinegar—cider and distilled white
Lemon and lime juice (in small plastic fruit-shaped bottles, found in produce section)
Diet lemon-lime soda pop—*Diet Mountain Dew Caffeine Free*
Instant fruit beverage mixes—*Crystal Light*
Reduced calorie chocolate syrup—*Hershey's Sugar-Free Syrup*
Sugar-free and fat-free ice cream—*Wells' Blue Bunny*

Remember, these are my suggestions. You are always free to use other national or local brands. Just keep in mind that if your choice is higher in fats and carbs, then you must adjust the recipe nutritional data accordingly.

If you keep your pantry stocked with these products, you can whip up any recipe in this cookbook. I suggest you start a running list, and whenever you use up anything (or start to run low), remember to make a note of it. Your shopping trips will become quicker and thriftier!

Kitchen Equipment Needed
When Cooking for Two

While you don't *need* a 6-quart slow cooker when preparing a stew for only two, a two-quart version sure comes in handy. And even though you won't be using a 12-cup muffin pan with these recipes, you'll often reach for your 6-cup one. So to help you stock your kitchen with, as Goldilocks would say, the "just right"–size equipment, I've compiled this list of what I used when testing all these recipes. A quick glance will reassure you that there's nothing strange or hard to find on this list.

Good-quality nonstick skillets (*medium and large*)
Good-quality saucepans (*small and medium*)
Glass mixing bowls (*small and medium*)
Sharp knives (*paring, chef, butcher*)
Rubber spatulas
Wire whisk
Measuring spoons (*get good-quality ones with the amount
   printed in a bold bright color, and be sure that the set includes
   a 1½ tablespoon measure*)
Measuring cups (*separate ones for liquid and dry measurements*)
Covered jar (*a pint-size fat-free mayo jar works just fine*)
Vegetable parer
Grater
Electric mixer
Electric blender
Cooking timer
Two or two-and-a-half quart slow cooker
Double-sided electric grill

Electric toaster oven *(to conserve energy when only one item is being baked, or for a recipe that calls for a short baking time)*
Wire racks for cooling baked goods
Oven- and microwave-safe custard cups *(10-ounce and 12-ounce)*
Petite loaf pan (measures 5¾ by 3⅛ by 2⅛ inches)
8-by-8-inch glass baking dishes
Cookie sheet *(good-quality nonstick)*
Muffin tin *(6-cup)*
Plastic colander
Cutting board
Square-shaped pie or cake server
Can opener

JoAnna's Ten Commandments of Successful Cooking

A very important part of any journey is knowing where you are going and the best way to get there. If you plan and prepare before you start to cook, you should reach mealtime with foods to write home about!

1. **Read the entire recipe from start to finish** and be sure you understand the process involved. Check that you have all the equipment you will need *before* you begin.

2. **Check the ingredient list** and be sure you have *everything* and in the amounts required. Keep cooking sprays handy—while they're not listed as ingredients, I use them all the time (just a quick squirt!).

3. **Set out *all* the ingredients and equipment needed** to prepare the recipe on the counter near you *before* you start. Remember that old saying *A stitch in time saves nine?* It applies in the kitchen, too.

4. **Do as much advance preparation as possible** before actually cooking. Chop, cut, grate, or do whatever is

needed to prepare the ingredients and have them ready before you start to mix. Turn the oven on at least ten minutes before putting food in to bake, to allow the oven to preheat to the proper temperature.

5. **Use a kitchen timer** to tell you when the cooking or baking time is up. Because stove temperatures vary slightly by manufacturer, you may want to set your timer for five minutes less than the suggested time just to prevent overcooking. Check the progress of your dish at that time, then decide if you need the additional minutes or not.

6. **Measure carefully.** Use glass measures for liquids and metal or plastic cups for dry ingredients. My recipes are based on standard measurements. Unless I tell you it's a scant or full cup, measure the cup level.

7. **For best results, follow the recipe instructions exactly.** Feel free to substitute ingredients that *don't tamper* with the basic chemistry of the recipe, but be sure to leave key ingredients alone. For example, you could substitute sugar-free instant chocolate pudding for sugar-free instant butterscotch pudding, but if you used a six-serving package when a four-serving package was listed in the ingredients, or you used instant when cook-and-serve is required, you won't get the right result.

8. **Clean up as you go.** It is much easier to wash a few items at a time than to face a whole counter of dirty dishes later. The same is true for spills on the counter or floor.

9. **Be careful about doubling or halving a recipe.** Though many recipes can be altered successfully to serve more or fewer people, *many cannot.* This is especially true when it comes to spices and liquids. If you try to double a recipe that calls for 1 teaspoon pumpkin-pie spice, for example, and you double the spice, you may end up with a too-spicy taste. I usually suggest increasing spices or liquid by 1½ times when doubling a recipe. If it tastes a little bland to you, you can increase the spice to 1¾ times the origi-

nal amount the next time you prepare the dish. Remember: You can always add more, but you can't take it out after it's stirred in.

The same is true with liquid ingredients. If you wanted to **triple** a main dish recipe because you were planning to serve a crowd, you might think you should use three times as much of every ingredient. Don't, or you could end up with soup instead! If the original recipe calls for 1¾ cups tomato sauce, I'd suggest using 3½ cups when you **triple** the recipe (or 2¾ cups if you **double** it). You'll still have a good-tasting dish that won't run all over the plate.

10. **Write your reactions next to each recipe once you've served it.** Yes, that's right, I'm giving you permission to write in this book. It's yours, after all. Ask yourself: Did everyone like it? Did you have to add another half teaspoon of chili seasoning to please your family, who like to live on the spicier side of the street? You may even want to rate the recipe on a scale of 1☆ to 4☆, depending on what you thought of it. (Four stars would be the top rating—and I hope you'll feel that way about many of my recipes.) Jotting down your comments while they are fresh in your mind will help you personalize the recipe to your own taste the next time you prepare it.

The Recipes

How to Read a Healthy Exchanges Recipe

The Healthy Exchanges Nutritional Analysis

Before using these recipes, you may wish to consult your physician or health-care provider to be sure they are appropriate for you. The information in this book is not intended to take the place of any medical advice. It reflects my experiences, studies, research, and opinions regarding healthy eating.

Each recipe includes nutritional information calculated in three ways:

Healthy Exchanges Weight Loss Choices™ or Exchanges
Calories; Fat, Protein, Carbohydrates, and Fiber in grams;
  Sodium and Calcium in milligrams
Diabetic Exchanges
Carb Choices for those who prefer to count their carbs

In every Healthy Exchanges recipe, the Diabetic Exchanges have been calculated by a registered dietitian. All the other calculations were done by computer, using the Food Processor II software.

When the ingredient listing gives more than one choice, the first ingredient listed is the one used in the recipe analysis. Due to inevitable variations in the ingredients you choose to use, the nutritional values should be considered approximate.

The annotation "(limited)" following Protein counts in some recipes indicates that consumption of whole eggs should be limited to four per week.

Please note the following symbols:

☆ This star means read the recipe's directions carefully for special instructions about **division** of ingredients.

❋ This symbol indicates **FREEZES WELL.**

Sumptuous Soups

à Deux (For Two)

Whether a fierce north wind is keeping you and your kids indoors on a Saturday afternoon, or you're drying off from a day spent swimming in your backyard pool, soup is a comforting choice for lunch, supper, or a healthy snack. But when you're cooking for one or two, homemade soup may seem like just too much trouble, and instead you decide to open a can of "store-bought."

At least, that's how it *used* to be—but no longer! This collection of soups for two might just revolutionize how you think about this culinary option that makes a splendid appetizer or a hearty main dish, depending on the recipe and the serving size. So whether you've invited a best friend for Sunday supper or you're reading the paper and enjoying a bit of solitude, there's bound to be a recipe here to tempt your taste buds!

On warm afternoons, there is nothing more appealing than my Easy Gazpacho, *full of the best of the summer harvest and brimming with vitamins in every sip. But when you're feeling a bit ravenous and bundled up in a cozy sweater against the chill, I recommend some* Old-Fashioned Potato Soup *served with a piece of crusty bread or some favorite crackers. And for a delectable splurge in flavor but not in fat or calories, fix my* Golden Broccoli Bisque—*and enjoy the applause.*

Summer Gazpacho

When the afternoon is hot enough to fry eggs on the sidewalk, here's the perfect post-work cooler! It's rich in antioxidants, but it's even richer in fresh flavors. ◐ Serves 2 (1 cup)

> 1 cup reduced-sodium tomato juice
> 2 tablespoons Kraft Fat Free Catalina Dressing
> ¼ teaspoon chili seasoning
> ⅛ teaspoon black pepper
> ½ cup chopped unpeeled cucumber
> ½ cup peeled and chopped fresh tomato
> ¼ cup chopped onion
> 2 tablespoons chopped green bell pepper
> 2 teaspoons chopped fresh parsley or ½ teaspoon dried
>   parsley flakes

In a medium bowl, combine tomato juice, Catalina dressing, chili seasoning, and black pepper. Add cucumber, tomato, onion, and green pepper. Mix well to combine. Stir in parsley. Cover and refrigerate for at least 30 minutes. Gently stir again just before serving.

Each serving equals:

HE: 2¼ Vegetable • 17 Optional Calories

64 Calories • 0 gm Fat • 2 gm Protein • 14 gm Carbohydrate • 237 mg Sodium • 37 mg Calcium • 2 gm Fiber

DIABETIC EXCHANGES: 2 Vegetable

CARB CHOICES: 1

Chunky Creamy Mushroom Soup

Talk about luscious, and you've got to be raving about this spectacularly good homemade mushroom soup! With lots of real mushrooms in every spoonful, this is a classic you'll prepare again and again. ◐ Serves 2 (1 cup)

> 2 cups finely chopped fresh mushrooms
> ¼ cup finely chopped onion
> ⅓ cup Carnation Nonfat Dry Milk Powder
> 3 tablespoons Bisquick Heart Smart Baking Mix
> 1½ cups water
> ¼ teaspoon dried minced garlic
> 1 teaspoon dried parsley flakes
> ⅛ teaspoon black pepper
> 2 teaspoons I Can't Believe It's Not Butter! Light Margarine

In a medium saucepan sprayed with butter-flavored cooking spray, sauté mushrooms and onion for 6 to 8 minutes. In a covered jar, combine dry milk powder, baking mix, and water. Shake well to blend. Stir milk mixture into mushroom mixture. Add garlic, parsley flakes, and black pepper. Mix well to combine. Stir in margarine. Lower heat and simmer for 5 to 6 minutes or until mixture thickens and is heated through, stirring often.

Each serving equals:

HE: 1¼ Vegetable • ½ Fat Free Milk • ½ Bread • ½ Fat

127 Calories • 3 gm Fat • 7 gm Protein • 18 gm Carbohydrate •
242 mg Sodium • 171 mg Calcium • 1 gm Fiber

DIABETIC EXCHANGES: 1 Vegetable • ½ Fat Free Milk • ½ Starch • ½ Fat

CARB CHOICES: 1

Adobe Cream of Tomato Soup

You've never had tomato soup like this sensational southwestern delight! It might just be the creamiest, rosiest soup you've ever tasted—and it's a beautiful starter for any meal for two.

○ Serves 2 (1¼ cups)

> ⅓ cup Carnation Nonfat Dry Milk Powder
> 1½ tablespoons all-purpose flour
> ¾ cup water
> 1 (15-ounce) can diced tomatoes, undrained
> ¼ cup Land O Lakes Fat Free Half & Half
> 1 tablespoon Splenda Granular
> 1½ teaspoons chili seasoning
> 1 teaspoon dried parsley flakes
> ⅛ teaspoon black pepper

In a covered jar, combine dry milk powder, flour, and water. Shake well to blend. Pour mixture into a medium saucepan sprayed with butter-flavored cooking spray. Add undrained tomatoes, half & half, Splenda, chili seasoning, parsley flakes, and black pepper. Mix well to combine. Cook over medium heat for 6 to 8 minutes or until mixture thickens and is heated through, stirring often.

Each serving equals:

HE: 2 Vegetable • ½ Fat Free Milk • ¼ Bread • ¼ Slider • 1 Optional Calorie

128 Calories • 0 gm Fat • 7 gm Protein • 25 gm Carbohydrate •
396 mg Sodium • 221 mg Calcium • 4 gm Fiber

DIABETIC EXCHANGES: 2 Vegetable • ½ Fat Free Milk • ½ Starch

CARB CHOICES: 2

Chunky Rice and Tomato Soup

Research continues to show that people who start their meals with soup are usually less ravenous and make healthier choices. Here's a recipe that can help transform the way you eat!

○ Serves 2 (1½ cups)

½ cup chopped onion
⅓ cup Carnation Nonfat Dry Milk Powder
¾ cup water
1 (15-ounce) can diced tomatoes, undrained
1 tablespoon Splenda Granular
1 teaspoon dried basil
⅛ teaspoon black pepper
⅓ cup uncooked instant rice
2 teaspoons I Can't Believe It's Not Butter! Light Margarine

In a medium saucepan sprayed with butter-flavored cooking spray, sauté onion for 5 minutes. In a covered jar, combine dry milk powder and water. Shake well to blend. Stir milk mixture into onion. Add undrained tomatoes, Splenda, basil, and black pepper. Mix well to combine. Stir in uncooked rice and margarine. Lower heat, cover, and simmer for 5 to 6 minutes or until rice is tender, stirring occasionally.

Each serving equals:

HE: 2½ Vegetable • ½ Fat Free Milk • ½ Bread • ½ Fat • 3 Optional Calories

174 Calories • 2 gm Fat • 7 gm Protein • 32 gm Carbohydrate •
381 mg Sodium • 209 mg Calcium • 4 gm Fiber

DIABETIC EXCHANGES: 2 Vegetable • 1 Starch • ½ Fat Free Milk • ½ Fat

CARB CHOICES: 2

Tomato and Green Bean Soup

I love to pick a fresh ripe tomato right from my garden when I prepare this delightful dish, but even if you "pick" your tomatoes at the local farm stand or supermarket, you're bound to smile during each and every sip! ☻ Serves 2 (1½ cups)

> 1 cup peeled and finely chopped fresh tomato
> 2 tablespoons chopped onion
> 1 (10¾-ounce) can Healthy Request Tomato Soup
> 1 cup fat-free milk
> 1 (8-ounce) can French-style green beans, rinsed and
>   drained
> ⅛ teaspoon black pepper

In a medium saucepan sprayed with butter-flavored cooking spray, sauté tomato and onion for 5 minutes. Stir in tomato soup. Add milk, green beans, and black pepper. Mix well to combine. Continue cooking for 5 to 6 minutes or until mixture is heated through, stirring often.

Each serving equals:

HE: 2 Vegetable • ½ Fat Free Milk • 1 Slider • 10 Optional Calories

194 Calories • 2 gm Fat • 7 gm Protein • 37 gm Carbohydrate •
908 mg Sodium • 187 mg Calcium • 4 gm Fiber

DIABETIC EXCHANGES: 2 Vegetable • 1 Starch/Carbohydrate • ½ Fat Free Milk

CARB CHOICES: 2½

Country Garden Soup

What a lovely dream, to sit in the midst of greenery and serve this as part of a light lunch! Whenever I've been traveling for days on end, I find myself recalling happy meals in my own country garden—and longing for home. ☻ Serves 2 (1½ cups)

> 1 (14-ounce) can Swanson Lower Sodium Fat Free Chicken
>   Broth
> 1 cup chopped zucchini
> 1 cup chopped carrots
> ¾ cup chopped celery
> ¼ cup chopped onion
> ¼ teaspoon dried dill weed
> ⅛ teaspoon black pepper

In a medium saucepan, combine chicken broth, zucchini, carrots, celery, and onion. Stir in dill weed and black pepper. Bring mixture to a boil. Lower heat, cover, and simmer for 10 to 12 minutes or until vegetables are tender, stirring occasionally.

Each serving equals:

HE: 3 Vegetable • 14 Optional Calories

60 Calories • 0 gm Fat • 4 gm Protein • 11 gm Carbohydrate • 394 mg Sodium • 64 mg Calcium • 4 gm Fiber

DIABETIC EXCHANGES: 2 Vegetable

CARB CHOICES: 1

Old-Fashioned Potato Soup

Here's a family classic you can stir up anytime, with any potatoes that catch your fancy! It's perfect with plain old spuds of the Idaho kind, but why not surprise your family with some purple Peruvians or Yukon Gold potatoes one of these nights? American farmers are growing all kinds of potato varieties these days.

Serves 2 (1½ cups)

> 1½ cups peeled and diced raw potatoes
> ¾ cup chopped celery
> ½ cup chopped onion
> ½ cup hot water
> 1 cup fat-free milk
> ¼ cup Land O Lakes Fat Free Half & Half
> ½ teaspoon Worcestershire sauce
> ⅛ teaspoon black pepper
> 2 teaspoons I Can't Believe It's Not Butter! Light Margarine

In a medium saucepan, combine potatoes, celery, onion, and water. Cook over medium heat for 8 to 10 minutes or until vegetables are tender. Partially mash potatoes and vegetables in cooking liquid. Stir in milk, half & half, Worcestershire sauce, and black pepper. Add margarine. Mix well to combine. Continue cooking for 3 to 4 minutes or until mixture is heated through, stirring often.

Each serving equals:

HE: 1¼ Vegetable • ¾ Bread • ½ Fat Free Milk • ½ Fat • 18 Optional Calories

170 Calories • 2 gm Fat • 7 gm Protein • 31 gm Carbohydrate •
180 mg Sodium • 214 mg Calcium • 3 gm Fiber

DIABETIC EXCHANGES: 1 Vegetable • 1 Starch • ½ Fat Free Milk • ½ Fat

CARB CHOICES: 2

Golden Broccoli Bisque

If you've passed (with regrets) on the high-fat broccoli cheese soups served at some popular chain restaurants, here's good news: You don't have to resist temptation any longer! This version is luscious—try it and see! ☻ Serves 2 (1 cup)

1 cup finely chopped fresh or frozen broccoli, thawed
¼ cup finely chopped onion
¼ cup hot water
⅓ cup Carnation Nonfat Dry Milk Powder
1 tablespoon all-purpose flour
1 cup cold water
¼ cup Land O Lakes Fat Free Half & Half
½ teaspoon Worcestershire sauce
1 (2.5-ounce) jar sliced mushrooms, drained and chopped
½ cup diced Velveeta Light processed cheese

In a medium saucepan, combine broccoli, onion, and hot water. Cook over medium heat for 7 to 9 minutes or until broccoli is tender. In a covered jar, combine dry milk powder, flour, and cold water. Shake well to blend. Pour milk mixture into broccoli mixture. Add half & half, Worcestershire sauce, mushrooms, and Velveeta cheese. Mix well to combine. Continue cooking for 10 minutes or until mixture thickens and cheese melts, stirring often.

Each serving equals:

HE: 1¾ Vegetable • 1 Protein • ½ Fat Free Milk • 18 Optional Calories

188 Calories • 4 gm Fat • 14 gm Protein • 24 gm Carbohydrate •
705 mg Sodium • 382 mg Calcium • 4 gm Fiber

DIABETIC EXCHANGES: 1 Meat • 1 Vegetable • ½ Fat Free Milk •
½ Starch/Carbohydrate

CARB CHOICES: 1½

Cauliflower Cheese Soup

A chilly fall night, and you're just not in the mood to shop for fresh produce? This soup turns your freezer into a terrific kitchen partner, providing the veggie at the heart of this rich and cheesy soup.

❂ Serves 2 (full 1½ cups)

> ¼ cup chopped onion
> 1¾ cups chopped frozen cauliflower, thawed
> 1 (14-ounce) can Swanson Lower Sodium Fat Free Chicken
>   Broth
> ⅓ cup Carnation Nonfat Dry Milk Powder
> 3 tablespoons all-purpose flour
> ½ cup diced Velveeta Light processed cheese
> 2 teaspoons I Can't Believe It's Not Butter! Light Margarine
> ¼ teaspoon Worcestershire sauce
> ¼ teaspoon lemon pepper

In a medium saucepan sprayed with butter-flavored cooking spray, sauté onion for 5 minutes. Stir in cauliflower. Continue to sauté for 6 to 8 minutes. In a covered jar, combine chicken broth, dry milk powder, and flour. Shake well to blend. Pour broth mixture into cauliflower mixture. Add Velveeta cheese, margarine, Worcestershire sauce, and lemon pepper. Mix well to combine. Lower heat and simmer for 6 to 8 minutes or until mixture thickens and cheese melts, stirring occasionally.

Each serving equals:

HE: 2 Vegetable • 1 Protein • ½ Fat Free Milk • ½ Bread • ½ Fat •
14 Optional Calories

205 Calories • 5 gm Fat • 15 gm Protein • 25 gm Carbohydrate •
595 mg Sodium • 342 mg Calcium • 3 gm Fiber

DIABETIC EXCHANGES: 2 Vegetable • 1 Meat • ½ Fat Free Milk • ½ Starch •
½ Fat

CARB CHOICES: 1½

Onion Cheese Soup

Love the hearty flavor of French onion soup, but don't have *hours* to prepare it the old-fashioned way? This is a surprisingly scrumptious soup that comes together quickly and delivers loads of irresistible taste. ❂ Serves 2 (1 cup)

> 1 cup coarsely chopped onion
> 1½ cups fat-free milk
> 1½ tablespoons all-purpose flour
> ¾ cup diced Velveeta Light processed cheese
> 1 teaspoon dried parsley flakes
> ⅛ teaspoon black pepper
> 2 teaspoons I Can't Believe It's Not Butter! Light Margarine

In a medium saucepan sprayed with butter-flavored cooking spray, sauté onion for 6 to 8 minutes. In a covered jar, combine milk and flour. Shake well to blend. Pour milk mixture into onion mixture. Add Velveeta cheese, parsley flakes, and black pepper. Mix well to combine. Lower heat and simmer for 6 to 8 minutes or until mixture thickens and cheese melts, stirring often. Just before serving, stir in margarine.

Each serving equals:

HE: 1½ Protein • 1 Vegetable • ¾ Fat Free Milk • ½ Fat • ¼ Bread

222 Calories • 6 gm Fat • 16 gm Protein • 26 gm Carbohydrate •
756 mg Sodium • 495 mg Calcium • 1 gm Fiber

DIABETIC EXCHANGES: 1½ Meat • 1 Fat Free Milk • 1 Vegetable • ½ Fat

CARB CHOICES: 2

Creamy Fresh Tomato Soup

Surprised to find some Splenda in a recipe for tomato soup? Don't be! Remember that a tomato is a fruit, not a vegetable—and that it just loves a little touch of sweetness.

○ Serves 2 (1¼ cups)

2 cups peeled and chopped fresh tomatoes
2 tablespoons finely chopped onion
1 tablespoon Splenda Granular
⅛ teaspoon black pepper
1 tablespoon all-purpose flour
¼ teaspoon baking soda
1 cup fat-free milk
1 tablespoon I Can't Believe It's Not Butter! Light Margarine
¼ teaspoon dried basil

In a medium saucepan sprayed with butter-flavored cooking spray, combine tomatoes, onion, Splenda, and black pepper. Bring mixture to a boil. Lower heat, cover, and simmer for 10 minutes. Pour hot mixture into a blender container. Cover and process on BLEND for 30 seconds. Pour mixture back into saucepan. Add flour, baking soda, milk, and margarine. Mix well to combine using a wire whisk. Stir in basil. Lower heat and simmer for 6 to 8 minutes or until mixture thickens and is heated through, stirring often.

Each serving equals:

HE: 2 Vegetable • ¾ Fat • ½ Fat Free Milk • 17 Optional Calories

123 Calories • 3 gm Fat • 6 gm Protein • 18 gm Carbohydrate • 207 mg Sodium • 178 mg Calcium • 2 gm Fiber

DIABETIC EXCHANGES: 2 Vegetable • 1 Fat • ½ Fat Free Milk

CARB CHOICES: 1

Classic Clam Chowder

In a perfect world, we'd all get to feast on clam chowder in a small New England seaport town on a cool day—but some of us are geographically landlocked, or at least live far from the nearest ocean. No matter, canned clams and a little kitchen magic produce a charming classic! ☻ Serves 2 (¾ cup)

1 cup peeled and cubed raw potatoes
½ cup chopped onion
¾ cup water
½ cup fat-free milk
1 (4.5-ounce drained weight) can Chicken of the Sea
   chopped clams, drained
2 teaspoons I Can't Believe It's Not Butter! Light Margarine
½ teaspoon dried parsley flakes
⅛ teaspoon black pepper
1 tablespoon Oscar Mayer or Hormel Real Bacon Bits

In a medium saucepan, combine potatoes, onion, and water. Cook over medium heat for 10 minutes or until vegetables are tender. Do not drain. Stir in milk, clams, margarine, parsley flakes, and black pepper. Add bacon bits. Mix well to combine. Lower heat and simmer for 6 to 8 minutes or until mixture is heated through, stirring often.

Each serving equals:

HE: 2½ Protein • ½ Bread • ½ Fat • ½ Vegetable • ¼ Fat Free Milk

208 Calories • 4 gm Fat • 21 gm Protein • 22 gm Carbohydrate • 258 mg Sodium • 150 mg Calcium • 2 gm Fiber

DIABETIC EXCHANGES: 2½ Meat • 1 Starch • ½ Fat • ½ Vegetable

CARB CHOICES: 1

Tuna Vegetable Chowder

Instead of the traditional chicken soup, here's a dish sure to produce a smile on every tuna lover's lips! It couldn't be easier (frozen veggies by the bag, milk from the carton) or tastier—yum!

○ Serves 2 (1½ cups)

> ¼ cup chopped onion
> 1½ cups fat-free milk
> ¼ cup Land O Lakes Fat Free Half & Half
> 2 tablespoons all-purpose flour
> 1 cup frozen mixed vegetables, thawed
> 1 (6-ounce) can white tuna, packed in water, drained and
>   flaked
> 1 (2-ounce) jar sliced pimiento, drained
> 1 teaspoon dried parsley flakes
> 1 teaspoon lemon pepper

In a medium saucepan sprayed with butter-flavored cooking spray, sauté onion for 5 minutes. In a covered jar, combine milk, half & half, and flour. Shake well to blend. Stir milk mixture into onions. Add mixed vegetables, tuna, pimiento, parsley flakes, and lemon pepper. Mix well to combine. Lower heat and simmer for 5 to 6 minutes or until mixture thickens and is heated through, stirring often.

HINT: Thaw mixed vegetables by rinsing in a colander under hot water for 1 minute.

Each serving equals:

HE: 2 Protein • 1 Vegetable • ¾ Fat Free Milk • ¾ Bread • 18 Optional Calories

263 Calories • 3 gm Fat • 27 gm Protein • 32 gm Carbohydrate •
605 mg Sodium • 301 mg Calcium • 4 gm Fiber

DIABETIC EXCHANGES: 3 Meat • 1 Fat Free Milk • 1 Starch • 1 Vegetable

CARB CHOICES: 2

Turkey Rice Soup

Most soup recipes stir up quarts and quarts of soup that people with small kitchens and smaller appliances just can't handle. I think it's only right that minimalist cooks have a recipe for this post-Thanksgiving pleasure.   ☻   Serves 2 (2 cups)

> 1 (14-ounce) can Swanson Lower Sodium Fat Free Chicken
>   Broth
> ¾ cup water
> ½ cup chopped onion
> ½ cup shredded carrots
> ⅓ cup uncooked Minute Rice
> ¼ teaspoon dried basil
> 1 cup diced cooked turkey breast
> ½ cup frozen peas

In a medium saucepan, combine chicken broth, water, onion, carrots, uncooked instant rice, and basil. Bring mixture to a boil. Stir in turkey and peas. Lower heat, cover, and simmer for 10 minutes, or until rice is tender, stirring occasionally.

HINT: If you don't have leftovers, purchase a chunk of cooked turkey breast from your local deli.

Each serving equals:

HE: 2½ Protein • 1 Bread • 1 Vegetable • 14 Optional Calories

218 Calories • 2 gm Fat • 26 gm Protein • 24 gm Carbohydrate •
258 mg Sodium • 49 mg Calcium • 3 gm Fiber

DIABETIC EXCHANGES: 2½ Meat • 1 Starch • 1 Vegetable

CARB CHOICES: ½

Chicken Tetrazzini Soup

I actually didn't create this recipe while staring into my refrigerator at a bowl of leftover chicken tetrazzini—but I might have! Sometimes leftovers do inspire a new recipe, but in this case I started thinking about fun ways to reinvent chicken soup—and this came to me in a flash!   ☺   Serves 2 (2 cups)

½ cup chopped onion
1 (14-ounce) can Swanson Lower Sodium Fat Free Chicken
    Broth
½ cup water
⅓ cup Carnation Nonfat Dry Milk Powder
3 tablespoons all-purpose flour
1 (2.5-ounce) jar sliced mushrooms, drained and finely
    chopped
1 (2-ounce) jar chopped pimiento, drained
½ cup hot cooked spaghetti, rinsed and drained
1 (5-ounce) can chicken breast, packed in water, drained
    and flaked
¼ cup shredded Kraft reduced-fat Cheddar cheese
1 teaspoon dried parsley flakes
⅛ teaspoon black pepper

In a medium saucepan sprayed with butter-flavored cooking spray, sauté onion for 6 to 8 minutes. In a covered jar, combine chicken broth, water, dry milk powder, and flour. Shake well to blend. Stir broth mixture into onion. Add mushrooms, pimiento, and spaghetti. Mix well to combine. Stir in chicken, Cheddar cheese, parsley flakes, and black pepper. Lower heat and simmer for 5 minutes or until cheese melts and mixture thickens, stirring often.

Each serving equals:

HE: 3 Protein • 1 Bread • 1 Vegetable • ½ Fat Free Milk • 13 Optional Calories

321 Calories • 5 gm Fat • 36 gm Protein • 33 gm Carbohydrate •
730 mg Sodium • 295 mg Calcium • 4 gm Fiber

DIABETIC EXCHANGES: 3 Meat • 1 Starch • 1 Vegetable • ½ Fat Free Milk

CARB CHOICES: 2

Provençal Chicken Soup

Doctors have recommended a Mediterranean diet for its healthful properties, but whether you decide to change your menus occasionally or opt for mostly Med, this dish is a winner.

◐ Serves 2 (2 cups)

> 6 ounces skinned and boned uncooked chicken breast, cut
>   into bite-size pieces
> ½ cup chopped onion
> 1 (15-ounce) can diced tomatoes, undrained
> 1 (14-ounce) can Swanson Lower Sodium Fat Free Chicken
>   Broth
> 1 teaspoon Italian seasoning
> 2 teaspoons Splenda Granular
> ¾ cup uncooked noodles

In a medium saucepan sprayed with olive oil–flavored cooking spray, sauté chicken and onion for 5 minutes. Add undrained tomatoes, chicken broth, Italian seasoning, and Splenda. Mix well to combine. Bring mixture to a boil. Stir in uncooked noodles. Lower heat and simmer for 15 to 20 minutes, or until chicken and noodles are tender, stirring occasionally.

Each serving equals:

HE: 2½ Vegetable • 2¼ Protein • 1 Bread • 16 Optional Calories

280 Calories • 4 gm Fat • 27 gm Protein • 34 gm Carbohydrate •
637 mg Sodium • 73 mg Calcium • 5 gm Fiber

DIABETIC EXCHANGES: 2½ Vegetable • 2 Meat • 1 Starch

CARB CHOICES: 2

Speedy Veggie Beef Soup

Here's one of those "dump everything in a pot" recipes that busy cooks just love—don't you? Even when you're not cooking for a crowd, you still need fast, festive, and flavorful foods on your table.

◐ Serves 2 (1½ cups)

> 4 ounces extra-lean ground sirloin beef or turkey breast
> ½ cup chopped onion
> 1 (8-ounce) can stewed tomatoes, chopped and undrained
> 1½ cups water
> 1 teaspoon Wyler's Beef Granules Instant Bouillon
> 1 teaspoon dried parsley flakes
> ⅛ teaspoon black pepper
> 1 cup frozen mixed vegetables, thawed
> ⅓ cup uncooked elbow macaroni

In a medium saucepan sprayed with butter-flavored cooking spray, brown meat and onion. Stir in undrained stewed tomatoes, water, dry beef bouillon, parsley flakes, and black pepper. Add mixed vegetables and uncooked macaroni. Mix well to combine. Bring mixture to a boil. Lower heat and simmer for 15 minutes or until vegetables and macaroni are tender, stirring often.

HINT: Thaw mixed vegetables by rinsing in a colander under hot water for 1 minute.

Each serving equals:

HE: 1½ Protein • 2 Vegetable • 1 Bread • 5 Optional Calories

227 Calories • 3 gm Fat • 15 gm Protein • 35 gm Carbohydrate • 321 mg Sodium • 76 mg Calcium • 6 gm Fiber

DIABETIC EXCHANGES: 2 Vegetable • 1½ Meat • 1 Starch

CARB CHOICES: 2

Green Bean Chili

Okay, I admit it—chili with green beans is definitely not a Mexican standard! But I had a great reason for stirring it up . . . my husband, Cliff, loves green beans and Mexican food separately, so I figured: Why not holding hands in one tasty treat?

● Serves 2 (1½ cups)

> 4 ounces extra-lean ground sirloin beef or turkey breast
> ½ cup chopped onion
> 1 (10¾-ounce) can Healthy Request Tomato Soup
> ½ cup water
> 1 teaspoon chili seasoning
> ⅛ teaspoon black pepper
> 1 (8-ounce) can cut green beans, rinsed and drained

In a medium saucepan sprayed with butter-flavored cooking spray, brown meat and onion. Stir in tomato soup, water, chili seasoning, and black pepper. Add green beans. Mix well to combine. Lower heat, cover, and simmer for 15 minutes, stirring occasionally.

Each serving equals:

HE: 1½ Protein • 1½ Vegetable • 1 Slider • 10 Optional Calories

196 Calories • 4 gm Fat • 11 gm Protein • 29 gm Carbohydrate • 809 mg Sodium • 24 mg Calcium • 3 gm Fiber

DIABETIC EXCHANGES: 1½ Meat • 1½ Vegetable • 1 Starch/Carbohydrate

CARB CHOICES: 1½

Chili a Duo

Here's a tangy farmer's special that features a hearty surprise—pork & beans in every bite! I love it when I can grab a can from my pantry and mix it into a brand-new dish.

⚬ Serves 2 (1¾ cups)

> 4 ounces extra-lean ground sirloin beef or turkey breast
> 1 (8-ounce) can pork & beans, pork fat removed
> 1 (8-ounce) can Hunt's Tomato Sauce
> ½ cup chunky salsa (mild, medium, or hot)
> 1 cup water
> 1½ teaspoons chili seasoning
> ⅛ teaspoon black pepper
> 2 tablespoons Land O Lakes no-fat sour cream

In a medium saucepan sprayed with butter-flavored cooking spray, brown meat. Stir in pork & beans, tomato sauce, salsa, and water. Add chili seasoning and black pepper. Mix well to combine. Lower heat and simmer for 10 minutes, stirring occasionally. When serving, top each bowl with 1 tablespoon sour cream.

Each serving equals:

HE: 2½ Vegetable • 2 Protein • 1 Bread • 15 Optional Calories

223 Calories • 3 gm Fat • 15 gm Protein • 34 gm Carbohydrate • 989 mg Sodium • 91 mg Calcium • 5 gm Fiber

DIABETIC EXCHANGES: 2 Meat • 1½ Vegetable • 1 Starch

CARB CHOICES: 2

Mexicalli Beef and Noodle Soup

I never want you to have half-empty cans of this or that in your fridge, which is why I recommend tinier sizes than you may be used to purchasing. It's a trade-off, of course—a few cents more for little containers, but much less waste (when you don't have to throw away spoiled food). ◒ Serves 2 (1½ cups)

> ½ cup chopped onion
> 1 cup diced lean cooked roast beef
> 1 (14-ounce) can Swanson Lower Sodium Fat Free Beef
>   Broth
> 1 (8-ounce) can stewed tomatoes, diced and undrained
> ½ teaspoon dried minced garlic
> 1 teaspoon Worcestershire sauce
> 1 teaspoon chili seasoning
> ¾ cup uncooked noodles

In a medium saucepan sprayed with butter-flavored cooking spray, sauté onion for 5 minutes. Stir in roast beef, beef broth, undrained stewed tomatoes, garlic, Worcestershire sauce, and chili seasoning. Add uncooked noodles. Mix well to combine. Continue cooking for 6 to 8 minutes or until noodles are tender, stirring occasionally.

HINT: If you don't have leftovers, purchase a chunk of lean cooked roast beef from your local deli or use Healthy Choice Deli slices.

Each serving equals:

HE: 2½ Protein • 1½ Vegetable • 1 Bread • 14 Optional Calories

315 Calories • 7 gm Fat • 29 gm Protein • 34 gm Carbohydrate • 478 mg Sodium • 56 mg Calcium • 4 gm Fiber

DIABETIC EXCHANGES: 2½ Meat • 1½ Vegetable • 1½ Starch

CARB CHOICES: 2

Grandma's Cabbage Roll Soup

Inspired by a dish I remember my grandmother making in an enormous soup pot at her boardinghouse, here's a terrific recipe for just enough for two!   ☻   Serves 2 (full 1½ cups)

> 4 ounces extra-lean ground sirloin beef or turkey breast
> ½ cup chopped onion
> 1¾ cups water
> 1½ teaspoons Wyler's Beef Granules Instant Bouillon
> 2 tablespoons reduced-sodium ketchup
> ½ teaspoon Worcestershire sauce
> 1 tablespoon Splenda Granular
> ⅛ teaspoon black pepper
> 1 (8-ounce) can stewed tomatoes, undrained
> 1 cup shredded cabbage
> ⅓ cup uncooked Minute Rice

In a medium saucepan sprayed with butter-flavored cooking spray, sauté meat and onion for 5 minutes. Stir in water, beef bouillon, ketchup, Worcestershire sauce, Splenda, and black pepper. Add undrained stewed tomatoes, cabbage, and uncooked instant rice. Mix well to combine. Lower heat, cover, and simmer for 15 minutes or until cabbage and rice are tender, stirring occasionally.

Each serving equals:

HE: 2 Vegetable • 1½ Protein • ½ Bread • ¼ Slider • 3 Optional Calories

198 Calories • 2 gm Fat • 12 gm Protein • 33 gm Carbohydrate • 428 mg Sodium • 69 mg Calcium • 4 gm Fiber

DIABETIC EXCHANGES: 2 Vegetable • 1½ Protein • 1 Starch/Carbohydrate

CARB CHOICES: 2

Cheeseburger Chowder

This is one of those treats I label "for Tom"—my cheeseburger-lovin' son! He's passed his love for this American classic on to his children, who love this almost as much as he does.

● Serves 2 (full 1½ cups)

> 4 ounces extra-lean ground sirloin beef or turkey breast
> ¼ cup chopped onion
> 1½ cups fat-free milk
> 1½ tablespoons all-purpose flour
> ¾ cup cubed Velveeta Light processed cheese
> ¼ teaspoon Worcestershire sauce
> 1 cup frozen mixed vegetables, thawed
> 1 (2.5-ounce) jar sliced mushrooms, drained and chopped

In a medium saucepan sprayed with butter-flavored cooking spray, brown meat and onion. In a covered jar, combine milk and flour. Shake well to blend. Pour milk mixture into meat mixture. Add Velveeta cheese and Worcestershire sauce. Mix well to combine. Stir in mixed vegetables and mushrooms. Lower heat and simmer for 6 to 8 minutes or until vegetables are tender and cheese is melted, stirring occasionally.

HINT: Thaw mixed vegetables by rinsing in a colander under hot water for 1 minute.

Each serving equals:

HE: 3 Protein • 1½ Vegetable • ¾ Fat Free Milk • ½ Bread

304 Calories • 7 gm Fat • 26 gm Protein • 34 gm Carbohydrate • 979 mg Sodium • 548 mg Calcium • 4 gm Fiber

DIABETIC EXCHANGES: 3 Meat • 1 Fat Free Milk • 1 Vegetable • ½ Starch

CARB CHOICES: 2

Broccoli, Ham, and Cheddar Soup

Talk about your "lunch-in-a-mug"! When you mix the contents of a ham-and-cheese sandwich into a cozy broccoli-based soup, you'll save a fortune on mealtime takeout!

○ Serves 2 (1½ cups)

> ¼ cup chopped onion
> 1½ cups frozen chopped broccoli, thawed
> ⅔ cup Carnation Nonfat Dry Milk Powder
> 1½ cups water
> 3 tablespoons all-purpose flour
> ½ cup diced Velveeta Light processed cheese
> ¾ cup diced Dubuque 97% fat-free ham or any extra-lean
>   ham
> ½ teaspoon Worcestershire sauce
> ½ teaspoon dried parsley flakes
> ⅛ teaspoon black pepper

In a medium saucepan sprayed with butter-flavored cooking spray, sauté onion for 5 minutes. Stir in broccoli. In a covered jar, combine dry milk powder, water, and flour. Shake well to blend. Pour milk mixture into onion and broccoli mixture. Add Velveeta cheese and ham. Mix well to combine. Stir in Worcestershire sauce, parsley flakes, and black pepper. Lower heat and simmer for 10 minutes or until cheese melts and mixture thickens, stirring often.

HINT: Thaw broccoli by rinsing in a colander under hot water for 1 minute.

Each serving equals:

HE: 2½ Protein • 1½ Vegetable • 1 Fat Free Milk • ½ Bread

257 Calories • 5 gm Fat • 24 gm Protein • 29 gm Carbohydrate • 988 mg Sodium • 367 mg Calcium • 4 gm Fiber

DIABETIC EXCHANGES: 2½ Meat • 1½ Vegetable • 1 Fat Free Milk • ½ Starch

CARB CHOICES: 1½

Ham and Navy Bean Soup

Yes, I'm suggesting you buy one of those cans of beans you may never have tried before—but I'm confident you'll be pleased that you did! Shelves and shelves of beans fight for space in your supermarket, but if you're always picking up the same old kidney beans, it's time to try something new. ☺ Serves 2 (2 cups)

> 1 (15-ounce) can Bush's Navy or Great Northern Beans,
>   rinsed and drained
> ½ cup diced Dubuque 97% fat-free ham or any extra-lean
>   ham
> ½ cup chopped celery
> ¾ cup shredded carrots
> ¼ cup chopped onion
> ½ cup diced raw potatoes
> 1½ cups water
> 3 tablespoons reduced-sodium ketchup
> 1 teaspoon dried parsley flakes
> ⅛ teaspoon black pepper

In a medium saucepan, combine beans, ham, celery, carrots, onion, potatoes, and water. Bring mixture to a boil, stirring often. Add ketchup, parsley flakes, and black pepper. Mix well to combine. Lower heat, cover, and simmer for 15 minutes or until vegetables are tender, stirring occasionally.

Each serving equals:

HE: 3 Protein • 1½ Vegetable • 1 Bread • ¼ Slider • 3 Optional Calories

271 Calories • 3 gm Fat • 19 gm Protein • 42 gm Carbohydrate •
828 mg Sodium • 104 mg Calcium • 8 gm Fiber

DIABETIC EXCHANGES: 2 Starch • 1½ Meat • 1½ Vegetable

CARB CHOICES: 2

Corned Beef and Cabbage Stew

Planning a relaxed supper for two after the local St. Paddy's Day festivities? This is what I'd serve, maybe with a little green-tinted Diet Dew! Erin go gobble this one down! ☻ Serves 2 (2 cups)

1½ cups water
2 cups coarsely chopped cabbage
1 cup unpeeled coarsely chopped raw potatoes
1 cup frozen sliced carrots, thawed
½ cup coarsely chopped onion
1 (2.5-ounce) package Carl Buddig lean corned beef,
*   shredded*
1 tablespoon prepared horseradish sauce
1 tablespoon chopped fresh parsley or 1 teaspoon dried
*   parsley flakes*
⅛ teaspoon black pepper

In a medium saucepan, combine water, cabbage, potatoes, carrots, and onion. Stir in shredded corned beef, horseradish sauce, parsley, and black pepper. Bring mixture to a boil, stirring occasionally. Lower heat, cover, and simmer for 15 to 20 minutes or until vegetables are tender, stirring occasionally.

HINT: Thaw carrots by rinsing in a colander under hot water for 1
    minute.

Each serving equals:

HE: 2½ Vegetable • 1¼ Protein • ½ Bread • 5 Optional Calories

171 Calories • 3 gm Fat • 10 gm Protein • 26 gm Carbohydrate •
569 mg Sodium • 32 mg Calcium • 4 gm Fiber

DIABETIC EXCHANGES: 2½ Vegetable • 1 Meat • 1 Starch

CARB CHOICES: 1½

Splendid Salads

O ne of the real dangers when you've made a commitment to eating healthy for a lifetime is that you get stuck in a salad rut. You keep serving the same-old, same-old lettuce, tomato, and cucumber salads until you feel like a bored rabbit! If you don't do something about it, you're likely to swear off greens forever—but the solution is a simple one.

Over the years, I've created so many different kinds of salads, you could eat a different one every day for a year and never eat the same one twice. Of course, even I don't do *that* . . . but I do make an effort to vary the kinds of salads I prepare and serve. Now, with the recipes in this chapter, you can do the same!

Why not add Sassy Sauerkraut Salad to the menu when you're dishing up franks and beans on a cool autumn afternoon? Or stuff your garden-fresh tomatoes with something a little different by choosing Cabbage-Stuffed Tomatoes for a luncheon with a friend? And for a summer picnic or poolside buffet, bring out something new and tasty with Ranch Potato Salad. You'll be the most popular person in the room!

Fresh Fruit Salad

Here's a little secret about fruit salad you may not have known: adding a little liquid "glaze" makes all the delectable difference! This combo is refreshing and easy to fix for two—or a crowd.

◗ Serves 2 (1 cup)

> 1 cup chopped fresh strawberries
> 1 cup (1 medium) diced banana
> ½ cup seedless grapes
> 2 tablespoons unsweetened orange juice
> 2 tablespoons diet ginger ale

In a medium bowl, combine strawberries, banana, and grapes. Add orange juice and ginger ale. Mix gently to combine. Cover and refrigerate for at least 15 minutes. Gently stir again just before serving.

Each serving equals:

HE: 2 Fruit • 6 Optional Calories

136 Calories • 0 gm Fat • 2 gm Protein • 32 gm Carbohydrate • 6 mg Sodium • 22 mg Calcium • 4 gm Fiber

DIABETIC EXCHANGES: 2 Fruit

CARB CHOICES: 2

Cabbage-Stuffed Tomatoes

Instead of the same-old, same-old tradition of stuffing tomatoes with tuna, why not give your dish some real crunch? Cabbage is a great veggie to use when you want to add texture to a dish!

○ Serves 2

> 2 (large-size) ripe unpeeled tomatoes
> 3 tablespoons Kraft fat-free mayonnaise
> 1 teaspoon white distilled vinegar
> 1 teaspoon Splenda Granular
> 1 cup shredded cabbage
> 2 teaspoons chopped fresh parsley or ½ teaspoon dried
> parsley flakes

Cut tops off tomatoes. Cut tomatoes into quarters, being careful not to cut all the way through the bottom. Spread wedges slightly apart. In a small bowl, combine mayonnaise, vinegar, and Splenda. Add cabbage and parsley. Mix well to combine. Evenly spoon about ½ cup cabbage mixture into center of each tomato. Cover and refrigerate for at least 15 minutes.

Each serving equals:

HE: 1½ Vegetable • 16 Optional Calories

64 Calories • 0 gm Fat • 2 gm Protein • 14 gm Carbohydrate • 205 mg Sodium • 33 mg Calcium • 3 gm Fiber

DIABETIC EXCHANGES: 1½ Vegetable

CARB CHOICES: 1

Creamy Dilled Cucumbers

Talk about a dish that sure doesn't look or taste like "diet food"! This wonderfully luscious blend cozies up to those cucumbers like a fabulous fake fur coat on a chilly day.

◐ Serves 2 (1 cup)

> 3 tablespoons Land O Lakes no-fat sour cream
> 1 tablespoon Land O Lakes Fat Free Half & Half
> 2 teaspoons white distilled vinegar
> 1 tablespoon Splenda Granular
> ¼ teaspoon dried dill weed
> 2 cups thinly sliced unpeeled cucumbers
> ¼ cup finely chopped onion

In a medium bowl, combine sour cream, half & half, vinegar, Splenda, and dill weed. Add cucumbers and onion. Mix well to combine. Cover and refrigerate for at least 30 minutes. Gently stir again just before serving.

Each serving equals:

HE: 1¼ Vegetable • ¼ Slider • 9 Optional Calories

52 Calories • 0 gm Fat • 2 gm Protein • 11 gm Carbohydrate • 44 mg Sodium • 60 mg Calcium • 1 gm Fiber

DIABETIC EXCHANGES: 1 Vegetable • ½ Other Carbohydrate

CARB CHOICES: 1

Carrot Pineapple Salad

If you've got a food processor you absolutely love, or one of those Salad Shooters, then go ahead and grate your own carrots. But for ease of preparation, I suggest those handy packages you can find in your supermarket produce section. ◑ Serves 2 (1 cup)

> 1 (8-ounce) can crushed pineapple, packed in fruit juice,
>   drained and 1 tablespoon liquid reserved
> ¼ cup Kraft fat-free mayonnaise
> 1 tablespoon Splenda Granular
> 1½ cups grated carrots
> 2 tablespoons chopped pecans

In a medium bowl, combine reserved pineapple liquid, mayonnaise, and Splenda. Add carrots, pineapple, and pecans. Mix well to combine. Cover and refrigerate for at least 30 minutes. Gently stir again just before serving.

Each serving equals:

HE: 1½ Vegetable • 1 Fruit • 1 Fat • ¼ Slider • 3 Optional Calories

177 Calories • 5 gm Fat • 2 gm Protein • 31 gm Carbohydrate • 298 mg Sodium • 50 mg Calcium • 5 gm Fiber

DIABETIC EXCHANGES: 1½ Vegetable • 1 Fruit • 1 Fat • ½ Other Carbohydrate

CARB CHOICES: 2

Marinated Green Bean Salad

I like to think of good bottled salad dressing as my chef's assistant—and in this simple but flavorful combination, you can turn plain old canned green beans into a worthy and tasty chilled salad. ❂ Serves 2 (scant ½ cup)

> 2 tablespoons Kraft Fat Free Italian Dressing
> 1 teaspoon dried onion flakes
> 1 tablespoon Splenda Granular
> 1 (8-ounce) can French-style green beans, rinsed and
>   drained
> ¼ cup chopped celery

In a small bowl, combine Italian dressing, onion flakes, and Splenda. Add green beans and celery. Mix well to combine. Cover and refrigerate for at least 30 minutes. Gently stir again just before serving.

Each serving equals:

HE: 1 Vegetable • 13 Optional Calories

32 Calories • 0 gm Fat • 1 gm Protein • 7 gm Carbohydrate • 401 mg Sodium • 29 mg Calcium • 2 gm Fiber

DIABETIC EXCHANGES: 1 Vegetable

CARB CHOICES: ½

French Bean Salad

Some readers are surprised that I use real bacon bits instead of imitation, but it's an important part of my healthy eating philosophy: A small amount of the "real thing" keeps you from feeling deprived and truly improves the flavor of the dish.

◑ Serves 2 (¾ cup)

> 1 tablespoon Kraft Fat Free Ranch Dressing
> 1 tablespoon Land O Lakes no-fat sour cream
> ¼ cup finely chopped celery
> 1 tablespoon finely chopped onion
> 2 tablespoons Oscar Mayer or Hormel Real Bacon Bits
> 1 (8-ounce) can French-style green beans, rinsed and
>   drained

In a small bowl, combine Ranch dressing and sour cream. Stir in celery, onion, and bacon bits. Add green beans. Mix well to combine. Cover and refrigerate for at least 10 minutes. Gently stir again just before serving.

Each serving equals:

HE: 1 Vegetable • ½ Protein • 19 Optional Calories

61 Calories • 1 gm Fat • 4 gm Protein • 9 gm Carbohydrate • 604 mg Sodium • 41 mg Calcium • 2 gm Fiber

DIABETIC EXCHANGES: 1 Vegetable • ½ Meat

CARB CHOICES: 1

Italian Garden Vegetable Salad

The key to this *delicioso* treat is FRESH, FRESH, FRESH! Make it on an evening when you feel like chopping and shredding for a little while—and the reward will be in the smiles around your table.

♥ Serves 2

> 2 cups shredded lettuce
> ½ cup chopped zucchini
> ½ cup sliced fresh mushrooms
> ¼ cup chopped onion
> ¾ cup diced unpeeled fresh tomatoes
> ¼ cup Kraft Fat Free Italian Dressing
> 2 tablespoons Kraft fat-free mayonnaise
> 1 tablespoon Splenda Granular

Evenly arrange 1 cup lettuce on each of 2 salad plates. In a medium bowl, combine zucchini, mushrooms, and onion. Stir in tomatoes. Spoon about 1 cup vegetable mixture over lettuce on each plate. In same bowl, combine Italian dressing, mayonnaise, and Splenda using a wire whisk. Drizzle a full 2 tablespoons dressing mixture over top of each salad. Serve at once.

Each serving equals:

HE: 3 Vegetable • ¼ Slider • 14 Optional Calories

72 Calories • 0 gm Fat • 3 gm Protein • 15 gm Carbohydrate • 570 mg Sodium • 34 mg Calcium • 3 gm Fiber

DIABETIC EXCHANGES: 2 Vegetable • ½ Other Carbohydrate

CARB CHOICES: 1

Sassy Sauerkraut Salad

This is one of the prettiest sauerkraut-based salads I've ever created, with lively bits of green pepper, red onion, and those tangy caraway seeds throughout. It's popular with my "menfolk," and so I recommend trying it on yours!   ◐   Serves 2 (full ½ cup)

1 tablespoon apple cider vinegar
1 tablespoon Splenda Granular
2 teaspoons vegetable oil
⅛ teaspoon black pepper
1 (8-ounce) can sauerkraut, well drained
2 tablespoons chopped green bell pepper
2 tablespoons chopped red onion
¼ teaspoon caraway seeds

In a medium bowl, combine vinegar, Splenda, vegetable oil, and black pepper. Add sauerkraut, green pepper, and red onion. Mix well to combine. Stir in caraway seeds. Cover and refrigerate for at least 30 minutes. Gently stir again just before serving.

Each serving equals:

HE: 1¼ Vegetable • 1 Fat • 3 Optional Calories

69 Calories • 5 gm Fat • 0 gm Protein • 6 gm Carbohydrate • 581 mg Sodium • 6 mg Calcium • 4 gm Fiber

DIABETIC EXCHANGES: 1 Vegetable • 1 Fat

CARB CHOICES: ½

Pleasing Pea Salad

They just released one of those health studies as I was testing this recipe that said that peas are a "major inhibitor" on the pathway to cancer cell growth (meaning, they keep bad cells from growing). In other words, eat 'em because you like 'em, but also know you're doing something good for your body! ☻ Serves 2 (¾ cup)

¼ cup Kraft fat-free mayonnaise
2 tablespoons Land O Lakes no-fat sour cream
1 teaspoon prepared yellow mustard
2 teaspoons dried onion flakes
1 cup frozen peas, thawed
¼ cup finely chopped celery
¼ cup diced Velveeta Light processed cheese

In a medium bowl, combine mayonnaise, sour cream, mustard, and onion flakes. Add peas and celery. Mix well to combine. Stir in Velveeta cheese. Cover and refrigerate for at least 10 minutes. Gently stir again just before serving.

HINT: Thaw peas by rinsing in a colander under hot water for 1 minute.

Each serving equals:

HE: 1 Bread • ½ Protein • ¼ Vegetable • ¼ Slider • 15 Optional Calories

131 Calories • 3 gm Fat • 7 gm Protein • 19 gm Carbohydrate • 605 mg Sodium • 130 mg Calcium • 4 gm Fiber

DIABETIC EXCHANGES: 1 Starch/Carbohydrate • ½ Meat

CARB CHOICES: 1

French Pea and Radish Salad

Not everyone is a radish lover, but if that rosy vegetable often finds a spot on your menu, here's a pretty salad that tastes as scrumptious as it looks! I grow my own, but radishes are usually available in your supermarket year-round. ☻ Serves 2 (¾ cup)

1 cup frozen peas, thawed
¼ cup thinly sliced red radishes
2 tablespoons finely chopped onion
¼ cup Kraft Fat Free French Dressing
1 teaspoon dried parsley flakes

In a small bowl, combine peas, radishes, and onion. Add French dressing and parsley flakes. Mix well to combine. Cover and refrigerate for at least 15 minutes. Gently stir again just before serving.

HINT: Thaw peas by rinsing in a colander under hot water for 1 minute.

Each serving equals:

HE: 1 Bread • ¼ Vegetable • ½ Slider • 5 Optional Calories

104 Calories • 0 gm Fat • 4 gm Protein • 22 gm Carbohydrate •
350 mg Sodium • 23 mg Calcium • 5 gm Fiber

DIABETIC EXCHANGES: 1½ Starch/Carbohydrate

CARB CHOICES: 1

Small Slaw

If you've always believed it wasn't worth it to make fresh coleslaw when you were only cooking for one or two, I'd like to change your mind. I've done the testing—now, all you need to do is stir and dine! ☺ Serves 2 (1 cup)

> ¼ cup Kraft fat-free mayonnaise
> 1 tablespoon apple cider vinegar
> 1 tablespoon Splenda Granular
> 2 teaspoons dried onion flakes
> 1½ tablespoons chopped fresh parsley or ½ teaspoon dried
>   parsley flakes
> 2 cups purchased coleslaw mix

In a medium bowl, combine mayonnaise, vinegar, Splenda, onion flakes, and parsley. Add coleslaw mix. Mix well to combine. Cover and refrigerate for at least 30 minutes. Gently stir again just before serving.

HINT: 1¾ cups shredded cabbage and ¼ cup shredded carrots may be used in place of purchased coleslaw mix.

Each serving equals:

HE: 1 Vegetable • ¼ Slider • 3 Optional Calories

57 Calories • 1 gm Fat • 1 gm Protein • 11 gm Carbohydrate • 264 mg Sodium • 47 mg Calcium • 3 gm Fiber

DIABETIC EXCHANGES: 1 Vegetable • ½ Other Carbohydrate

CARB CHOICES: 1

Peanut Slaw

It's amazing how happy it makes us to find just a few chunks of crunchy peanuts in a main dish or salad. Why do peanuts have that cheering effect? Maybe because we feel like kids again, snacking on peanut butter or sneaking a treat! ◑ Serves 2 (¾ cup)

3 tablespoons Kraft fat-free mayonnaise
2 tablespoons Land O Lakes no-fat sour cream
1 teaspoon Splenda Granular
1½ teaspoons dried onion flakes
1 teaspoon dried parsley flakes
1½ cups purchased coleslaw mix
¼ cup chopped celery
2 tablespoons chopped dry-roasted peanuts

In a medium bowl, combine mayonnaise, sour cream, Splenda, onion flakes, and parsley flakes. Add coleslaw mix and celery. Mix well to combine. Stir in peanuts. Cover and refrigerate for at least 15 minutes. Gently stir again just before serving.

HINT: 1¼ cups shredded cabbage and ¼ cup shredded carrots may be used in place of purchased coleslaw mix.

Each serving equals:

HE: 1 Vegetable • ½ Fat • ¼ Protein • ¼ Slider • 11 Optional Calories

113 Calories • 5 gm Fat • 4 gm Protein • 13 gm Carbohydrate •
232 mg Sodium • 66 mg Calcium • 3 gm Fiber

DIABETIC EXCHANGES: 1 Fat • 1 Vegetable • ½ Starch/Carbohydrate

CARB CHOICES: 1

Tossed Salad à Deux

For the man who prefers a simple lettuce salad, treat him to a dish that looks like "the usual" but tastes like so much more! Once you find your favorite brand of pickle relish, stock up—you'll be glad you did.   ❍   Serves 2

¼ cup Kraft fat-free mayonnaise
1 tablespoon reduced-sodium ketchup
1 tablespoon sweet pickle relish
1 teaspoon dried onion flakes
1 teaspoon dried parsley flakes
4 cups shredded lettuce
2 tablespoons Oscar Mayer or Hormel Real Bacon Bits

In a small bowl, combine mayonnaise, ketchup, pickle relish, onion flakes, and parsley flakes. For each salad, place 2 cups lettuce on a plate, drizzle about ¼ cup dressing over lettuce, and sprinkle 1 tablespoon bacon bits over top.

Each serving equals:

HE: 2 Vegetable • ½ Protein • ¼ Slider • 18 Optional Calories

86 Calories • 2 gm Fat • 4 gm Protein • 13 gm Carbohydrate • 541 mg Sodium • 8 mg Calcium • 2 gm Fiber

DIABETIC EXCHANGES: 2 Vegetable • ½ Meat

CARB CHOICES: 1

Special Spinach Salad

Spinach salad is a culinary classic that never fails to please, but I am rarely satisfied with doing the same thing over and over. So I decided to "fiddle" a bit with the dressing, and the results were truly special! ◐ Serves 2 (2 cups)

> 3 cups torn fresh spinach leaves, stems removed and
>   discarded
> 1 cup finely chopped fresh mushrooms
> 1 hard boiled egg, chopped
> 2 tablespoons Oscar Mayer or Hormel Real Bacon Bits
> ¼ cup Kraft Fat Free Italian Dressing
> 1 tablespoon Splenda Granular
> ½ teaspoon Worcestershire sauce

In a large bowl, combine spinach, mushrooms, egg, and bacon bits. Cover and refrigerate for at least 15 minutes. Just before serving, in a small saucepan sprayed with butter-flavored cooking spray, combine Italian dressing, Splenda, and Worcestershire sauce. Cook over low heat for 5 minutes or until mixture is heated through, stirring often. Drizzle hot dressing evenly over cold spinach mixture. Toss gently to coat. Serve at once.

Each serving equals:

HE: 2 Vegetable • 1 Protein • ¼ Slider • 3 Optional Calories

108 Calories • 4 gm Fat • 8 gm Protein • 10 gm Carbohydrate • 758 mg Sodium • 56 mg Calcium • 2 gm Fiber

DIABETIC EXCHANGES: 2 Vegetable • 1 Meat

CARB CHOICES: 1

Old-Fashioned Macaroni Salad

Here's a family favorite "slimmed down" to serve just two. It has the same well-loved look and taste of the original you liked to make for a crowd, but now you won't be stuck with tons of leftovers if you're "between potlucks"! ● Serves 2 (¾ cup)

¼ cup Kraft fat-free mayonnaise
2 teaspoons Splenda Granular
2 teaspoons white distilled vinegar
½ teaspoon prepared yellow mustard
⅛ teaspoon black pepper
1 cup cooked elbow macaroni, rinsed and drained
¼ cup chopped celery
2 tablespoons chopped onion
1 hard-boiled egg, chopped

In a medium bowl, combine mayonnaise, Splenda, vinegar, mustard, and black pepper. Add macaroni, celery, and onion. Mix well to combine. Stir in chopped egg. Cover and refrigerate for at least 15 minutes. Gently stir again just before serving.

HINT: Usually ⅔ cup uncooked elbow macaroni cooks to about 1 cup.

Each serving equals:

HE: 1 Bread • ½ Protein • ¼ Vegetable • ¼ Slider • 2 Optional Calories

168 Calories • 4 gm Fat • 7 gm Protein • 26 gm Carbohydrate • 298 mg Sodium • 29 mg Calcium • 2 gm Fiber

DIABETIC EXCHANGES: 2 Starch/Carbohydrate • ½ Meat

CARB CHOICES: 2

Old-Time Potato Salad

It's true that Midwesterners love their old-fashioned cold salads—you won't attend a church supper or school picnic without spotting bowls of them on the buffet! We're proud of holding onto our culinary connection with the good old days—and you will be glad we did when you try this! ☻ Serves 2 (1 cup)

3 tablespoons Kraft fat-free mayonnaise
1 tablespoon sweet pickle relish
1 teaspoon prepared yellow mustard
1 teaspoon white distilled vinegar
2 teaspoons Splenda Granular
⅛ teaspoon black pepper
1¼ cups diced cooked potatoes
6 tablespoons chopped celery
2 tablespoons chopped onion

In a medium bowl, combine mayonnaise, sweet pickle relish, and mustard. Stir in vinegar, Splenda, and black pepper. Add potatoes, celery, and onion. Mix well to combine. Cover and refrigerate for at least 1 hour. Gently stir again just before serving.

Each serving equals:

HE: 1 Bread • ½ Vegetable • ¼ Slider • 7 Optional Calories

120 Calories • 0 gm Fat • 2 gm Protein • 28 gm Carbohydrate • 292 mg Sodium • 20 mg Calcium • 3 gm Fiber

DIABETIC EXCHANGES: 1½ Starch/Carbohydrate

CARB CHOICES: 2

Ranch Potato Salad

For a pleasant change that sends your taste buds on an excursion, stir up this Westernized version of a family favorite! It's cool, it's tangy, and oh so crunchy—what more could you ask?

♥ Serves 2 (1 cup)

> ¼ cup Kraft fat-free mayonnaise
> 2 tablespoons Kraft Fat Free Ranch Dressing
> 1 tablespoon chopped fresh parsley or 1 teaspoon dried
>   parsley flakes
> ⅛ teaspoon black pepper
> 1¼ cups diced cold cooked potatoes
> ½ cup chopped celery
> ¼ cup chopped unpeeled cucumber
> 2 tablespoons chopped green onion
> 1 hard-boiled egg, chopped

In a medium bowl, combine mayonnaise, Ranch dressing, parsley, and black pepper. Add potatoes, celery, cucumber, and green onion. Mix well to combine. Stir in chopped egg. Cover and refrigerate for at least 15 minutes. Gently stir again just before serving.

Each serving equals:

HE: 1 Bread • ¾ Vegetable • ½ Protein • ½ Slider • 4 Optional Calories

180 Calories • 4 gm Fat • 5 gm Protein • 31 gm Carbohydrate • 478 mg Sodium • 40 mg Calcium • 3 gm Fiber

DIABETIC EXCHANGES: 1½ Starch/Carbohydrate • ½ Vegetable • ½ Meat

CARB CHOICES: 2

Creamy German Potato Salad

So many ethnic traditions have a version of potato salad, you can travel the world night after night tasting each and every one! My ancestors brought their recipe from Bohemia in Eastern Europe, so this recipe honors their courage in traveling half a world away from home.   ○   Serves 2 (¾ cup)

> ¼ cup chopped onion
> ¼ cup water
> 1 tablespoon white distilled vinegar
> 1 tablespoon Splenda Granular
> 1 teaspoon all-purpose flour
> ⅛ teaspoon black pepper
> ¼ cup Land O Lakes no-fat sour cream
> 1¼ cups diced cooked potatoes
> ½ teaspoon dried parsley flakes
> 2 tablespoons Oscar Mayer or Hormel Real Bacon Bits

In a medium skillet sprayed with butter-flavored cooking spray, sauté onion for 5 minutes. Add water, vinegar, Splenda, flour, and black pepper. Mix well to combine. Continue cooking for 1 to 2 minutes or until mixture thickens, stirring often. Remove from heat and let cool for 5 minutes. Stir in sour cream. Add potatoes, parsley flakes, and bacon bits. Mix well to combine. Return skillet to heat and continue cooking for 2 to 3 minutes or until mixture is heated through, stirring often. Serve at once.

Each serving equals:

HE: 1 Bread • ½ Protein • ¼ Vegetable • ¼ Slider • 17 Optional Calories

145 Calories • 1 gm Fat • 6 gm Protein • 28 gm Carbohydrate •
269 mg Sodium • 52 mg Calcium • 2 gm Fiber

DIABETIC EXCHANGES: 1½ Starch/Carbohydrate • ½ Meat

CARB CHOICES: 2

Greek Cucumber Romaine Salad

I've never been to Greece, but I was thrilled when grocery stores around the country started carrying feta cheese! It's perfect for stirring into a crunchy and fresh-tasting salad like this one, giving it a little Mediterranean style you can't resist!

◑ Serves 2 (1¼ cups)

> 2 tablespoons Kraft Fat Free Ranch Dressing
> 2 tablespoons Kraft Fat Free Italian Dressing
> 2 teaspoons Splenda Granular
> ½ teaspoon dried basil
> 1 cup diced unpeeled cucumber
> 1½ cups torn Romaine lettuce
> ¼ cup diced fresh tomatoes
> ¼ cup crumbled feta cheese

In a medium bowl, combine Ranch dressing, Italian dressing, Splenda, and basil. Add cucumber and romaine lettuce. Mix well to combine. Stir in tomatoes and feta cheese. Cover and refrigerate for at least 10 minutes. Gently stir again just before serving.

Each serving equals:

HE: 1½ Vegetable • ½ Protein • ¼ Slider • 10 Optional Calories

97 Calories • 5 gm Fat • 4 gm Protein • 9 gm Carbohydrate • 549 mg Sodium • 130 mg Calcium • 2 gm Fiber

DIABETIC EXCHANGES: 1½ Vegetable • ½ Meat • ½ Other Carbohydrate

CARB CHOICES: 1

Mini Chef Salad

I've never met "the chef" who invented this restaurant classic, but I'm grateful to whoever tossed bits of this and that into a main dish salad. This petite version might be enough for a light lunch, but it also makes a fine side salad.   ☺   Serves 2

¼ cup Kraft fat-free mayonnaise
2 tablespoons Land O Lakes no-fat sour cream
1 tablespoon reduced-sodium ketchup
1 tablespoon sweet pickle relish
1 teaspoon dried onion flakes
4 cups torn lettuce
½ cup chopped Dubuque 97% fat-free ham or any extra-
     lean ham
1 hard-boiled egg, chopped

In a small bowl, combine mayonnaise, sour cream, ketchup, sweet pickle relish, and onion flakes. For each salad, place 2 cups lettuce on a plate, sprinkle ¼ cup ham over lettuce, arrange half of chopped egg over top, and drizzle about ¼ cup dressing mixture over top of each. Serve at once.

Each serving equals:

HE: 2 Vegetable • 1½ Protein • ½ Slider • 12 Optional Calories

161 Calories • 5 gm Fat • 12 gm Protein • 17 gm Carbohydrate •
702 mg Sodium • 37 mg Calcium • 2 gm Fiber

DIABETIC EXCHANGES: 2 Vegetable • 1½ Meat • ½ Other Carbohydrate

CARB CHOICES: 1

California Pasta Salad

It's the state where so many innovations in food have begun, so I offer this salute to the West Coast—and the hungry cooks who've let their creativity grow as tall as those famous redwoods!

○ Serves 2 (¾ cup)

> ¼ cup Kraft Fat Free Italian Dressing
> 2 tablespoons reduced-sodium ketchup
> ¼ teaspoon Worcestershire sauce
> ¾ cup cooked rotini pasta, rinsed and drained
> ¼ cup finely chopped cucumber
> ¼ cup finely shredded spinach
> ¼ cup finely chopped fresh tomatoes
> 2 tablespoons crumbled feta cheese

In a medium bowl, combine Italian dressing, ketchup, and Worcestershire sauce. Stir in rotini pasta. Add cucumber, spinach, tomatoes, and feta cheese. Mix well to combine. Cover and refrigerate for at least 10 minutes. Gently stir again just before serving.

HINT: Usually ½ cup uncooked rotini pasta cooks to about ¾ cup.

Each serving equals:

HE: ¾ Bread • ½ Vegetable • ¼ Protein • ¼ Slider • 5 Optional Calories

130 Calories • 2 gm Fat • 4 gm Protein • 24 gm Carbohydrate • 409 mg Sodium • 61 mg Calcium • 1 gm Fiber

DIABETIC EXCHANGES: 1½ Starch/Carbohydrate • ½ Vegetable

CARB CHOICES: 1½

Rising Sun Chicken Spaghetti Salad

The fancy "chef" vocabulary for blending the ingredients of different ethnic cuisines is "fusion," and this recipe blends several traditions in one tasty dish. It's colorful, flavorful, and a favorite of all ages. ☮ Serves 2 (1 cup)

> ¼ cup Kraft Fat Free French Dressing
> 1 tablespoon reduced-sodium soy sauce
> ½ teaspoon dried parsley flakes
> 1 cup cooked spaghetti, rinsed and drained
> ½ cup shredded carrots
> ¼ cup chopped celery
> ¼ cup chopped red onion
> 1 cup diced cooked chicken breast

In a medium bowl, combine French dressing, soy sauce, and parsley flakes. Add spaghetti, carrots, celery, and onion. Mix well to combine. Stir in chicken. Cover and refrigerate for at least 10 minutes. Gently stir again just before serving.

HINTS: 1. Usually ⅔ cup broken uncooked spaghetti cooks to about 1 cup.
2. If you don't have leftovers, purchase a chunk of cooked chicken breast from your local deli.

Each serving equals:

HE: 2½ Protein • 1 Bread • 1 Vegetable • ½ Slider • 5 Optional Calories

275 Calories • 3 gm Fat • 26 gm Protein • 36 gm Carbohydrate • 651 mg Sodium • 37 mg Calcium • 4 gm Fiber

DIABETIC EXCHANGES: 2½ Meat • 1½ Starch • 1 Vegetable

CARB CHOICES: 2

Hawaiian Chicken Pasta Salad

When the tropical breezes blow, they carry the luscious scents of whatever's cooking nearby. But this cold salad will require more detective work to discover its island delights—one good-sized forkful will do it!   ☉   Serves 2 (1½ cups)

> 1 (8-ounce) can crushed pineapple, packed in fruit juice, drained
> ¼ cup Kraft fat-free mayonnaise
> 2 teaspoons chopped fresh parsley or ½ teaspoon dried parsley flakes
> 1 (5-ounce) can chicken, packed in water, drained and flaked
> ¾ cup cooked rotini pasta, rinsed and drained
> 1 tablespoon chopped pecans
> 1 cup shredded lettuce

In a medium bowl, combine pineapple, mayonnaise, and parsley. Add chicken, rotini pasta, and pecans. Mix well to combine. Cover and refrigerate for at least 10 minutes. Just before serving, stir in lettuce.

HINT: Usually ½ cup uncooked rotini pasta cooks to about ¾ cup.

Each serving equals:

HE: 2½ Protein • 1 Fruit • ¾ Bread • ½ Vegetable • ½ Fat • ¼ Slider

282 Calories • 6 gm Fat • 25 gm Protein • 32 gm Carbohydrate • 298 mg Sodium • 32 mg Calcium • 3 gm Fiber

DIABETIC EXCHANGES: 2½ Meat • 1 Fruit • 1 Starch/Carbohydrate • ½ Vegetable • ½ Fat

CARB CHOICES: 2

Broccoli, Ham, and Cheese Toss

Few vegetables deliver more bite and crunch than fresh broccoli, so I've made it the heart of this main dish salad! It's a great solution when you're not in the mood for a ham-and-cheese sandwich but still want to enjoy those flavors. ☻ Serves 2 (1 cup)

> 2 tablespoons Kraft Fat Free Ranch Dressing
> ¼ cup Kraft fat-free mayonnaise
> 1 teaspoon dried onion flakes
> 1½ teaspoons Grey Poupon Country Style Dijon Mustard
> 1 cup chopped fresh broccoli
> ¾ cup cooked rotini pasta, rinsed and drained
> ½ cup diced Dubuque 97% fat-free ham or any extra-lean ham
> 2 (¾-ounce) slices Kraft reduced-fat Swiss cheese, shredded

In a medium bowl, combine Ranch dressing, mayonnaise, onion flakes, and mustard. Add broccoli, rotini pasta, and ham. Mix well to combine. Stir in Swiss cheese. Cover and refrigerate for at least 15 minutes. Gently stir again just before serving.

HINT: Usually ½ cup uncooked rotini pasta cooks to about ¾ cup.

Each serving equals:

HE: 2 Protein • 1 Vegetable • ¾ Bread • ½ Slider • 6 Optional Calories

251 Calories • 7 gm Fat • 18 gm Protein • 29 gm Carbohydrate • 961 mg Sodium • 222 mg Calcium • 2 gm Fiber

DIABETIC EXCHANGES: 2 Meat • 1½ Starch/Carbohydrate • ½ Vegetable

CARB CHOICES: 2

Layered Spinach and Ham Salad

If you don't already have a pretty glass bowl, this recipe should inspire you to pick one up at your local thrift store or neighborhood garage sale! Food that looks appetizing and pretty tastes even better, so it's worth taking the time to layer these ingredients in a super-duper salad "parfait"! ☺ Serves 2 (1½ cups)

> 2 cups torn fresh spinach, stems removed and discarded
> 1 hard-boiled egg, chopped
> ½ cup diced Dubuque 97% fat-free ham or any extra-lean ham
> ¼ cup chopped red onion
> ½ cup frozen peas, thawed
> ¼ cup Kraft fat-free mayonnaise
> 2 tablespoons Land O Lakes no-fat sour cream
> 2 tablespoons Oscar Mayer or Hormel Real Bacon Bits

In a clear glass medium bowl, layer half of the spinach, half of the chopped egg, half of the ham, half of the onion, and half of the peas. Repeat layers. In a small bowl, combine mayonnaise and sour cream. Carefully spread mayonnaise mixture over top of salad. Sprinkle bacon bits over top. Cover and refrigerate for at least 1 hour. When serving, evenly spoon salad mixture onto serving plates.

Each serving equals:

HE: 1½ Protein • 1¼ Vegetable • ½ Bread • ¼ Slider • 15 Optional Calories

182 Calories • 6 gm Fat • 16 gm Protein • 16 gm Carbohydrate • 847 mg Sodium • 78 mg Calcium • 3 gm Fiber

DIABETIC EXCHANGES: 1½ Meat • 1 Vegetable • 1 Starch/Carbohydrate

CARB CHOICES: 1

Vegetable Combos

The fashion police tell us not to wear stripes with plaids or polka dots with paisley (until some hot foreign designer decides it's *new* and *cool!*). Well, you won't find me playing kitchen police and telling you what vegetables you can and can't combine—that's always up to you.

But I enjoy thinking about unusual pairings when it comes to food, combining textures (crunchy, soft) and colors (red, yellow, green) along with flavors (tangy, sweet, spicy) and temperatures (mild, medium, or hot-hot-hot!). If variety is the spice of life, it's also the name of the game when designing veggie dishes that don't just fill up space on a big white plate!

Tired of basic carrots? Go for Sweet and Sour Carrots, Parslied Carrots, or Zucchini Carrot Sauté! *Done with good old reliable green beans? Stir up* Parmesan Green Beans, Thai Green Beans, or—oh, yes, Deviled Green Beans! *Ready to retire all those cans of corn? Don't do it—serve* Fiesta Corn or Tex-Mex Tomato Corn Sauté *tonight!*

Green Beans with Water Chestnuts

Whenever I create recipes, I think a lot about texture—and crunch in particular. Eating satisfaction isn't just about flavor, and a dish like this one satisfies in part because of the chopped bits of water chestnut. ☺ Serves 2 (1 full cup)

2 cups frozen cut green beans, thawed
¼ cup chopped onion
2 tablespoons water
1 (8-ounce) can water chestnuts, rinsed, drained, and
    chopped
1 (2-ounce) jar chopped pimiento, drained
2 teaspoons Splenda Granular
2 teaspoons I Can't Believe It's Not Butter! Light Margarine
⅛ teaspoon black pepper

In a medium skillet sprayed with butter-flavored cooking spray, combine green beans, onion, and water. Cover and cook over medium heat for 8 to 10 minutes, stirring occasionally. Add water chestnuts, pimiento, Splenda, margarine, and black pepper. Mix well to combine. Continue cooking, uncovered, for 5 minutes or until mixture is heated through and most of liquid is absorbed, stirring occasionally.

HINT: Thaw green beans by rinsing in a colander under hot water for 1 minute.

Each serving equals:

HE: 2¾ Vegetable • ½ Fat • 2 Optional Calories

90 Calories • 2 gm Fat • 3 gm Protein • 15 gm Carbohydrate • 64 mg Sodium •
42 mg Calcium • 4 gm Fiber

DIABETIC EXCHANGES: 3 Vegetable • ½ Fat

CARB CHOICES: ½

Green Beans with Mushrooms

Here's a veggie dish that is sure to become a regular on your evening menu! It's simple, it's flavorful, and it looks as if you've fussed for ages over a hot stove to make the creamy sauce. (I won't tell if you won't!)   ☻   Serves 2 (1 cup)

> 2 cups frozen cut green beans, thawed
> ½ cup sliced fresh mushrooms
> ¼ cup chopped onion
> 2 teaspoons I Can't Believe It's Not Butter! Light Margarine
> 2 tablespoons Land O Lakes Fat Free Half & Half
> ½ teaspoon lemon pepper

In a medium skillet sprayed with butter-flavored cooking spray, sauté green beans, mushrooms, and onion for 8 to 10 minutes. Stir in margarine, half & half, and lemon pepper. Continue cooking for 2 to 3 minutes or until mixture is heated through, stirring often.

HINT: Thaw green beans by rinsing in a colander under hot water for 1 minute.

Each serving equals:

HE: 2½ Vegetable • ½ Fat • 9 Optional Calories

---

82 Calories • 2 gm Fat • 3 gm Protein • 13 gm Carbohydrate • 195 mg Sodium • 87 mg Calcium • 4 gm Fiber

---

DIABETIC EXCHANGES: 2½ Vegetable • ½ Fat

CARB CHOICES: 1

Kraut and Green Beans

Are you surprised to find a dish that combines sauerkraut—an ingredient usually eaten on its own—with good old green beans? I thought, we love sauerkraut, and we also love green beans, so why not partner them up for a change of pace?

○ Serves 2 (¾ cup)

> ¼ cup chopped onion
> 1 (8-ounce) can sauerkraut, well drained
> 1 (8-ounce) can cut green beans, rinsed and drained
> 2 tablespoons water
> 2 tablespoons reduced-sodium ketchup
> 2 teaspoons Splenda Granular
> ⅛ teaspoon black pepper

In a medium saucepan sprayed with butter-flavored cooking spray, sauté onion for 5 minutes. Stir in sauerkraut, green beans, and water. Add ketchup, Splenda, and black pepper. Mix well to combine. Lower heat and simmer for 5 minutes, stirring occasionally.

Each serving equals:

HE: 2¼ Vegetable • 17 Optional Calories

64 Calories • 0 gm Fat • 1 gm Protein • 15 gm Carbohydrate • 589 mg Sodium • 23 mg Calcium • 2 gm Fiber

DIABETIC EXCHANGES: 2 Vegetable

CARB CHOICES: 1

Piquant Green Beans

Don't let the name puzzle you—the word *piquant* is from the French and means pleasantly tart or sharp. This dish has a tangy flavor that will definitely awaken your taste buds and fill your mouth with a bit of sizzle!   ☻   Serves 2 (¾ cup)

¼ *cup finely chopped onion*
1 (15-ounce) can cut green beans, rinsed and drained
1 tablespoon white distilled vinegar
1 tablespoon Splenda Granular
1 teaspoon Worcestershire sauce
⅛ *teaspoon black pepper*
2 tablespoons Oscar Mayer or Hormel Real Bacon Bits

In a medium saucepan sprayed with butter-flavored cooking spray, sauté onion for 5 minutes. Stir in green beans. Add vinegar, Splenda, Worcestershire sauce, and black pepper. Mix well to combine. Continue cooking for 5 minutes or until mixture is heated through, stirring often. Just before serving, stir in bacon bits.

Each serving equals:

HE: 2 Vegetable • ½ Protein • 3 Optional Calories

69 Calories • 1 gm Fat • 5 gm Protein • 10 gm Carbohydrate • 807 mg Sodium • 45 mg Calcium • 4 gm Fiber

DIABETIC EXCHANGES: 2 Vegetable • ½ Meat

CARB CHOICES: 1

Deviled Green Beans

Why should deviled eggs get all the praise when you add your dish to the table at a family potluck? These spicy beans offer a wonderful contrast to smooth or cool dishes like cold chicken or traditional potato salads. ☻ Serves 2 (¾ cup)

> 2 teaspoons Grey Poupon County Style Dijon Mustard
> 2 tablespoons Land O Lakes Fat Free Half & Half
> ½ teaspoon Worcestershire sauce
> 1 (15-ounce) can cut green beans, rinsed and drained
> 1 tablespoon dried onion flakes
> 2 teaspoons I Can't Believe It's Not Butter! Light Margarine

In a medium saucepan, combine mustard, half & half, and Worcestershire sauce. Add green beans, onion flakes, and margarine. Mix well to combine. Cook over medium heat for 5 to 6 minutes or until mixture is heated through, stirring occasionally. Serve at once.

Each serving equals:

HE: 2 Vegetable • ½ Fat • 9 Optional Calories

70 Calories • 2 gm Fat • 3 gm Protein • 10 gm Carbohydrate • 611 mg Sodium • 51 mg Calcium • 3 gm Fiber

DIABETIC EXCHANGES: 2 Vegetable • ½ Fat

CARB CHOICES: 1

Catalina Isle Green Beans

Named for the glorious island off the Southern California coast where the wealthy went to play, this sunny dish is a bright and colorful gift to your dinner guests! ☻ Serves 2 (½ cup)

> 2 tablespoons Kraft Fat Free Catalina Dressing
> ½ teaspoon Worcestershire sauce
> 1½ teaspoons dried onion flakes
> 1 (15-ounce) can whole green beans, rinsed and drained
> 1 (2-ounce) jar chopped pimiento, drained

In a medium saucepan, combine Catalina dressing, Worcestershire sauce, and onion flakes. Add green beans and pimiento. Mix well to combine. Cook over medium heat for 5 to 7 minutes or until mixture is heated through, stirring often.

Each serving equals:

HE: 2 Vegetable • 17 Optional Calories

56 Calories • 0 gm Fat • 2 gm Protein • 12 gm Carbohydrate • 588 mg Sodium • 35 mg Calcium • 4 gm Fiber

DIABETIC EXCHANGES: 2 Vegetable

CARB CHOICES: 1

Thai Green Beans

Even if your chances of vacationing in Bangkok are slim to none, you don't have to miss out on this irresistible cuisine, which combines colorful veggies with a peanut-soy glaze that tempts you to head for Asia with every bite! ☻ Serves 2 (scant 1 cup)

> 2 cups fresh or frozen cut green beans, thawed
> ½ cup water
> ½ cup coarsely chopped red bell pepper
> ¼ cup coarsely chopped green onion
> 1 tablespoon Peter Pan reduced-fat creamy peanut butter
> 1 tablespoon reduced-sodium soy sauce
> 1 tablespoon Splenda Granular
> 2 tablespoons coarsely chopped dry-roasted peanuts

In a medium saucepan, combine green beans and water. Cover and cook for 8 to 10 minutes or just until beans are tender. Drain well. Meanwhile, in a medium skillet sprayed with butter-flavored cooking spray, sauté red pepper and green onion for 5 minutes. Stir in drained green beans. Continue to sauté for 3 to 4 minutes. Add peanut butter, soy sauce, and Splenda. Mix well to combine. Continue to sauté for 2 to 3 minutes or until mixture is heated through and peanut butter is melted, stirring often. When serving, sprinkle 1 tablespoon peanuts over top of each serving.

HINT: Thaw green beans by rinsing in a colander under hot water for 1 minute.

Each serving equals:

HE: 2¾ Vegetable • 1 Fat • ¾ Protein • 3 Optional Calories

155 Calories • 7 gm Fat • 6 gm Protein • 17 gm Carbohydrate • 812 mg Sodium • 44 mg Calcium • 5 gm Fiber

DIABETIC EXCHANGES: 2½ Vegetable • 1 Fat • ½ Meat

CARB CHOICES: 1

Parmesan Green Beans

No time to cook, and ravenous as all get-out? Put a sticky note on this page of the cookbook, so you'll always be ready to get something tasty on the table in under 10 minutes! You'll be glad you did.

● Serves 2 (¾ cup)

1 (15-ounce) can cut green beans, rinsed and drained
½ teaspoon Italian seasoning
2 teaspoons Splenda Granular
2 teaspoons I Can't Believe It's Not Butter! Light Margarine
¼ cup Kraft Reduced Fat Parmesan Style Grated Topping ☆

In a small saucepan sprayed with butter-flavored cooking spray, combine green beans, Italian seasoning, and Splenda. Add margarine and 2 tablespoons Parmesan cheese. Mix gently just to combine. Cook over medium heat for 5 minutes or until mixture is heated through, stirring often. When serving, top each with 1 tablespoon Parmesan cheese.

Each serving equals:

HE: 1¾ Vegetable • ½ Protein • ½ Fat • 2 Optional Calories

109 Calories • 5 gm Fat • 3 gm Protein • 13 gm Carbohydrate •
285 mg Sodium • 139 mg Calcium • 3 gm Fiber

DIABETIC EXCHANGES: 2 Vegetable • ½ Meat • ½ Fat

CARB CHOICES: 1

Sweet and Sour Carrots

As vegetables go, carrots have a naturally higher sugar content than others, which means it makes a perfect pair when combined with a sweetener like Splenda. But to counteract all that sweetness, I added a touch of sour/tangy flavor using vinegar. The combination? A real winner! ☻ Serves 2 (¾ cup)

½ cup chopped onion
1 (15-ounce) can sliced carrots, rinsed and drained
2 tablespoons white distilled vinegar
2 tablespoons Splenda Granular
2 teaspoons I Can't Believe It's Not Butter! Light Margarine
1 teaspoon dried parsley flakes
⅛ teaspoon black pepper

In a medium saucepan sprayed with butter-flavored cooking spray, sauté onion for 5 minutes. Stir in carrots. Add vinegar, Splenda, margarine, parsley flakes, and black pepper. Mix well to combine. Lower heat and simmer for 6 to 8 minutes, stirring occasionally.

Each serving equals:

HE: 2½ Vegetable • ½ Fat • 6 Optional Calories

70 Calories • 2 gm Fat • 1 gm Protein • 12 gm Carbohydrate • 212 mg Sodium • 39 mg Calcium • 2 gm Fiber

DIABETIC EXCHANGES: 2½ Vegetable • ½ Fat

CARB CHOICES: 1

Carrot and Apple Medley

Here's a delightful accompaniment to a hearty meal of pork or turkey, both of which pair up beautifully with the sweetness of carrots and apples. The maple syrup perks up the fruit, while the onion keeps it a veggie dish, not a dessert.

Serves 2 (¾ cup)

½ cup chopped onion
1½ cups shredded carrots
1 cup (1 medium) unpeeled and diced tart cooking apples
2 tablespoons Log Cabin Sugar Free Maple Syrup
2 teaspoons I Can't Believe It's Not Butter! Light Margarine

In a large skillet sprayed with butter-flavored cooking spray, sauté onion for 5 minutes. Stir in carrots and apples. Continue to sauté for 5 minutes. Add maple syrup and margarine. Mix well to combine. Lower heat and simmer for 2 to 3 minutes or until mixture is heated through, stirring occasionally.

Each serving equals:

HE: 2 Vegetable • ½ Fruit • ½ Fat • 9 Optional Calories

106 Calories • 2 gm Fat • 1 gm Protein • 21 gm Carbohydrate • 129 mg Sodium • 40 mg Calcium • 4 gm Fiber

DIABETIC EXCHANGES: 2 Vegetable • ½ Fruit • ½ Fat

CARB CHOICES: 1

Parslied Carrots

If there's too much "white" on your dinner plate, whether you're serving chicken breast or turkey, or even pork, here's a great antidote to "pale"—bright orange carrots that look snazzy with parsley sprinkled on top!   ☯   Serves 2 (¾ cup)

> 1 (15-ounce) can sliced carrots, rinsed and drained
> 1 tablespoon I Can't Believe It's Not Butter! Light Margarine
> 1 tablespoon chopped fresh parsley or 1 teaspoon dried
>   parsley flakes

In a medium saucepan sprayed with butter-flavored cooking spray, combine carrots, margarine, and parsley flakes. Cook over medium heat for 5 minutes or until mixture is heated through, stirring often.

Each serving equals:

HE: 2 Vegetable • ¾ Fat

75 Calories • 3 gm Fat • 2 gm Protein • 10 gm Carbohydrate • 406 mg Sodium • 39 mg Calcium • 3 gm Fiber

DIABETIC EXCHANGES: 2 Vegetable • ½ Fat

CARB CHOICES: 1

Zucchini Carrot Sauté

An easy skillet vegetable dish is great to have on hand when you walk in the door exhausted after a long day at work. Plug in your food processor, shred those carrots and zucchini in just a few bursts, and you've almost got food on the table!

◐ Serves 2 (1 cup)

> ½ cup chopped onion
> 1½ cups shredded carrots
> 1 cup shredded zucchini
> 2 teaspoons I Can't Believe It's Not Butter! Light Margarine
> 2 tablespoons Kraft Fat Free Catalina Dressing

In a medium saucepan sprayed with butter-flavored cooking spray, sauté onion for 5 minutes. Stir in carrots and zucchini. Add margarine and Catalina dressing. Mix well to combine. Continue to sauté for 5 to 6 minutes or just until vegetables are tender.

Each serving equals:

HE: 3 Vegetable • ½ Fat • 17 Optional Calories

98 Calories • 2 gm Fat • 2 gm Protein • 18 gm Carbohydrate • 269 mg Sodium • 46 mg Calcium • 4 gm Fiber

DIABETIC EXCHANGES: 2½ Vegetable • ½ Fat

CARB CHOICES: 1

Simmered Carrots and Corn

Terrific teammates, carrots and corn are a recipe for sweet satisfaction—and this pantry pleaser can be prepared from foods you keep on hand in cabinet and freezer. White or yellow corn? You decide! ☺ Serves 2 (full ½ cup)

> ½ cup frozen whole-kernel corn, thawed
> 1 (8-ounce) can sliced carrots, rinsed and drained
> 1 tablespoon water
> 2 teaspoons dried onion flakes
> ½ teaspoon lemon pepper
> 2 teaspoons I Can't Believe It's Not Butter! Light Margarine

In a small saucepan sprayed with butter-flavored cooking spray, combine corn, carrots, and water. Stir in onion flakes and lemon pepper. Add margarine. Mix well to combine. Cook over medium-low heat for 8 to 10 minutes or until mixture is heated through, stirring often.

HINT: Thaw corn by rinsing in a colander under hot water for 1 minute.

Each serving equals:

HE: 1 Vegetable • ½ Bread • ½ Fat

90 Calories • 2 gm Fat • 2 gm Protein • 16 gm Carbohydrate • 382 mg Sodium • 26 mg Calcium • 3 gm Fiber

DIABETIC EXCHANGES: 1 Vegetable • ½ Starch • ½ Fat

CARB CHOICES: 1

Chinese Cabbage

I could give you a bunch of reasons why I serve cabbage often, but I only need one, and this recipe provides it: cabbage is delicious! (And nutritious, too!) ☉ Serves 2 (1 cup)

> 1 tablespoon + 1 teaspoon I Can't Believe It's Not Butter!
>   Light Margarine
> 1½ cups shredded cabbage
> ½ cup chopped celery
> ½ cup chopped green bell pepper
> ½ cup chopped onion
> 2 tablespoons reduced-sodium soy sauce
> ⅛ teaspoon black pepper

In a medium skillet sprayed with butter-flavored cooking spray, melt margarine. Add cabbage, celery, green pepper, and onion. Mix well to combine. Cover and cook over medium-low heat for 5 minutes or just until vegetables are tender, stirring occasionally. Stir in soy sauce and black pepper. Serve at once.

Each serving equals:

HE: 2¼ Vegetable • 1 Fat

96 Calories • 4 gm Fat • 3 gm Protein • 12 gm Carbohydrate • 662 mg Sodium • 60 mg Calcium • 3 gm Fiber

DIABETIC EXCHANGES: 2 Vegetable • 1 Fat

CARB CHOICES: 1

Sautéed Peas and Cabbage

It's been such fun making creamy sauces using the wonderful fat-free half & half products on the market. If you love cream sauce but have denied yourself the pleasure for health or dietary reasons, join me on a journey to the land of culinary delight . . . and enjoy what you love. ☻ Serves 2 (1 cup)

> 1½ cups shredded cabbage
> ¾ cup frozen peas, thawed
> 2 tablespoons Land O Lakes Fat Free Half & Half
> 2 teaspoons I Can't Believe It's Not Butter! Light Margarine
> 1 teaspoon dried parsley flakes
> ½ teaspoon lemon pepper

In a medium skillet sprayed with butter-flavored cooking spray, sauté cabbage for 5 minutes. Add peas. Mix well to combine. Stir in half & half, margarine, parsley flakes, and lemon pepper. Continue cooking for 4 to 5 minutes or until mixture is heated through, stirring often.

HINT: Thaw peas by rinsing in a colander under hot water for 1 minute.

Each serving equals:

HE: ¾ Bread • ¾ Vegetable • ½ Fat • 9 Optional Calories

82 Calories • 2 gm Fat • 4 gm Protein • 12 gm Carbohydrate • 230 mg Sodium • 60 mg Calcium • 4 gm Fiber

DIABETIC EXCHANGES: 1 Starch • ½ Vegetable • ½ Fat

CARB CHOICES: 1

Creamed Peas and Carrots

Are you one of the many people who've given up your favorite creamed veggie dishes because you're watching your cholesterol and keeping life low-fat? Then I'm thrilled to bring you this luscious dish that looks and tastes sinful but is actually good for you!

○ Serves 2 (¾ cup)

½ cup fat-free milk
¼ cup Land O Lakes Fat Free Half & Half
1 tablespoon all-purpose flour
1½ cups frozen peas & carrots, thawed
1 teaspoon dried parsley flakes
⅛ teaspoon black pepper
2 teaspoons I Can't Believe It's Not Butter! Light Margarine

In a covered jar, combine milk, half & half, and flour. Shake well to blend. Pour mixture into a medium saucepan sprayed with butter-flavored cooking spray. Add peas & carrots, parsley flakes, and black pepper. Mix well to combine. Cook over medium heat for 5 minutes or until mixture thickens and is heated through, stirring often. Just before serving, stir in margarine.

HINT: Thaw peas & carrots by rinsing in a colander under hot water for 1 minute.

Each serving equals:

HE: 1 Vegetable • ½ Bread • ½ Fat • ¼ Fat Free Milk • 18 Optional Calories

127 Calories • 3 gm Fat • 6 gm Protein • 19 gm Carbohydrate •
183 mg Sodium • 132 mg Calcium • 3 gm Fiber

DIABETIC EXCHANGES: 1 Vegetable • 1 Starch • ½ Fat

CARB CHOICES: 1

Italian Corn

Stirring up your own saucy sides is easier when you start with a favorite salad dressing! This dish is brightly colored *and* brightly flavored, too. *Bravo* to the cook! ☻ Serves 2 (½ cup)

>1 cup frozen whole-kernel corn, thawed
>1 (2.5-ounce) jar sliced mushrooms, chopped and drained
>1 (2-ounce) jar chopped pimiento, drained
>2 tablespoons Kraft Fat Free Italian Dressing
>1 teaspoon Splenda Granular
>⅛ teaspoon black pepper

In a medium saucepan sprayed with butter-flavored cooking spray, combine corn, mushrooms, and pimiento. Add Italian dressing, Splenda, and black pepper. Mix well to combine. Cook over medium heat for 5 to 7 minutes or until mixture is heated through, stirring occasionally.

HINT: Thaw corn by rinsing in a colander under hot water for 1 minute.

Each serving equals:

HE: 1 Bread • ½ Vegetable • 11 Optional Calories

112 Calories • 0 gm Fat • 4 gm Protein • 24 gm Carbohydrate • 387 mg Sodium • 16 mg Calcium • 4 gm Fiber

DIABETIC EXCHANGES: 1 Starch • ½ Vegetable

CARB CHOICES: 1½

Fiesta Corn

Strike up the band, break out the buffet, and party 'til everyone collapses into a chair! This festive dish is so simple to prepare, you're sure to make it a regular on your table all year-round.

● Serves 2 (½ cup)

¼ cup chopped onion
½ cup chunky salsa (mild, medium, or hot)
2 teaspoons Splenda Granular
½ teaspoon chili seasoning
1 cup frozen whole-kernel corn, thawed

In a medium saucepan sprayed with butter-flavored cooking spray, sauté onion for 5 minutes. Stir in salsa, Splenda, and chili seasoning. Add corn. Mix well to combine. Continue cooking for 5 to 7 minutes or until mixture is heated through, stirring often.

HINT: Thaw corn by rinsing in a colander under hot water for 1 minute.

Each serving equals:

HE: 1 Bread • ¾ Vegetable • 2 Optional Calories

112 Calories • 0 gm Fat • 3 gm Protein • 25 gm Carbohydrate •
450 mg Sodium • 8 mg Calcium • 3 gm Fiber

DIABETIC EXCHANGES: 1 Starch • ½ Vegetable

CARB CHOICES: 2

Deviled Corn

It wouldn't be an Iowan's cookbook without lots of tasty corn dishes, and this is one of my taste testers' new favorites. (Yes, they were all from Iowa, so maybe they were a bit biased in favor of this local love!) It's sweet and tangy, creamy and rich—and it's ready in no time at all. ☻ Serves 2 (½ cup)

> 2 teaspoons Grey Poupon Country Style Dijon Mustard
> 2 teaspoons I Can't Believe It's Not Butter! Light Margarine
> 1 tablespoon Land O Lakes Fat Free Half & Half
> 2 teaspoons Splenda Granular
> 1 teaspoon dried onion flakes
> 1 teaspoon dried parsley flakes
> 1 cup frozen whole-kernel corn, thawed

In a small saucepan, combine mustard, margarine, and half & half. Add Splenda, onion flakes, and parsley flakes. Mix well to combine. Stir in corn. Cover and cook on medium-low heat for 5 to 7 minutes or until mixture is heated through, stirring occasionally.

HINT: Thaw corn by rinsing in a colander under hot water for 1 minute.

Each serving equals:

HE: 1 Bread • ½ Fat • 6 Optional Calories

110 Calories • 2 gm Fat • 3 gm Protein • 20 gm Carbohydrate • 180 mg Sodium • 13 mg Calcium • 2 gm Fiber

DIABETIC EXCHANGES: 1 Starch • ½ Fat

CARB CHOICES: 1

Tex-Mex Tomato Corn Sauté

I'm always careful not to create recipes that leave you with inconvenient leftovers in the fridge, and this one is no exception. You don't have to purchase the tiniest peppers or onions out there—just chop up the whole pepper, then bag up what you don't need, and freeze it!　◐　Serves 2 (¾ cup)

¼ cup chopped green bell pepper
¼ cup chopped red bell pepper
¼ cup chopped onion
1½ cups peeled and chopped fresh tomatoes
1 cup fresh or frozen whole-kernel corn, thawed
2 tablespoons Splenda Granular
¾ teaspoon chili seasoning
⅛ teaspoon black pepper

In a medium skillet sprayed with butter-flavored cooking spray, sauté green pepper, red pepper, and onion for 5 minutes. Add tomatoes, corn, Splenda, chili seasoning, and black pepper. Mix well to combine. Lower heat and simmer for 12 to 14 minutes, stirring occasionally.

HINT: Thaw corn by rinsing in a colander under hot water for 1 minute.

Each serving equals:

HE: 2¼ Vegetable • 1 Bread • 6 Optional Calories

136 Calories • 0 gm Fat • 4 gm Protein • 30 gm Carbohydrate • 41 mg Sodium • 25 mg Calcium • 4 gm Fiber

DIABETIC EXCHANGES: 2 Vegetable • 1 Starch

CARB CHOICES: 2

San Antonio Mixed Veggies

I've experimented with lots of brands of mixed vegetables over the years, and I've liked some more than others. I'm leaving it up to you which kind you prefer, so you can take advantage of store sales and family favorites.   ☻   Serves 2 (½ cup)

1½ cups frozen mixed vegetables, thawed
¼ cup water
1 tablespoon I Can't Believe It's Not Butter! Light Margarine
2 teaspoons Splenda Granular
¼ teaspoon chili seasoning

In a medium saucepan, combine mixed vegetables and water. Cook over medium heat for 6 to 8 minutes or just until vegetables are tender, stirring occasionally. Drain well and return vegetables to saucepan. Add margarine, Splenda, and chili seasoning. Mix well to combine. Continue cooking for 3 to 4 minutes or until mixture is heated through, stirring often.

HINT: Thaw mixed vegetables by rinsing in a colander under hot water for 1 minute.

Each serving equals:

HE: 1 Vegetable • ¾ Fat • ½ Bread • 2 Optional Calories

115 Calories • 3 gm Fat • 4 gm Protein • 18 gm Carbohydrate •
117 mg Sodium • 36 mg Calcium • 6 gm Fiber

DIABETIC EXCHANGES: 1 Vegetable • 1 Fat • ½ Starch

CARB CHOICES: 1

Parmesan Stewed Tomatoes

This dish may surprise you with its scrumptious combination of flavors, from the sweetness of the tomatoes (deftly partnered with Splenda) to the savory blend of Italian seasoning and Parmesan cheese. *Delicioso!*   ☻   Serves 2 (1 cup)

½ cup chopped onion
1 (15-ounce) can diced tomatoes, undrained
2 teaspoons I Can't Believe It's Not Butter! Light Margarine
½ teaspoon Italian seasoning
1 tablespoon Splenda Granular
2 slices reduced-calorie Italian or white bread, torn into
    large pieces
2 tablespoons Kraft Reduced Fat Parmesan Style Grated
    Topping

In a medium skillet sprayed with olive oil–flavored cooking spray, sauté onion for 5 minutes. Stir in undrained tomatoes, margarine, Italian seasoning, and Splenda. Add bread pieces and Parmesan cheese. Mix well to combine. Lower heat and simmer for 5 to 6 minutes, stirring occasionally.

Each serving equals:

HE: 2½ Vegetable • ½ Bread • ½ Fat • ¼ Protein • 3 Optional Calories

143 Calories • 3 gm Fat • 5 gm Protein • 24 gm Carbohydrate •
507 mg Sodium • 106 mg Calcium • 4 gm Fiber

DIABETIC EXCHANGES: 2½ Vegetable • ½ Starch • ½ Fat

CARB CHOICES: 1½

Stove Top Onion au Gratin

Cheesy and lush, this combo of melted cheese and onions offers a terrific contrast to grilled meats. It's also incredibly good, reheated the next day, on top of leftover beef or pork as a sandwich topping . . . sort of a cousin to the Philly cheesesteak.

☻ Serves 2 (¾ cup)

> 1½ cups coarsely chopped onion
> ½ cup fat-free milk
> 1 tablespoon all-purpose flour
> ½ cup diced Velveeta Light processed cheese
> 1 teaspoon dried parsley flakes
> ⅛ teaspoon black pepper

In a large skillet sprayed with butter-flavored cooking spray, sauté onion for 6 to 8 minutes. In a covered jar, combine milk and flour. Shake well to blend. Pour milk mixture into onion. Add Velveeta cheese, parsley flakes, and black pepper. Mix well to combine. Lower heat and simmer for 5 to 6 minutes or until mixture thickens and cheese melts, stirring occasionally.

Each serving equals:

HE: 1½ Vegetable • 1 Protein • ¼ Fat Free Milk • 15 Optional Calories

147 Calories • 3 gm Fat • 9 gm Protein • 21 gm Carbohydrate •
479 mg Sodium • 268 mg Calcium • 2 gm Fiber

DIABETIC EXCHANGES: 1½ Vegetable • 1 Meat • ½ Starch/Carbohydrate

CARB CHOICES: 1

Vegetable Bake

Here's the clever thing—individually baked servings look so special, and yet it's the easiest way to prepare just the right amount for two diners. They also take up less room in your fridge or freezer (if you make two but eat just one tonight)! ☻ Serves 2

¼ cup chopped onion
¼ cup chopped red bell pepper
½ cup chopped unpeeled zucchini
½ cup frozen chopped broccoli, thawed
1 cup frozen sliced carrots, thawed
½ cup fat-free milk
¼ cup Land O Lakes Fat Free Half & Half
2 tablespoons all-purpose flour
⅛ teaspoon black pepper
¼ cup shredded Kraft reduced-fat Cheddar cheese
2 teaspoons I Can't Believe It's Not Butter! Light
    Margarine
2 Ritz Reduced Fat Crackers, made into crumbs

Preheat oven to 350 degrees. Spray two (10-ounce) ovenproof custard cups with butter-flavored cooking spray. In a medium skillet sprayed with butter-flavored cooking spray, sauté onion, red pepper, and zucchini for 3 minutes. Stir in broccoli and carrots. Continue to sauté for 2 to 3 minutes. Evenly spoon vegetables into prepared custard cups. In a covered jar, combine milk, half & half, flour, and black pepper. Shake well to blend. Pour milk mixture into same skillet vegetables were sautéed in. Add Cheddar cheese and margarine. Mix well to combine. Cook over medium heat for 2 to 3 minutes or until mixture thickens and cheese melts, stirring often. Evenly spoon sauce over vegetables. Sprinkle cracker crumbs evenly over top. Place prepared custard cups on a baking sheet. Bake for 20 to 25 minutes.

HINT: Thaw broccoli and carrots by rinsing in a colander under
    hot water for 1 minute.

Each serving equals:

HE: 2½ Vegetable • ½ Bread • ½ Protein • ½ Fat • ¼ Fat Free Milk • ¼ Slider • 19 Optional Calories

209 Calories • 5 gm Fat • 12 gm Protein • 29 gm Carbohydrate • 331 mg Sodium • 277 mg Calcium • 4 gm Fiber

DIABETIC EXCHANGES: 2 Vegetable • 1 Starch/Carbohydrate • ½ Meat • ½ Fat

CARB CHOICES: 2

Succulent Succotash

There are dozens of recipes for this Native American specialty, but I think you'll agree (after a bite or three) that this one might just be the richest and creamiest of all! Even if you're not a lima bean lover, give this a chance. Lima beans are loaded with good nutrition, and change is good for the soul! ☻ Serves 2 (½ cup)

> ½ cup frozen whole-kernel corn, thawed
> ½ cup frozen baby lima beans, thawed
> ¼ cup water
> 2 tablespoons Land O Lakes Fat Free Half & Half
> 1 tablespoon Land O Lakes no-fat sour cream
> 1 tablespoon I Can't Believe It's Not Butter! Light Margarine
> 2 teaspoons Splenda Granular
> 1 teaspoon dried parsley flakes
> ⅛ teaspoon black pepper

In a medium saucepan, combine corn, lima beans, and water. Cook over medium heat for 5 minutes or just until vegetables are tender. Drain well and return to saucepan. Add half & half, sour cream, margarine, Splenda, parsley flakes, and black pepper. Mix well to combine. Continue cooking for 5 to 6 minutes or until mixture is heated through, stirring occasionally.

HINT: Thaw corn and lima beans by rinsing in a colander under hot water for one minute.

Each serving equals:

HE: 1 Bread • ¾ Fat • 19 Optional Calories

131 Calories • 3 gm Fat • 5 gm Protein • 21 gm Carbohydrate •
122 mg Sodium • 43 mg Calcium • 3 gm Fiber

DIABETIC EXCHANGES: 1 Starch • 1 Fat

CARB CHOICES: 1

Two "Sides" To
Every Story

For many cooks, side dishes are just an afterthought, something you deal with once the main dish is decided. But I've always believed that sides are an integral part of any meal, especially when you're dealing with dietary concerns or health issues. Why? Because you might be eating a much smaller piece of meat, for example, or even none at all. How do you keep from feeling deprived? By celebrating with side dishes that dazzle the senses and delight the palate!

Now, are you one of those diners who eat all of one food before moving to the next part of the plate, or do you "eat around," tasting a bit of everything until it's all finished? We develop these habits in childhood, and it takes some extra effort to change what you've always done. But I believe you'll find that training yourself to eat a little of each element will produce more satisfaction at meal's end.

Mmm-mm, what should you choose from this slate of "supporting actors"? Grande Vegetable Pilaf *is a pretty choice to go with lots of different entrees;* Parmesan Noodles *is another dish worth absolutely every carb it "costs"! And if potatoes are your splurge of choice, dig into* Potato Broccoli Bake *or* Creamy Scalloped Potatoes, *and forgive yourself for any extra-loud "oohs and ahhs"!*

Fruit Stuffing

With holiday time just around the corner (as I'm writing this book), I had such fun creating this yummy stuffing that doesn't need to be baked inside any bird! It gets beautifully crusty in the oven and makes an ordinary weekday dinner seem like a party.

● Serves 2

½ cup finely chopped celery
¼ cup finely chopped onion
3 slices reduced-calorie white bread, torn into pieces
1 tablespoon seedless raisins
½ cup (1 small) cored, peeled, and chopped cooking apple
¼ cup unsweetened apple juice
¼ cup water
1 tablespoon Splenda Granular
1 teaspoon dried parsley flakes
½ teaspoon ground cinnamon

Preheat oven to 350 degrees. Spray 2 (12-ounce) ovenproof custard cups with butter-flavored cooking spray. In a medium skillet sprayed with butter-flavored cooking spray, sauté celery and onion for 5 minutes. In a medium bowl, combine bread pieces, raisins, and apple. Stir in celery and onion mixture. Add apple juice, water, Splenda, parsley flakes, and cinnamon. Mix gently just to combine. Evenly pat mixture into prepared custard cups. Cover each with aluminum foil. Place filled custard cups on a baking sheet. Bake for 30 minutes. Uncover and continue baking for 15 minutes. Place cups on a wire rack and let set for 2 to 3 minutes.

Each serving equals:

HE: 1 Fruit • ¾ Bread • ¾ Vegetable • 3 Optional Calories

116 Calories • 0 gm Fat • 4 gm Protein • 25 gm Carbohydrate • 199 mg Sodium • 55 mg Calcium • 2 gm Fiber

DIABETIC EXCHANGES: 1 Fruit • ½ Starch • ½ Vegetable

CARB CHOICES: 1½

Vegetable Pilaf

Why settle for plain old rice when a vividly colorful blend of rice and veggies is so easy to fix? What makes this rice special is the savory flavor that cooking it in bouillon adds!

● Serves 2 (1 cup)

> ¾ cup water
> 1 teaspoon Wyler's Chicken Granules Instant Bouillon
> ⅔ cup uncooked Minute Rice
> 1 tablespoon dried onion flakes
> ½ teaspoon dried parsley flakes
> 1 cup frozen mixed vegetables, thawed
> 1 tablespoon I Can't Believe It's Not Butter! Light Margarine

In a medium saucepan, combine water and dry chicken bouillon. Bring mixture to a boil. Stir in uncooked instant rice, onion flakes, parsley flakes, and mixed vegetables. Add margarine. Mix well to combine. Lower heat, cover, and simmer for 6 to 8 minutes or until rice and vegetables are tender and liquid is absorbed, stirring occasionally.

HINT: Thaw mixed vegetables by rinsing in a colander under hot water for 1 minute.

Each serving equals:

HE: 1¼ Bread • 1 Vegetable • ¾ Fat • 5 Optional Calories

191 Calories • 3 gm Fat • 5 gm Protein • 36 gm Carbohydrate • 289 mg Sodium • 40 mg Calcium • 4 gm Fiber

DIABETIC EXCHANGES: 1½ Starch • 1 Vegetable • ½ Fat

CARB CHOICES: 2

Grande Vegetable Pilaf

I'm a fan of easy preparation in the kitchen, so here's a suggestion for busy cooks everywhere: When you make the time to shred some veggies (carrots and zucchini, in this case) or chop some onions, save time for another night by shredding and chopping extra. For those nights when even a few minutes of work seems like too much, having veggies ready to use is a gift!

☻ Serves 2 (1 cup)

> ¾ cup shredded unpeeled zucchini
> ½ cup shredded carrots
> ¼ cup finely chopped onion
> 1 cup water
> 1 teaspoon Wyler's Beef Granules Instant Bouillon
> ½ teaspoon chili seasoning
> ⅛ teaspoon black pepper
> 1 tablespoon chopped fresh parsley or 1 teaspoon dried
>   parsley flakes
> ⅔ cup uncooked Minute Rice

In a medium skillet sprayed with butter-flavored cooking spray, sauté zucchini, carrots, and onion for 5 minutes. Add water, dry beef bouillon, chili seasoning, black pepper, and parsley. Mix well to combine. Stir in uncooked instant rice. Bring mixture to a boil. Lower heat, cover, and simmer for 8 to 10 minutes or until rice is tender and most of liquid is absorbed, stirring occasionally.

Each serving equals:

HE: 1½ Vegetable • 1 Bread • 5 Optional Calories

145 Calories • 1 gm Fat • 6 gm Protein • 28 gm Carbohydrate • 70 mg Sodium • 37 mg Calcium • 2 gm Fiber

DIABETIC EXCHANGES: 1½ Starch • 1 Vegetable

CARB CHOICES: 2

Broccoli Rice Side Dish

Do you usually toss out the stems of the fresh broccoli you buy and just use the fluffy tops? Many cooks do, but there's so much nutrition in those stems, I want to suggest you give them another chance. Chopped finely (or sliced thin in other dishes), they will cook at the same pace as the rest of the vegetables.

☻ Serves 2 (¾ cup)

> ¼ cup finely chopped onion
> ½ cup finely chopped fresh or frozen broccoli, thawed
> ¾ cup water
> ¼ teaspoon dried minced garlic
> ¼ teaspoon Italian seasoning
> ⅛ teaspoon black pepper
> ⅔ cup uncooked Minute Rice
> 2 tablespoons Kraft Reduced Fat Parmesan Style Grated
>   Topping
> 1 tablespoon Land O Lakes Fat Free Half & Half
> 2 teaspoons I Can't Believe It's Not Butter! Light Margarine

In a medium saucepan sprayed with butter-flavored cooking spray, sauté onion and broccoli for 5 minutes. Add water, garlic, Italian seasoning, and black pepper. Mix well to combine. Stir in uncooked instant rice. Lower heat, cover, and simmer for 6 to 8 minutes or until rice is tender and liquid is absorbed, stirring occasionally. Add Parmesan cheese, half & half, and margarine. Mix well to combine. Serve at once.

HINT: Thaw broccoli by rinsing in a colander under hot water for 1 minute.

Each serving equals:

HE: 1 Bread • ¾ Vegetable • ½ Fat • ¼ Protein • 4 Optional Calories

147 Calories • 3 gm Fat • 4 gm Protein • 26 gm Carbohydrate •
182 mg Sodium • 81 mg Calcium • 2 gm Fiber

DIABETIC EXCHANGES: 1½ Starch • ½ Vegetable • ½ Fat

CARB CHOICES: 2

Creamy Baked Rice and Peas

Here's a great idea for using up that leftover rice from the Chinese restaurant, though of course you can prepare some just for this dish. I recommend purchasing frozen peas by the bag instead of the box, for ease of measuring out just the amount you require.

🌣 Serves 2

⅓ cup Carnation Nonfat Dry Milk Powder
¼ cup water
2 tablespoons Land O Lakes Fat Free Half & Half
2 tablespoons Land O Lakes no-fat sour cream
½ cup cooked rice
½ cup frozen peas, thawed
1 (2.5-ounce) jar sliced mushrooms, drained and chopped
2 teaspoons dried onion flakes
⅛ teaspoon black pepper

Preheat oven to 350 degrees. Spray 2 (10-ounce) ovenproof custard cups with butter-flavored cooking spray. In a medium bowl, combine dry milk powder, water, half & half, and sour cream. Stir in rice, peas, and mushrooms. Add onion flakes and black pepper. Mix well to combine. Place filled custard cups on a baking sheet. Bake for 20 to 25 minutes. Place cups on a wire rack and let set 2 to 3 minutes.

HINTS: 1. Usually ⅓ cup uncooked instant or ¼ cup regular rice cooks to about ½ cup.
   2. Thaw peas by rinsing in a colander under hot water for 1 minute.

Each serving equals:

HE: 1 Bread • ½ Fat Free Milk • ½ Vegetable • ¼ Slider • 4 Optional Calories

136 Calories • 0 gm Fat • 8 gm Protein • 26 gm Carbohydrate •
295 mg Sodium • 203 mg Calcium • 3 gm Fiber

DIABETIC EXCHANGES: 1 Starch • ½ Fat Free Milk

CARB CHOICES: 1½

Italian Rice Side Dish

What's in Italian seasoning, you may wonder? In most cases, oregano and basil are combined in just the right proportions with bits of other flavors (marjoram, sage) to give that lively flavor you recognize as "That's Italian!" ☺ Serves 2 (¾ cup)

½ cup finely chopped onion
1 cup tomato juice
1 teaspoon olive oil
1 teaspoon Italian seasoning
1 tablespoon Splenda Granular
2 tablespoons water
⅔ cup uncooked Minute Rice
2 tablespoons Kraft Reduced Fat Parmesan Style Grated
    Topping

In a medium saucepan sprayed with olive oil–flavored cooking spray, sauté onion for 5 minutes. Stir in tomato juice, olive oil, Italian seasoning, and Splenda. Bring mixture to a boil, stirring occasionally. Add water, uncooked instant rice, and Parmesan cheese. Mix well to combine. Lower heat, cover, and simmer for 6 to 8 minutes or until rice is tender and liquid is absorbed, stirring often.

Each serving equals:

HE: 1½ Vegetable • 1 Bread • ½ Fat • ¼ Protein • 3 Optional Calories

196 Calories • 4 gm Fat • 4 gm Protein • 36 gm Carbohydrate •
180 mg Sodium • 83 mg Calcium • 2 gm Fiber

DIABETIC EXCHANGES: 1½ Vegetable • 1½ Starch • ½ Fat

CARB CHOICES: 2

Grande Rice

Grande means "big" in Spanish, which makes it the right name for a side dish with big flavor—and this one's got it! You choose the level of heat, so no one at the table has to pass this by.

○ Serves 2 (¾ cup)

> ¼ cup chopped onion
> 1 cup reduced-sodium tomato juice
> ¼ cup chunky salsa (mild, medium, or hot)
> 1 tablespoon Splenda Granular
> ½ teaspoon chili seasoning
> ⅔ cup uncooked Minute Rice
> 2 teaspoons I Can't Believe It's Not Butter! Light Margarine

In a medium skillet sprayed with olive oil–flavored cooking spray, sauté onion for 5 minutes. Stir in tomato juice, salsa, Splenda, and chili seasoning. Add uncooked instant rice. Mix well to combine. Lower heat, cover, and simmer for 6 to 8 minutes or until rice is tender, stirring occasionally. Just before serving, stir in margarine.

Each serving equals:

HE: 1½ Vegetable • 1 Bread • ½ Fat • ¼ Protein • 3 Optional Calories

146 Calories • 2 gm Fat • 3 gm Protein • 29 gm Carbohydrate •
359 mg Sodium • 26 mg Calcium • 1 gm Fiber

DIABETIC EXCHANGES: 1½ Vegetable • 1½ Starch • ½ Fat

CARB CHOICES: 2

French Onion–Mushroom Rice Casserole

What gives French onion soup its deep, dark flavor? The broth is cooked for *hours* on top of the stove. Lucky for you, you can get that rich taste by combining good canned broth with other ingredients, for a dish that tastes as if it's been cooked "long and slow."

Serves 2

1 cup chopped onion
1 (14-ounce) can Swanson Lower Sodium Fat Free Beef Broth
1 teaspoon dried parsley flakes
⅔ cup uncooked Minute Rice
1 (2.5-ounce) jar sliced mushrooms, drained
¼ cup shredded Kraft reduced-fat mozzarella cheese

Preheat oven to 350 degrees. Spray 2 (12-ounce) ovenproof custard cups with butter-flavored cooking spray. In a large skillet sprayed with butter-flavored cooking spray, sauté onion for 5 minutes. Add beef broth, parsley flakes, and uncooked instant rice. Mix well to combine. Stir in mushrooms. Bring mixture to a boil, stirring often. Continue cooking for 6 to 8 minutes or until rice is tender and most of liquid is absorbed, stirring occasionally. Evenly spoon mixture into prepared custard cups. Sprinkle 2 tablespoons mozzarella cheese over top of each. Place filled custard cups on a baking sheet. Bake for 15 minutes. Place custard cups on a wire rack and let set for 2 to 3 minutes.

Each serving equals:

HE: 1½ Vegetable • 1 Bread • ½ Protein • 18 Optional Calories

179 Calories • 3 gm Fat • 10 gm Protein • 28 gm Carbohydrate • 509 mg Sodium • 145 mg Calcium • 3 gm Fiber

DIABETIC EXCHANGES: 1½ Starch • 1 Vegetable • ½ Meat

CARB CHOICES: 2

Cheesy Baked Rice with Carrots ❄

This is one of the recipes that most pleased my grandchildren, and I suspect that kids everywhere will gobble it up with pleasure! The carrots give it color, and the cheese makes it downright irresistible!

◐ Serves 2

⅓ cup Carnation Nonfat Dry Milk Powder
½ cup water
2 teaspoons Splenda Granular
1 egg, or equivalent in egg substitute
½ teaspoon prepared yellow mustard
1 teaspoon dried onion flakes
1 teaspoon dried parsley flakes
⅛ teaspoon black pepper
1 cup cooked rice
1 cup shredded carrots
¼ cup shredded Kraft reduced-fat Cheddar cheese

Preheat oven to 350 degrees. Spray 2 (12-ounce) ovenproof custard cups with butter-flavored cooking spray. In a medium bowl, combine dry milk powder and water. Stir in Splenda, egg, mustard, onion flakes, parsley flakes, and black pepper. Add rice, carrots, and Cheddar cheese. Mix well to combine. Evenly spoon mixture into prepared custard cups. Place filled custard cups on a baking sheet and bake for 30 to 35 minutes. Place cups on a wire rack and let set for 2 to 3 minutes.

HINT: Usually ⅔ cup uncooked instant or ½ cup regular rice cooks to about 1 cup.

Each serving equals:

HE: 1 Bread • 1 Protein • 1 Vegetable • ½ Fat Free Milk • 2 Optional Calories

217 Calories • 5 gm Fat • 13 gm Protein • 30 gm Carbohydrate • 268 mg Sodium • 293 mg Calcium • 2 gm Fiber

DIABETIC EXCHANGES: 1½ Starch • 1 Meat • 1 Vegetable • ½ Fat Free Milk

CARB CHOICES: 2

Parmesan Noodles

Instead of driving to the nearest Italian restaurant, you can enjoy a luscious taste of Rome at home! Break out the bottle of Chianti, light some candles, and pretend you're dining in the Eternal City.

Serves 2 (½ cup)

1 cup hot cooked noodles, rinsed and drained
¼ cup Kraft Reduced Fat Parmesan Style Grated Topping
¼ cup Land O Lakes Fat Free Half & Half
¼ cup fat-free milk
2 teaspoons I Can't Believe It's Not Butter! Light Margarine
1 tablespoon chopped fresh parsley or 1 teaspoon dried parsley flakes
⅛ teaspoon black pepper

In a medium saucepan, combine noodles, Parmesan cheese, half & half, and milk. Add margarine, parsley, and black pepper. Mix well to combine. Cook over medium heat for 3 to 5 minutes or until mixture is heated through, stirring often.

HINT: Usually ¾ cup uncooked noodles cooks to about 1 cup.

Each serving equals:

HE: 1 Bread • ½ Protein • ½ Fat • ¼ Slider • 7 Optional Calories

202 Calories • 6 gm Fat • 7 gm Protein • 30 gm Carbohydrate • 320 mg Sodium • 171 mg Calcium • 1 gm Fiber

DIABETIC EXCHANGES: 2 Starch • ½ Meat • ½ Fat

CARB CHOICES: 2

Italian Noodle Side Dish

Sure, it may seem easier to heat up a frozen side dish instead of stirring one up on your stovetop. But eating well is an important part of living well, and taking the time to fix a flavorful dish like this one will make you feel good all over. ☻ Serves 2 (¾ cup)

> 1 cup hot cooked noodles, rinsed and drained
> ¼ cup Kraft Reduced Fat Parmesan Style Grated Topping
> 3 tablespoons Land O Lakes Fat Free Half & Half
> 1 tablespoon Land O Lakes no-fat sour cream
> 1½ teaspoons olive oil
> ¼ teaspoon Italian seasoning
> ⅛ teaspoon black pepper
> 2 tablespoons chopped ripe olives

In a medium saucepan sprayed with olive oil–flavored cooking spray, combine noodles, Parmesan cheese, half & half, and sour cream. Add olive oil, Italian seasoning, and black pepper. Mix well to combine. Stir in olives. Cook over medium heat for 4 to 5 minutes, stirring often.

HINT: Usually ¾ cup uncooked noodles cook to about 1 cup.

Each serving equals:

HE: 1 Bread • 1 Fat • ½ Protein • ¼ Slider • 1 Optional Calorie

221 Calories • 9 gm Fat • 6 gm Protein • 29 gm Carbohydrate • 333 mg Sodium • 140 mg Calcium • 1 gm Fiber

DIABETIC EXCHANGES: 1½ Starch • 1½ Fat • ½ Meat

CARB CHOICES: 2

Salsa Noodles

Put on some Latin-inspired music and fix a spicy noodle dish that is oh-so-creamy, too! This takes so little time to prepare, you'll have a few minutes for a relaxing glass of sparkling water or wine with your favorite dinner guest.   ☻   Serves 2 (¾ cup)

> ¼ cup chunky salsa (mild, medium, or hot)
> ¼ cup Land O Lakes no-fat sour cream
> 1 teaspoon Splenda Granular
> 1 teaspoon dried parsley flakes
> ⅛ teaspoon black pepper
> 1 cup hot cooked noodles, rinsed and drained

In a small saucepan sprayed with butter-flavored cooking spray, combine salsa, sour cream, Splenda, parsley flakes, and black pepper. Stir in noodles. Cook over low heat for 5 to 6 minutes or until mixture is heated through, stirring often.

HINT: Usually ¾ cup uncooked noodles cook to about 1 cup.

Each serving equals:

HE: 1 Bread • ¼ Vegetable • ¼ Slider • 11 Optional Calories

141 Calories • 1 gm Fat • 5 gm Protein • 28 gm Carbohydrate •
266 mg Sodium • 51 mg Calcium • 1 gm Fiber

DIABETIC EXCHANGES: 1½ Starch

CARB CHOICES: 1½

Pasta and Cabbage Side Dish

Talk about a marriage of textures and flavors—this dish has got happy honeymoon written all over it! Crunchy cabbage, curly pasta, tangy sauce—and smiling diners—make this supremely satisfying. ☺ Serves 2 (1½ cups)

> 2 cups shredded cabbage
> 1 cup cooked rotini pasta, rinsed and drained
> 1 (2-ounce) jar chopped pimiento, drained
> ¼ cup Kraft Reduced Fat Parmesan Style Grated Topping
> 2 teaspoons I Can't Believe It's Not Butter! Light Margarine
> 2 tablespoons Land O Lakes Fat Free Half & Half
> ⅛ teaspoon black pepper

In a medium skillet sprayed with butter-flavored cooking spray, sauté cabbage for 6 to 8 minutes or just until tender. Stir in rotini pasta and pimiento. Add Parmesan cheese, margarine, half & half, and black pepper. Mix well to combine. Lower heat and simmer for 3 to 4 minutes or until mixture is heated through, stirring occasionally.

HINT: Usually ¾ cup uncooked rotini pasta cooks to about 1 cup.

Each serving equals:

HE: 1 Bread • 1 Vegetable • ½ Protein • ½ Fat • 9 Optional Calories

205 Calories • 5 gm Fat • 7 gm Protein • 33 gm Carbohydrate • 300 mg Sodium • 155 mg Calcium • 3 gm Fiber

DIABETIC EXCHANGES: 1½ Starch • 1 Vegetable • ½ Meat • ½ Fat

CARB CHOICES: 2

Basil Pasta Pronto

In Italy, basil really is the "spice of life"—and this pasta delight shows it off with ease and grace. I love rotini because it holds sauce so beautifully, but feel free to try this with any other favorite pasta shape. (My friend Barbara loves one called *campanelle*—bellflowers!) ☺ Serves 2 (½ cup)

> 1 cup hot cooked rotini pasta, rinsed and drained
> 2 teaspoons I Can't Believe It's Not Butter! Light Margarine
> ¼ cup Land O Lakes Fat Free Half & Half
> 1½ teaspoons dried basil
> ½ teaspoon dried parsley flakes
> ½ teaspoon minced garlic
> ¼ cup Kraft Reduced Fat Parmesan Style Grated Topping

In a medium saucepan sprayed with butter-flavored cooking spray, combine rotini pasta, margarine, and half & half. Add basil, parsley flakes, garlic, and Parmesan cheese. Mix well to combine. Cook over medium heat for 3 to 4 minutes or until mixture is heated through, stirring occasionally. Serve at once.

HINT: Usually ¾ cup uncooked rotini pasta cooks to about 1 cup.

Each serving equals:

HE: 1 Bread • ½ Protein • ½ Fat • 18 Optional Calories

185 Calories • 5 gm Fat • 6 gm Protein • 29 gm Carbohydrate • 303 mg Sodium • 163 mg Calcium • 1 gm Fiber

DIABETIC EXCHANGES: 1½ Starch • ½ Meat • ½ Fat

CARB CHOICES: 2

Cheesy Macaroni Bake

Are casseroles like this cozy, cheesy one old-fashioned? Maybe. But since everything old is new again when it comes to fashion, I suspect that young people all over the country will happily hop on the comfort food bandwagon! 🖤 Serves 2

⅓ cup Carnation Nonfat Dry Milk Powder
½ cup water
2 teaspoons I Can't Believe It's Not Butter! Light Margarine
¾ cup diced Velveeta Light processed cheese
1 cup hot cooked elbow macaroni, rinsed and drained
⅛ teaspoon black pepper

Preheat oven to 350 degrees. Spray 2 (12-ounce) ovenproof custard cups with butter-flavored cooking spray. In a medium saucepan sprayed with butter-flavored cooking spray, combine dry milk powder, water, and margarine. Stir in Velveeta cheese. Cook over medium heat until cheese melts, stirring often. Add macaroni and black pepper. Mix well to combine. Evenly spoon mixture into prepared custard cups. Place filled custard cups on a baking sheet. Bake for 30 minutes. Place cups on a wire rack and let set for 2 to 3 minutes.

HINT: Usually ⅔ cup uncooked elbow macaroni cooks to about 1 cup.

Each serving equals:

HE: 1½ Protein • 1 Bread • ½ Fat Free Milk • ½ Fat

247 Calories • 7 gm Fat • 16 gm Protein • 30 gm Carbohydrate •
783 mg Sodium • 400 mg Calcium • 1 gm Fiber

DIABETIC EXCHANGES: 1½ Meat • 1½ Starch • ½ Fat Free Milk • ½ Fat

CARB CHOICES: 2

Far East Spaghetti Side Dish

I was raised by a mother who knew an endless number of "tricks" to feed her family well and on a modest budget. I think she would approve of this Asian-inspired, inexpensive pantry pleaser that coaxes a delicious meal from ingredients we all keep on hand.

◐ Serves 2 (1 cup)

> 1½ cups purchased fresh or frozen stir-fry vegetables, thawed
> 1 cup hot cooked spaghetti, rinsed and drained
> ¼ cup reduced-sodium ketchup
> 2 tablespoons Land O Lakes Fat Free Half & Half
> 1 teaspoon reduced-sodium soy sauce
> ½ teaspoon dried parsley flakes
> ⅛ teaspoon black pepper

In a medium skillet sprayed with butter-flavored cooking spray, sauté vegetables for 5 minutes. Add spaghetti, ketchup, and half & half. Mix well to combine. Stir in soy sauce, parsley flakes, and black pepper. Lower heat, cover, and simmer for 5 minutes or until vegetables are tender and mixture is heated through, stirring occasionally.

HINT: Usually ¾ cup broken uncooked spaghetti cooks to about 1 cup.

Each serving equals:

HE: 1½ Vegetable • 1 Bread • ¼ Slider • 19 Optional Calories

198 Calories • 2 gm Fat • 7 gm Protein • 38 gm Carbohydrate • 518 mg Sodium • 75 mg Calcium • 2 gm Fiber

DIABETIC EXCHANGES: 2 Starch/Carbohydrate • 1½ Vegetable

CARB CHOICES: 2½

Cheesy Potato Green Bean Bake ❄

My truck drivin' husband, Cliff, spends many days on the road, driving coast to coast in his big rig. When he comes home hungry, I like to give him the foods he most craves when he's away—hearty, homecooked dishes like this one that features his beloved green beans (as well as cheesy, creamy potatoes!). ◑ Serves 2

¼ cup Land O Lakes Fat Free Half & Half
2 tablespoons Land O Lakes no-fat sour cream
1½ tablespoons all-purpose flour
1 tablespoon dried onion flakes
1 teaspoon dried parsley flakes
⅛ teaspoon black pepper
2¼ cups frozen loose-packed shredded hash brown potatoes
1 cup frozen cut green beans, thawed
½ cup diced Velveeta Light processed cheese

Preheat oven to 350 degrees. Spray 2 (12-ounce) ovenproof custard cups with butter-flavored cooking spray. In a medium bowl, combine half & half, sour cream, and flour. Stir in onion flakes, parsley flakes, and black pepper. Add potatoes, green beans, and Velveeta cheese. Mix well to combine. Evenly spoon mixture into prepared custard cups. Place filled custard cups on a baking sheet. Bake for 45 to 50 minutes. Place cups on a wire rack and let set for 2 to 3 minutes.

HINTS: 1. Mr. Dell's frozen shredded potatoes are a good choice or raw shredded potatoes, rinsed and patted dry, may be used in place of frozen potatoes.
2. Thaw green beans by rinsing in a colander under hot water for 1 minute.

Each serving equals:

HE: 1 Bread • 1 Protein • 1 Vegetable • ¼ Slider • 13 Optional Calories

208 Calories • 4 gm Fat • 11 gm Protein • 32 gm Carbohydrate •
519 mg Sodium • 261 mg Calcium • 3 gm Fiber

DIABETIC EXCHANGES: 1½ Starch • 1 Meat • 1 Vegetable

CARB CHOICES: 2

Potato Broccoli Bake

If you've got kids who turn their noses up at vegetables, try slipping a few past them in this scrumptious baked casserole. They'll be so busy gobbling potatoes in a creamy, cheesy sauce, they may just not notice the broccoli they're eating!   ♥   Serves 2

½ cup fat-free milk
¼ cup Land O Lakes Fat Free Half & Half
1 tablespoon all-purpose flour
2½ cups frozen loose-packed shredded hash brown potatoes
1 cup frozen cut broccoli, thawed and finely chopped
1 (2.5-ounce) jar sliced mushrooms, drained
¼ cup diced Velveeta Light processed cheese
⅛ teaspoon black pepper

Preheat oven to 350 degrees. Spray 2 (12-ounce) ovenproof custard cups with butter-flavored cooking spray. In a medium bowl, combine milk, half & half, and flour using a wire whisk. Add potatoes, broccoli, and mushrooms. Mix well to combine. Stir in Velveeta cheese and black pepper. Evenly spoon mixture into prepared custard cups. Place filled custard cups on a baking sheet. Bake for 55 to 65 minutes. Place cups on a wire rack and let set for 2 to 3 minutes.

HINTS: 1. Mr. Dell's frozen shredded potatoes are a good choice or raw shredded potatoes, rinsed and patted dry, may be used in place of frozen potatoes.
2. Thaw broccoli by rinsing in a colander under hot water for 1 minute.

Each serving equals:

HE: 1½ Vegetable • 1 Bread • ½ Protein • ¼ Fat Free Milk • 18 Optional Calories

194 Calories • 2 gm Fat • 12 gm Protein • 32 gm Carbohydrate • 469 mg Sodium • 232 mg Calcium • 4 gm Fiber

DIABETIC EXCHANGES: 2 Starch/Carbohydrate • 1 Vegetable • ½ Meat

CARB CHOICES: 2

Potato Cheese Casserole

I still get letters and e-mails from readers wanting to know why I don't lower the fat further by using fat-free cheeses. My answer is always the same: I don't think they taste good enough nor do I feel they look sufficiently appealing when they are melted on top of my recipes. (Some don't melt at all!) So I choose reduced-fat cheese instead—because I'm eating in a healthy way for a lifetime.

Serves 2

> 2¼ cups frozen loose-packed shredded hash brown potatoes
> ¼ cup finely chopped onion
> ¼ cup Kraft fat-free mayonnaise
> 2 tablespoons Land O Lakes no-fat sour cream
> ½ teaspoon Worcestershire sauce
> 1 teaspoon dried parsley flakes
> ⅛ teaspoon black pepper
> ½ cup shredded Kraft reduced-fat Cheddar cheese

Preheat oven to 350 degrees. Spray 2 (12-ounce) ovenproof custard cups with butter-flavored cooking spray. In a medium bowl, combine potatoes and onion. Stir in mayonnaise, sour cream, Worcestershire sauce, parsley flakes, and black pepper. Add Cheddar cheese. Mix well to combine. Evenly spoon mixture into prepared custard cups. Cover each with aluminum foil. Place filled custard cups on a baking sheet. Bake for 45 minutes. Uncover and continue baking for 15 minutes. Place cups on a wire rack and let set for 2 to 3 minutes.

Each serving equals:

HE: 1 Protein • ¾ Bread • ¼ Vegetable • ¼ Slider • 15 Optional Calories

190 Calories • 6 gm Fat • 11 gm Protein • 23 gm Carbohydrate • 521 mg Sodium • 241 mg Calcium • 2 gm Fiber

DIABETIC EXCHANGES: 1½ Starch/Carbohydrate • 1 Meat

CARB CHOICES: 1½

Creamy Scalloped Potatoes

Fat-free dairy products have given us so much culinary pleasure in recent years, I'm constantly cheering the companies who've made it possible to eat rich and creamy foods without the fat! Join me in saying "Thank you" by enjoying every single bite of these dairy delights! ☉ Serves 2

1 cup fat-free milk
1½ tablespoons all-purpose flour
2 tablespoons Land O Lakes Fat Free Half & Half
2 tablespoons finely chopped onion
2¼ cups frozen loose-packed shredded hash brown potatoes
2 teaspoons I Can't Believe It's Not Butter! Light Margarine
2 tablespoons Land O Lakes no-fat sour cream
1 teaspoon dried parsley flakes
⅛ teaspoon black pepper

Preheat oven to 350 degrees. Spray 2 (12-ounce) ovenproof custard cups with butter-flavored cooking spray. In a covered jar, combine milk and flour. Shake well to blend. Pour mixture into a medium saucepan sprayed with butter-flavored cooking spray. Stir in half & half and onion. Cook over medium heat for 6 to 8 minutes or until mixture thickens, stirring often. Remove from heat. Add potatoes, margarine, sour cream, parsley flakes, and black pepper. Mix well to combine. Evenly spoon mixture into prepared custard cups. Place filled custard cups on a baking sheet. Bake for 30 to 35 minutes. Place cups on a wire rack and let set for 2 to 3 minutes.

HINT: Mr. Dell's frozen shredded potatoes are a good choice or raw shredded potatoes, rinsed and patted dry, may be used in place of frozen potatoes.

Each serving equals:

HE: 1 Bread • ½ Fat Free Milk • ½ Fat • ¼ Slider • 4 Optional Calories

166 Calories • 2 gm Fat • 8 gm Protein • 29 gm Carbohydrate •
139 mg Sodium • 202 mg Calcium • 1 gm Fiber

DIABETIC EXCHANGES: 1½ Starch • ½ Fat Free Milk • ½ Fat

CARB CHOICES: 2

Baked Potato–Corn Side Dish

I know, I know, it's downright decadent to combine two spectacular starches in one recipe—but living well is the best revenge, don't they say? Corn and potatoes provide lots of good-for-you nutrition, and enjoyed in moderation can be part of a healthy eating plan. Think of it—you can lose weight eating corn and potatoes! Life is good.   ○ Serves 2

1 egg, or equivalent in egg substitute

¼ cup Land O Lakes no-fat sour cream

2 tablespoons Land O Lakes Fat Free Half & Half

1½ cups frozen loose-packed shredded hash brown potatoes

½ cup frozen whole-kernel corn, thawed

1 (2-ounce) jar chopped pimiento, drained

2 teaspoons dried onion flakes

1½ teaspoons dried parsley flakes

1 teaspoon Splenda Granular

⅛ teaspoon black pepper

Preheat oven to 350 degrees. Spray 2 (12-ounce) custard cups with butter-flavored cooking spray. In a medium bowl, combine egg, sour cream, and half & half. Add potatoes, corn, and pimiento. Mix well to combine. Stir in onion flakes, parsley flakes, Splenda, and black pepper. Evenly spoon mixture into prepared custard cups. Place filled custard cups on a baking sheet. Bake for 30 to 35 minutes. Place cups on a wire rack and let set for 2 to 3 minutes.

HINTS: 1. Mr. Dell's frozen shredded potatoes are a good choice or raw shredded potatoes, rinsed and patted dry, may be used in place of frozen potatoes.
2. Thaw corn by rinsing in a colander under hot water for 1 minute.

Each serving equals:

HE: 1 Bread • ½ Protein • ¼ Slider • 19 Optional Calories

171 Calories • 3 gm Fat • 8 gm Protein • 28 gm Carbohydrate • 103 mg Sodium • 83 mg Calcium • 2 gm Fiber

DIABETIC EXCHANGES: 1½ Starch • ½ Meat

CARB CHOICES: 1½

Cheesy Veggie Side Dish

So how do you choose the right zucchini for the job? If I'm going to be shredding it, I don't mind using the bigger zukes, but in a dish like this, I like to have a little green peel showing on each chunk and choose a slimmer one.   ☻   Serves 2 (1 cup)

1 cup chopped unpeeled zucchini
¾ cup diced cooked potatoes
1 cup frozen peas & carrots, thawed
⅓ cup Carnation Nonfat Dry Milk Powder
½ cup water
1 tablespoon all-purpose flour
½ cup shredded Kraft reduced-fat Cheddar cheese
½ teaspoon dried parsley flakes
⅛ teaspoon black pepper

In a medium saucepan sprayed with butter-flavored cooking spray, sauté zucchini and potatoes for 5 minutes. Stir in peas & carrots. In a covered jar, combine dry milk powder, water, and flour. Shake well to blend. Add milk mixture to vegetable mixture. Mix well to combine. Stir in Cheddar cheese, parsley flakes, and black pepper. Continue cooking for 4 to 5 minutes or until mixture thickens and cheese melts, stirring often.

HINT: Thaw peas & carrots by rinsing in a colander under hot water for 1 minute.

Each serving equals:

HE: 1½ Vegetable • 1 Bread • 1 Protein • ½ Fat Free Milk • 15 Optional Calories

237 Calories • 5 gm Fat • 16 gm Protein • 32 gm Carbohydrate •
385 mg Sodium • 386 mg Calcium • 4 gm Fiber

DIABETIC EXCHANGES: 1½ Vegetable • 1 Starch • 1 Meat • ½ Fat Free Milk

CARB CHOICES: 2

Rosemary "Fried" Potatoes and Onions

Doesn't just the name of this recipe get your taste buds excited? I'll bet it does. By using my special "technique," you get the flavor of fried without all the oil and calories! And the rosemary makes these incredibly tempting. ◑ Serves 2 (¾ cup)

> 2 teaspoons I Can't Believe It's Not Butter! Light Margarine
> 1½ cups diced raw potatoes, rinsed and drained
> ¼ cup finely chopped onion
> ½ teaspoon dried rosemary

In a medium skillet sprayed with butter-flavored cooking spray, melt margarine. Evenly arrange potatoes and onion in skillet. Cover and cook on medium for 10 minutes. Lightly spray top with butter-flavored cooking spray. Carefully turn potatoes. Evenly sprinkle rosemary over top. Re-cover and continue cooking for 15 minutes or until potatoes are browned on the outside and tender inside, stirring occasionally.

Each serving equals:

HE: ¾ Bread • ½ Fat

106 Calories • 2 gm Fat • 2 gm Protein • 20 gm Carbohydrate • 49 mg Sodium • 13 mg Calcium • 2 gm Fiber

DIABETIC EXCHANGES: 1 Starch • ½ Fat

CARB CHOICES: 1

Simmered Potato and Green Bean Skillet

Stovetop cooking is fast and uncomplicated, but it's important to have your ingredients ready before you turn on the heat. It's not just for the cooking shows that it makes sense to have each item measured and preset—try it and see! ☺ Serves 2 (1 cup)

> 2 cups thinly sliced unpeeled raw potatoes
> ½ cup chopped onion
> 1 (8-ounce) can cut green beans, rinsed and drained
> ¼ cup Land O Lakes Fat Free Half & Half
> ⅛ teaspoon black pepper
> 2 teaspoons I Can't Believe It's Not Butter! Light Margarine

In a medium skillet sprayed with butter-flavored cooking spray, combine potatoes and onion. Cover and cook over medium-low heat for 5 minutes, stirring occasionally. Add green beans, half & half, and black pepper. Mix well to combine. Re-cover and continue simmering for 10 minutes, stirring occasionally. Stir in margarine. Serve at once.

Each serving equals:

HE: 1½ Vegetable • 1 Bread • 18 Optional Calories

170 Calories • 2 gm Fat • 4 gm Protein • 34 gm Carbohydrate • 404 mg Sodium • 64 mg Calcium • 4 gm Fiber

DIABETIC EXCHANGES: 1½ Vegetable • 1½ Starch

CARB CHOICES: 2

Creamy Potatoes and Peas

When you dice potatoes for a dish like this one, it's important to get the pieces close to the same size, so they all cook at about the same pace. This might take practice, but the finished dish will convince you it's worth trying to do well. ○ Serves 2 (¾ cup)

> 1¼ cups diced raw potatoes
> ¼ cup frozen peas, thawed
> ½ cup water
> ½ cup fat-free milk
> 2 tablespoons Land O Lakes Fat Free Half & Half
> 1 tablespoon all-purpose flour
> 1 tablespoon I Can't Believe It's Not Butter! Light Margarine
> 1 teaspoon Splenda Granular
> ½ teaspoon dried parsley flakes
> ⅛ teaspoon black pepper

In a medium saucepan, combine potatoes, peas, and water. Cook over medium heat for 12 minutes or just until potatoes are tender. Drain and return potatoes and peas to saucepan. In a covered jar, combine milk, half & half, and flour. Shake well to blend. Pour milk mixture into saucepan with potatoes. Return pan to heat. Continue cooking for 3 to 5 minutes or until mixture thickens, stirring often. Add margarine, Splenda, parsley flakes, and black pepper. Mix gently to combine. Continue cooking for 2 to 3 minutes, stirring often.

HINT: Thaw peas by rinsing in a colander under hot water for 30 seconds.

Each serving equals:

HE: 1 Bread • ¾ Fat • ¼ Fat Free Milk • 10 Optional Calories

151 Calories • 3 gm Fat • 5 gm Protein • 26 gm Carbohydrate •
131 mg Sodium • 102 mg Calcium • 2 gm Fiber

DIABETIC EXCHANGES: 1½ Starch • 1 Fat

CARB CHOICES: 1½

Main Dish Duets

W hether I'm demonstrating dishes at the State Fair or visiting with readers in a bookstore or on the phone at QVC, people who live alone or whose kids are grown and gone often tell me that making dinner every night has become a dreaded chore. It's even truer for couples in which one partner has health concerns like diabetes or high cholesterol. "He says that everything tastes bland and boring," one woman told me about her husband's struggle to follow his doctor's recommendations for a low-fat diet. "And he hates leftovers!"

This chapter (and this whole book, of course) is for her, and for all of you who feel the same. You won't be stuck with lots of leftovers if you are cooking for one or two; you'll be delighted by the easy preparation and cleanup; and most of all, you'll find lots of great choices for entrees that offer intense flavor, old-fashioned comfort, and plenty of variety. Eat—and enjoy!

Did you ever imagine you could enjoy lasagna without making a huge pan of it? Lazy Lasagna has your name on it. And how about an Asian adventure just for two? Chicken Cashew Stir-Fry will transport you to exotic locales (if only culinarily)! You'll finally be able to fix just enough meat loaf (Tomato-Basil Meat Loaf) and "just right" skillet specials (Stove Top BBQ Steak and Mushrooms). Whether you're hungry for pork, beef, chicken, turkey, or fish, you'll find it right here!

Impossible Italian Summer Pies

Nothing's impossible when you are determined—I've proved that to myself lots of times, whether the challenge was recipes or staying healthy! Here I've got some help from Bisquick in making an elegant entrée. ◐ Serves 2

> ¼ cup fat-free milk
> ½ teaspoon white distilled vinegar
> ¾ cup finely chopped unpeeled zucchini
> ½ cup peeled and finely chopped fresh tomato
> ¼ cup finely chopped onion
> ¼ cup Bisquick Heart Smart Baking Mix
> ¼ cup Kraft Reduced Fat Parmesan Style Grated Topping
> 1 egg, or equivalent in egg substitute
> ½ teaspoon Italian seasoning
> 2 tablespoons shredded Kraft reduced-fat mozzarella cheese

Preheat oven to 375 degrees. In a small bowl, combine milk and vinegar. Set aside. Spray 2 (12-ounce) ovenproof custard cups with olive oil–flavored cooking spray. In a medium bowl, combine zucchini, tomato, and onion. Evenly spoon vegetable mixture into prepared custard cups. In same bowl, combine baking mix, Parmesan cheese, egg, milk mixture, and Italian seasoning. Mix gently just to combine using a wire whisk. Pour mixture evenly over vegetables. Sprinkle 1 tablespoon mozzarella cheese over top of each. Place filled custard cups on a baking sheet. Bake for 22 to 26 minutes or until a knife inserted in center comes out clean. Place cups on a wire rack and let set for 2 to 3 minutes.

Each serving equals:

HE: 1½ Vegetable • 1¼ Protein • ⅔ Bread • 10 Optional Calories

153 Calories • 5 gm Fat • 9 gm Protein • 18 gm Carbohydrate •
282 mg Sodium • 134 mg Calcium • 2 gm Fiber

DIABETIC EXCHANGES: 1 Vegetable • 1 Meat • ½ Starch

CARB CHOICES: 1

Pasta with Tomatoes and Olives

Everyone says that a Mediterranean diet is healthy, but here's the best part: You still get to enjoy hearty, filling, and flavorful pasta dishes like this one! I love using canned diced tomatoes in my recipes—they are thisclose to the taste of fresh off the vine.

● Serves 2 (1 cup)

½ cup chopped onion
1 (15-ounce) can diced tomatoes, undrained
2 tablespoons Splenda Granular
1 teaspoon dried basil
¾ cup cooked rotini pasta, rinsed and drained
¼ cup sliced ripe olives
¼ cup Kraft Reduced Fat Parmesan Style Grated Topping

In a medium skillet sprayed with olive oil–flavored cooking spray, sauté onion for 5 minutes. Stir in undrained tomatoes, Splenda, and basil. Add rotini pasta, olives, and Parmesan cheese. Mix well to combine. Lower heat and simmer for 5 to 6 minutes, stirring occasionally.

HINT: Usually ½ cup uncooked rotini pasta cooks to about ¾ cup.

Each serving equals:

HE: 2½ Vegetable • ¾ Bread • ½ Protein • ½ Fat • 6 Optional Calories

217 Calories • 5 gm Fat • 7 gm Protein • 36 gm Carbohydrate •
631 mg Sodium • 162 mg Calcium • 5 gm Fiber

DIABETIC EXCHANGES: 2½ Vegetable • 1 Starch • ½ Meat • ½ Fat

CARB CHOICES: 2

Lazy Lasagna

Love the taste of lasagna but don't have room in the refrigerator for a standard pan of this Italian favorite? Here's a great way to enjoy what you love without ending up with tons of leftovers.

● Serves 2

> 1 (8-ounce) can Hunt's Tomato Sauce
> 1 tablespoon Splenda Granular
> 1 teaspoon Italian seasoning
> ½ cup fat-free cottage cheese
> ½ cup shredded Kraft reduced-fat mozzarella cheese
> 1 cup hot cooked mini lasagna noodles, rinsed and drained
> 2 tablespoons Kraft Reduced Fat Parmesan Style Grated
>   Topping

Preheat oven to 375 degrees. Spray 2 (12-ounce) ovenproof custard cups with olive oil–flavored cooking spray. In a medium skillet sprayed with olive oil–flavored cooking spray, combine tomato sauce, Splenda, and Italian seasoning. Add cottage cheese and mozzarella cheese. Mix well to combine. Stir in noodles. Evenly spoon mixture into prepared custard cups. Place filled custard cups on a baking sheet. Sprinkle 1 tablespoon Parmesan cheese over top of each. Bake for 20 minutes. Serve at once.

HINT: Usually ¾ cup uncooked lasagna noodles cook to about 1 cup.

Each serving equals:

HE: 2 Vegetable • 1¾ Protein • 1 Bread • 3 Optional Calories

291 Calories • 7 gm Fat • 22 gm Protein • 35 gm Carbohydrate • 953 mg Sodium • 317 mg Calcium • 3 gm Fiber

DIABETIC EXCHANGES: 2 Vegetable • 2 Meat • 1½ Starch

CARB CHOICES: 2

Green Bean and Fish Almondine

If you're looking for easy ways to put more fish on the menu, this recipe is a great start. You can choose any kind of white fish you like (sole or flounder are popular choices) and then jazz it up with tasty beans and crunchy nuts! ◐ Serves 2

> 8 ounces frozen white fish, thawed and cut into 2 pieces
> 1 cup water
> 1 tablespoon lemon juice
> 1½ cups frozen French-style green beans, thawed
> ¼ cup Land O Lakes Fat Free Half & Half
> 1 tablespoon all-purpose flour
> 2 teaspoons I Can't Believe It's Not Butter! Light Margarine
> ½ teaspoon lemon pepper
> 2 tablespoons sliced almonds, toasted

In a medium skillet sprayed with butter-flavored cooking spray, evenly arrange fish pieces. Pour water and lemon juice over fish. Bring mixture to a boil. Lower heat and simmer for 10 to 12 minutes or until fish flakes easily. Meanwhile, in another medium skillet sprayed with butter-flavored cooking spray, sauté green beans for 2 to 3 minutes. Add half & half, flour, margarine, and lemon pepper. Mix well to combine. Lower heat and simmer while fish continues cooking, stirring occasionally. When serving, remove fish from skillet with a slotted spoon, place 1 piece of fish on each plate, spoon a full ½ cup green bean mixture over fish, and sprinkle 1 tablespoon almonds over top of each.

HINT: Thaw green beans by rinsing in a colander under hot water for 1 minute.

Each serving equals:

HE: 2½ Protein • 1½ Vegetable • 1 Fat • ¼ Slider • 12 Optional Calories

211 Calories • 7 gm Fat • 21 gm Protein • 16 gm Carbohydrate • 163 mg Sodium • 140 mg Calcium • 3 gm Fiber

DIABETIC EXCHANGES: 3 Meat • 1½ Vegetable • 1 Fat

CARB CHOICES: 1

California Tuna Bake

Yes, it's time for a new version of tuna casserole that serves just a pair! This creamy blend is simple to prepare any night of the week.

◐   Serves 2

> ¼ cup Land O Lakes no-fat sour cream
> 3 tablespoons Land O Lakes Fat Free Half & Half
> 2 teaspoons dried onion flakes
> 1 teaspoon dried parsley flakes
> ⅛ teaspoon black pepper
> ¾ cup cooked rotini pasta, rinsed and drained
> ¼ cup frozen peas, thawed
> 2 tablespoons sliced ripe olives
> 1 (2-ounce) jar chopped pimiento, drained
> 1 (6-ounce) can white tuna, packed in water, drained and
>   flaked

Preheat oven to 350 degrees. Spray 2 (12-ounce) ovenproof custard cups with butter-flavored cooking spray. In a medium bowl, combine sour cream, half & half, onion flakes, parsley flakes, and black pepper. Stir in rotini pasta, peas, olives, and pimiento. Add tuna. Mix well to combine. Evenly spoon mixture into prepared custard cups. Place filled custard cups on a baking sheet. Bake for 20 to 25 minutes. Place cups on a wire rack and let set for 2 to 3 minutes.

HINTS: 1. Usually a scant ½ cup uncooked rotini pasta cooks to about ¾ cup.

2. Thaw peas by rinsing in a colander under hot water for 30 seconds.

Each serving equals:

HE: 2 Protein • 1 Bread • ¼ Fat • ½ Slider • 3 Optional Calories

244 Calories • 4 gm Fat • 25 gm Protein • 27 gm Carbohydrate • 491 mg Sodium • 95 mg Calcium • 2 gm Fiber

DIABETIC EXCHANGES: 3 Meat • 1½ Starch/Carbohydrate

CARB CHOICES: 1½

Creamy Tuna and Chips

If you love the tradition of a crunchy top on your baked tuna dishes, you're sure to enjoy this tasty treat! You can choose from several different flavors of Lay's Light chips for a refreshing change of pace. ☺ Serves 2

1 (6-ounce) can white tuna, packed in water, drained and
   flaked
½ cup frozen peas, thawed
1 (2.5-ounce) jar sliced mushrooms, drained and finely
   chopped
1 (2-ounce) jar chopped pimiento, drained
1 tablespoon dried onion flakes
¼ cup Land O Lakes no-fat sour cream
2 tablespoons Kraft fat-free mayonnaise
½ cup crushed Lay's Light Fat Free potato chips ☆
½ teaspoon dried parsley flakes
⅛ teaspoon black pepper

Preheat oven to 350 degrees. Spray 2 (12-ounce) ovenproof custard cups with butter-flavored cooking spray. In a medium bowl, combine tuna, peas, and mushrooms. Add pimiento, onion flakes, sour cream, and mayonnaise. Mix well to combine. Stir in ¼ cup potato chips, parsley flakes, and black pepper. Evenly spoon mixture into prepared custard cups. Sprinkle remaining crushed potato chips evenly over top of each. Place custard cups on a baking sheet. Bake for 25 to 30 minutes. Place cups on a wire rack and let set for 2 to 3 minutes.

HINT: Thaw peas by rinsing in a colander under hot water for 30
   seconds.

Each serving equals:

HE: 2 Protein • 1 Bread • ½ Vegetable • ½ Slider • 1 Optional Calorie

219 Calories • 3 gm Fat • 25 gm Protein • 23 gm Carbohydrate •
650 mg Sodium • 73 mg Calcium • 4 gm Fiber

DIABETIC EXCHANGES: 3 Meat • 1½ Starch/Carbohydrate • ½ Vegetable

CARB CHOICES: 1½

Creamed Tuna and Peas with Dill

Check your spice jars, and if your dill has been sitting there for months, treat yourself to a new jar for this recipe. Even if you keep your spices in a cool, dark place, they do lose some of their sparkle as time passes. ☾ Serves 2 (1 cup)

> 1 cup fat-free milk
> 2 tablespoons Land O Lakes Fat Free Half & Half
> 1½ tablespoons all-purpose flour
> 1 (6-ounce) can white tuna, packed in water, drained and
> flaked
> ¾ cup frozen peas, thawed
> ½ teaspoon dill weed
> ⅛ teaspoon black pepper

In a covered jar, combine milk, half & half, and flour. Shake well to blend. Pour mixture into a medium saucepan sprayed with butter-flavored cooking spray. Add tuna, peas, dill weed, and black pepper. Mix well to combine. Cook over medium heat for 6 to 8 minutes or until mixture thickens and is heated through, stirring often.

HINTS: 1. Thaw peas by rinsing in a colander under hot water for
1 minute.
2. Serve over toast, English muffins, pasta, rice, or potato.

Each serving equals:

HE: 2 Protein • 1 Bread • ½ Fat Free Milk • 9 Optional Calories

215 Calories • 3 gm Fat • 28 gm Protein • 19 gm Carbohydrate •
402 mg Sodium • 196 mg Calcium • 3 gm Fiber

DIABETIC EXCHANGES: 3 Meat • 1 Starch • ½ Fat Free Milk

CARB CHOICES: 1

Salmon Patties with Dill Pea Sauce

Salmon is a great healthy alternative to canned tuna or chicken. Want a splash of color on the plate, along with lots of good nutrition? Fix this festive recipe sometime soon. ☻ Serves 2

1 (6-ounce) can Chicken of the
    Sea pink salmon, packed
    in water, drained and
    flaked
7 small fat-free saltine
    crackers, made into
    crumbs
1 tablespoon egg substitute
1 teaspoon onion flakes
⅛ teaspoon black pepper

1 cup fat-free milk
1½ tablespoons all-purpose
    flour
¼ cup frozen peas, thawed
2 teaspoons I Can't Believe It's
    Not Butter! Light
    Margarine
1 teaspoon Splenda Granular
½ teaspoon dill weed

In a medium bowl, combine salmon, cracker crumbs, egg substitute, onion flakes, and black pepper. Mix well to combine. Evenly form into 2 patties. Place patties in a medium skillet sprayed with butter-flavored cooking spray. Brown patties for 5 to 6 minutes on each side. Meanwhile, in a covered jar, combine milk and flour. Shake well to blend. Pour mixture into a medium saucepan sprayed with butter-flavored cooking spray. Add peas, margarine, Splenda, and dill weed. Mix well to combine. Cook over medium heat for 5 to 6 minutes or until mixture thickens, stirring often. Lower heat and simmer until patties are done. When serving, place 1 patty on a plate and spoon a full ⅓ cup sauce over top.

HINT: Thaw peas by rinsing in a colander under hot water for 30
    seconds.

Each serving equals:

HE: 2½ Protein • 1 Bread • ½ Fat Free Milk • ½ Fat • 1 Optional Calorie

244 Calories • 8 gm Fat • 21 gm Protein • 22 gm Carbohydrate •
555 mg Sodium • 281 mg Calcium • 1 gm Fiber

DIABETIC EXCHANGES: 3 Meat • 1½ Starch • ½ Fat

CARB CHOICES: 1½

Chunky Chicken Salad Wrap

Think of all the money you can save in a month or a year when you bring your lunch to work instead of ordering in. You won't feel deprived when you dig into this spectacular wrapped sandwich!

○ Serves 2

¼ cup Kraft fat-free mayonnaise
2 teaspoons lemon juice
2 teaspoons Splenda Granular
2 teaspoons chopped fresh parsley or ½ teaspoon dried
    parsley flakes
1 (5-ounce) can chicken breast, packed in water, drained
    and flaked
½ cup (1 small) cored, unpeeled, and finely chopped Red
    Delicious apple
¼ cup finely chopped celery
2 tablespoons chopped pecans
2 (6-inch) flour tortillas
4 Romaine or lettuce leaves

In a medium bowl, combine mayonnaise, lemon juice, Splenda, and parsley. Add chicken, apple, and celery. Mix well to combine. Stir in pecans. For each serving, place 1 tortilla on center of plate, arrange 2 Romaine leaves on tortilla, and spoon about ¼ cup chicken mixture over top. Roll up tortillas. Serve at once or cover and refrigerate until ready to serve.

Each serving equals:

HE: 2½ Protein • 1 Bread • ½ Fruit • ½ Fat • ½ Vegetable • ¼ Slider • 2 Optional Calories

290 Calories • 10 gm Fat • 25 gm Protein • 25 gm Carbohydrate • 305 mg Sodium • 34 mg Calcium • 3 gm Fiber

DIABETIC EXCHANGES: 2½ Meat • 1 Bread • 1 Fat • ½ Fruit • ½ Vegetable

CARB CHOICES: 1½

Chicken BLT Sandwich

Is your double-sided electric grill gathering dust lately? Put it to work at lunchtime by preparing this tasty grilled treat. With fresh tomato and lettuce and a touch of bacon, it's a winner anytime.

❍ Serves 2

> 2 (4-ounce) skinned and boned uncooked chicken breasts
> 2 tablespoons Kraft Fat Free Italian Dressing
> ¼ cup Kraft fat-free mayonnaise
> 2 tablespoons Oscar Mayer or Hormel Real Bacon Bits
> ½ teaspoon Italian seasoning
> 4 slices reduced-calorie white bread, toasted
> 2 lettuce leaves
> 1 small tomato, sliced

Plug in and generously spray both sides of double-sided electric contact grill with butter-flavored cooking spray and preheat for 5 minutes. Flatten chicken pieces with a meat cleaver. Place chicken pieces on prepared grill. Spread 1 tablespoon Italian dressing over top of each. Close lid and grill for 5 to 6 minutes or until chicken is cooked through. Meanwhile, in a small bowl, combine mayonnaise, bacon bits, and Italian seasoning. For each sandwich, spread about 1½ tablespoons dressing mixture on 1 slice of toast, arrange lettuce over dressing mixture, place chicken on lettuce, top with tomato slices, and place remaining slice of toast over top. Serve at once.

Each serving equals:

HE: 3½ Protein • 1 Bread • ½ Vegetable • ¼ Slider • 8 Optional Calories

274 Calories • 6 gm Fat • 35 gm Protein • 20 gm Carbohydrate • 874 mg Sodium • 64 mg Calcium • 2 gm Fiber

DIABETIC EXCHANGES: 3½ Meat • 1½ Starch/Carbohydrate • ½ Vegetable

CARB CHOICES: 1

Chicken à la Cozy

When it's cold outside, baby, warm yourself up inside and out with this easy skillet entrée. Canned chicken is a terrific pantry partner in getting dinner on the table fast!   ☻   Serves 2 (1¼ cups)

> 1½ cups fat-free milk
> 3 tablespoons all-purpose flour
> ½ teaspoon Wyler's Chicken Granules Instant Bouillon
> 1 (2.5-ounce) jar sliced mushrooms, drained and chopped
> 2 tablespoons chopped green onion
> 1 (5-ounce) can white chicken breast, packed in water,
>   drained and flaked
> ½ cup frozen peas, thawed
> 1 (2-ounce) jar chopped pimiento, drained

In a covered jar, combine milk, flour, and chicken bouillon. Shake well to blend. Pour mixture into a medium saucepan sprayed with butter-flavored cooking spray. Stir in mushrooms, green onion, chicken, peas, and pimiento. Cook over medium heat for 5 minutes or until mixture thickens, stirring often.

HINTS: 1. Thaw peas by rinsing in a colander under hot water for 1 minute.
2. Serve over biscuits, noodles, rice, or potato.

Each serving equals:

HE: 2½ Protein • 1 Bread • ¾ Fat Free Milk • ½ Vegetable • 5 Optional Calories

263 Calories • 3 gm Fat • 32 gm Protein • 27 gm Carbohydrate •
401 mg Sodium • 257 mg Calcium • 4 gm Fiber

DIABETIC EXCHANGES: 2½ Meat • 1 Starch • 1 Fat Free Milk • ½ Vegetable

CARB CHOICES: 2

Easy Chicken Alfredo

I bet my daughter-in-law Pam would find this quick main dish a pleasure, especially if she didn't have to do the cooking! It's luscious and creamy, full of flavor, and it's ready fast.

⟳ Serves 2 (1 cup)

> 1 cup diced cooked chicken breast
> 1 cup hot cooked fettuccine, rinsed and drained
> ½ cup frozen peas, thawed
> ⅓ cup fat-free milk
> 2 tablespoons Land O Lakes Fat Free Half & Half
> 2 teaspoons I Can't Believe It's Not Butter! Light Margarine
> ¼ cup Kraft Reduced Fat Parmesan Style Grated Topping
> ¼ teaspoon dried minced garlic
> ⅛ teaspoon black pepper

In a medium skillet sprayed with butter-flavored cooking spray, sauté chicken for 5 minutes. Stir in fettuccine and peas. Add milk, half & half, and margarine. Mix well to combine. Stir in Parmesan cheese, garlic, and black pepper. Continue cooking for 4 to 5 minutes or until mixture is heated through, stirring often.

HINTS: 1. If you don't have leftovers, purchase a chunk of cooked chicken breast from your local deli.
2. Usually ¾ cup broken uncooked fettuccine cooks to about 1 cup.
3. Thaw peas by rinsing in a colander under hot water for 1 minute.

Each serving equals:

HE: 3 Protein • 1½ Bread • ½ Fat • ¼ Slider • 3 Optional Calories

302 Calories • 6 gm Fat • 30 gm Protein • 32 gm Carbohydrate •
272 mg Sodium • 137 mg Calcium • 3 gm Fiber

DIABETIC EXCHANGES: 3 Meat • 2 Starch • ½ Fat

CARB CHOICES: 2

Chicken Cashew Stir Fry

Why do we love stir-fried supper dishes so much? I think it's the colorful variety of ingredients, coupled with the varied textures, from tender chicken to crunchy nuts and carrots.

◐ Serves 2 (1½ cups)

> *8 ounces skinned and boned uncooked chicken breast, cut*
> *into bite-size pieces*
> *1 cup baby carrots, cut in half lengthwise*
> *1 cup coarsely chopped onion*
> *½ cup coarsely chopped red bell pepper*
> *½ teaspoon dried minced garlic*
> *½ cup unsweetened orange juice*
> *1 tablespoon cornstarch*
> *1 cup snow peas*
> *2 tablespoons coarsely chopped cashews*

In a large skillet sprayed with butter-flavored cooking spray, sauté chicken pieces, carrots, onion, and red pepper for 6 to 8 minutes or until chicken is cooked through and vegetables are just tender. Stir in garlic. In a covered jar, combine orange juice and cornstarch. Shake well to blend. Pour orange juice mixture into chicken mixture. Add snow peas. Mix well to combine. Continue cooking for 1 to 2 minutes or until mixture thickens, stirring often. Remove from heat. Stir in cashews.

HINT: Good as is or spooned over rice.

Each serving equals:

HE: 3½ Protein • 3 Vegetable • ½ Fruit • ½ Fat • 15 Optional Calories

295 Calories • 7 gm Fat • 27 gm Protein • 31 gm Carbohydrate • 92 mg Sodium • 67 mg Calcium • 4 gm Fiber

DIABETIC EXCHANGES: 3 Meat • 3 Vegetable • 1 Fat • ½ Fruit

CARB CHOICES: 2

Chicken Veggie Sauté

If you enjoy zucchini as much as I do, this healthy skillet supper is a splendid choice for lunch or dinner all year round. I make it more often at summer's end, when the zukes threaten to take over the kitchen!   ◐   Serves 2 (1 cup)

8 ounces skinned and boned uncooked chicken breast, cut
   into bite-size pieces
1½ cups diced unpeeled zucchini
¼ cup chopped onion
1 cup frozen mixed vegetables, thawed
1 (2-ounce) jar chopped pimiento, drained
¼ cup Land O Lakes Fat Free Half & Half
¼ cup fat-free milk
1 tablespoon all-purpose flour
¼ teaspoon dried basil
⅛ teaspoon black pepper

In a large skillet sprayed with butter-flavored cooking spray, sauté chicken pieces for 5 minutes. Add zucchini, onion, and mixed vegetables. Mix well to combine. Continue to sauté for 5 to 7 minutes or until chicken and vegetables are tender. Stir in pimiento. In a small bowl, combine half & half, milk, and flour. Mix well using a wire whisk. Add milk mixture to chicken mixture. Mix well to combine. Stir in basil and black pepper. Continue cooking for 3 to 5 minutes or until mixture thickens, stirring often.

HINTS: 1. Thaw mixed vegetables by rinsing in a colander under
             hot water for 1 minute.
         2. Good as is or spooned over pasta or rice.

Each serving equals:

HE: 3 Protein • 1½ Vegetable • ¼ Bread • ¼ Slider • 8 Optional Calories

268 Calories • 4 gm Fat • 33 gm Protein • 25 gm Carbohydrate •
165 mg Sodium • 126 mg Calcium • 5 gm Fiber

DIABETIC EXCHANGES: 3 Meat • 1½ Vegetable • ½ Starch

CARB CHOICES: 1

Chicken and Carrots
with Rosemary

Kitchen magic sometimes requires selecting ingredients that you'd *never* use when preparing a main dish. In this case, I grabbed some juice and some spreadable fruit—and the result is sweet and succulent.   ◐   Serves 2

> 2 (4-ounce) skinned and boned uncooked chicken breasts
> 1½ tablespoons all-purpose flour
> ½ cup chopped onion
> 1½ cups frozen sliced carrots, thawed
> ½ cup unsweetened orange juice
> 1½ tablespoons orange marmalade spreadable fruit
> 2 teaspoons I Can't Believe It's Not Butter! Light Margarine
> ½ teaspoon dried rosemary

Flatten chicken breasts to ½-inch thickness using a meat cleaver. Spray a medium skillet with butter-flavored cooking spray. Place flour in a shallow saucer. Coat chicken breasts in flour, then arrange coated chicken pieces in prepared pan. Brown chicken for 4 to 5 minutes on each side. Meanwhile, in a small saucepan sprayed with butter-flavored cooking spray, sauté onion and carrots for 5 to 6 minutes. Stir in orange juice, spreadable fruit, margarine, rosemary, and any remaining flour. Continue cooking for 3 to 4 minutes or until chicken is browned and cooked through, stirring occasionally. For each serving, place 1 piece of chicken on a plate and spoon about ¾ cup carrot mixture over top.

HINT: Thaw carrots by rinsing in a colander under hot water for
1 minute.

Each serving equals:

HE: 3 Protein • 2 Vegetable • 1 Fruit • ½ Fat • ¼ Bread

273 Calories • 5 gm Fat • 25 gm Protein • 32 gm Carbohydrate •
170 mg Sodium • 65 mg Calcium • 3 gm Fiber

DIABETIC EXCHANGES: 3 Meat • 2 Vegetable • 1 Fruit • ½ Fat • ½ Starch

CARB CHOICES: 2

Chicken and Rice with Apricots

Dried fruit isn't just for compotes or snacking on, and this recipe proves my point! Cooking brings out deep flavors in these dried apricots, which are a perfect complement to the chicken and rice.

◑ Serves 2

> 8 ounces skinned and boned uncooked chicken breast, cut
>   into bite-size pieces
> ¼ cup chopped green onion
> ½ cup water
> ¼ cup Kraft Fat Free Catalina Dressing
> ¼ cup chopped dried apricots
> 1 teaspoon dried parsley flakes
> 1 cup hot cooked rice

In a medium skillet sprayed with butter-flavored cooking spray, sauté chicken pieces and green onion for 5 to 6 minutes. Stir in water and Catalina dressing. Add apricots and parsley flakes. Mix well to combine. Lower heat, cover, and simmer for 5 to 6 minutes or until chicken is cooked through and apricots are tender, stirring occasionally. For each serving, place ½ cup rice on a plate and spoon about ½ cup chicken mixture over top.

HINT: Usually ⅔ cup uncooked instant or ½ regular rice cooks to
    about 1 cup.

Each serving equals:

HE: 3 Protein • 1 Bread • 1 Fruit • ¼ Vegetable • ¼ Slider •
15 Optional Calories

271 Calories • 3 gm Fat • 25 gm Protein • 36 gm Carbohydrate •
381 mg Sodium • 26 mg Calcium • 4 gm Fiber

DIABETIC EXCHANGES: 3 Meat • 1½ Starch • 1 Fruit

CARB CHOICES: 2½

Chicken Cacciatore Sauté

Cacciatore means "hunter" in Italian, but the good news is, you won't have to spend hours searching for the ingredients for this Italian classic. Prepared by simmering in a tomato sauce, this dish is a great choice whether you're dining alone or sharing supper with a friend. ☺ Serves 2 (1½ cups)

> 8 ounces skinned and boned uncooked chicken breast, cut
> into bite-size pieces
> ¼ cup chopped onion
> ¼ cup chopped green bell pepper
> 1 (8-ounce) can stewed tomatoes, chopped and undrained
> ¼ cup reduced-sodium ketchup
> 1 teaspoon Italian seasoning
> 1 (2.5-ounce) jar sliced mushrooms, drained
> 1 cup cooked rotini pasta, rinsed and drained
> 2 tablespoons sliced ripe olives

In a medium skillet sprayed with olive oil–flavored cooking spray, sauté chicken pieces, onion, and green pepper for 6 to 8 minutes. Stir in undrained stewed tomatoes, ketchup, and Italian seasoning. Add mushrooms, rotini pasta, and olives. Mix well to combine. Continue cooking for 5 minutes or until mixture is heated through, stirring often.

HINT: Usually ¾ cup uncooked rotini pasta cooks to about 1 cup.

Each serving equals:

HE: 3 Protein • 2 Vegetable • 1 Bread • ¼ Fat • ¼ Slider • 10 Optional Calories

316 Calories • 4 gm Fat • 32 gm Protein • 38 gm Carbohydrate •
558 mg Sodium • 78 mg Calcium • 4 gm Fiber

DIABETIC EXCHANGES: 3 Meat • 2 Vegetable • 1½ Starch • ½ Fat

CARB CHOICES: 2½

Chicken and Noodles
in Mornay Sauce

Did you know that the earliest chefs invented flavorful sauces in part to cover up the taste of meat that had been around a little too long? Nowadays, sauces make the ordinary a little bit special—or a lot, like this one. ○ Serves 2 (1¼ cups)

> 1 cup fat-free milk
> 1 tablespoon all-purpose flour
> 2 tablespoons Kraft Reduced Fat Parmesan Style Grated
>   Topping
> 2 (¾-ounce) slices Kraft reduced-fat Swiss cheese, shredded
> 1 cup diced cooked chicken breast
> 1 (2.5-ounce) jar sliced mushrooms, drained and chopped
> 1 cup hot cooked noodles, rinsed and drained

In a covered jar, combine milk and flour. Shake well to blend. Pour milk mixture into a medium skillet sprayed with butter-flavored cooking spray. Add Parmesan cheese and Swiss cheese. Mix well to combine. Cook over medium heat until mixture thickens and cheese melts, stirring often. Add chicken and mushrooms. Mix well to combine. Stir in noodles. Lower heat and simmer for 5 to 6 minutes or until mixture is heated through, stirring often.

HINT: Usually ¾ cup uncooked noodles cook to about 1 cup.

Each serving equals:

HE: 3¾ Protein • 1 Bread • ½ Fat Free Milk • ½ Vegetable •
14 Optional Calories

334 Calories • 6 gm Fat • 38 gm Protein • 32 gm Carbohydrate •
436 mg Sodium • 428 mg Calcium • 2 gm Fiber

DIABETIC EXCHANGES: 3½ Meat • 2 Starch • ½ Fat Free Milk

CARB CHOICES: 2

French Baked Chicken

Just think of how many delectable choices your supermarket salad dressing shelf offers—and then imagine preparing a plain old chicken breast with each one. This one will have you dancing the can-can as soon as dinner's over! ◐ Serves 2

> 2 (4-ounce) skinned and boned uncooked chicken breasts
> ½ cup finely chopped celery
> ¼ cup finely chopped onion
> 1 (4-ounce) jar sliced mushrooms, drained
> ¼ cup Kraft Fat Free French Dressing
> 2 tablespoons chopped fresh parsley or 2 teaspoons dried
>   parsley flakes

Preheat oven to 350 degrees. Spray an 8-by-8-inch baking dish with butter-flavored cooking spray. In a medium skillet sprayed with butter-flavored cooking spray, brown chicken breasts for 4 to 5 minutes on each side. Meanwhile, in a medium saucepan sprayed with butter-flavored cooking spray, sauté celery and onion for 5 to 6 minutes. Stir in mushrooms. Add French dressing and parsley. Mix well to combine. Lower heat and simmer while chicken is browning. Place browned chicken pieces in prepared baking dish. Evenly spoon vegetable mixture over top. Cover and bake for 20 minutes. Uncover and continue baking for 10 to 15 minutes. When serving, evenly spoon vegetable mixture over chicken.

Each serving equals:

HE: 3 Protein • 1¾ Vegetable • ½ Slider • 5 Optional Calories

215 Calories • 3 gm Fat • 29 gm Protein • 18 gm Carbohydrate • 701 mg Sodium • 42 mg Calcium • 4 gm Fiber

DIABETIC EXCHANGES: 3 Meat • 1½ Vegetable • ½ Other Carbohydrate

CARB CHOICES: 1

Baked Italian Chicken

The flavors of Italy are celebrated in this simple yet delicious chicken dish, which brings out the best in each of its main ingredients—the chicken is tender, the tomatoes are sweet *and* savory, and the olives assert their tangy magic in every bite!

● Serves 2

> 2 (4-ounce) skinned and boned uncooked chicken breasts
> 1 (8-ounce) can stewed tomatoes, chopped and undrained
> 1 (2.5-ounce) jar sliced mushrooms, drained
> 2 tablespoons sliced ripe olives
> 1 teaspoon Italian seasoning
> 2 teaspoons Splenda Granular

Preheat oven to 350 degrees. Spray an 8-by-8-inch baking dish with olive oil–flavored cooking spray. Evenly arrange chicken breasts in prepared baking dish. In a small bowl, combine undrained stewed tomatoes, mushrooms, olives, Italian seasoning, and Splenda. Spoon tomato mixture evenly over chicken breasts. Bake for 35 to 40 minutes or until chicken is cooked through. Place baking dish on a wire rack and let set for 5 minutes. When serving, evenly spoon tomato mixture over chicken.

Each serving equals:

HE: 3 Protein • 1½ Vegetable • ¼ Fat • 2 Optional Calories

176 Calories • 4 gm Fat • 25 gm Protein • 10 gm Carbohydrate • 575 mg Sodium • 66 mg Calcium • 2 gm Fiber

DIABETIC EXCHANGES: 3 Meat • 1 Vegetable • ½ Fat

CARB CHOICES: 1

Creamy Chicken and Rice Bake

There must be dozens of ways to prepare chicken with rice, and each one has its own special charms. This one is so luscious, you can serve it to guests without anyone suspecting that you're serving a heart-healthy entrée! ☻ Serves 2

¼ cup Land O Lakes no-fat sour cream
3 tablespoons Kraft fat-free mayonnaise
1 tablespoon Land O Lakes Fat Free Half & Half
¼ cup finely chopped celery
¼ cup finely chopped onion
1 cup cooked rice
1 (2.5-ounce) jar sliced mushrooms, drained and chopped
1 (5-ounce) can chicken breast, packed in water, drained
    and flaked
1 teaspoon dried parsley flakes
⅛ teaspoon black pepper

Preheat oven to 350 degrees. Spray 2 (12-ounce) ovenproof custard cups with butter-flavored cooking spray. In a medium bowl, combine sour cream, mayonnaise, and half & half. Stir in celery and onion. Add rice, mushrooms, chicken, parsley flakes, and black pepper. Mix well to combine. Evenly spoon mixture into prepared custard cups. Place filled custard cups on a baking sheet. Bake for 25 to 30 minutes. Place cups on a wire rack and let set for 5 minutes.

HINT: Usually ⅔ cup uncooked instant or ½ cup regular rice cooks to about 1 cup.

Each serving equals:

HE: 2½ Protein • 1 Bread • 1 Vegetable • ½ Slider • 10 Optional Calories

255 Calories • 3 gm Fat • 26 gm Protein • 31 gm Carbohydrate •
434 mg Sodium • 82 mg Calcium • 2 gm Fiber

DIABETIC EXCHANGES: 2½ Meat • 2 Starch/Carbohydrate • ½ Vegetable

CARB CHOICES: 2

Turkey Supreme

If the Supreme Court is the highest and most powerful in the land, then a turkey recipe named "Supreme" must be something spectacular! I think you'll agree that this easy-to-fix, easier-to-eat dish makes a beautiful luncheon centerpiece when you're entertaining a close friend. ● Serves 2

> 1 cup diced cooked turkey breast
> 1 cup finely chopped celery
> 2 tablespoons slivered almonds
> ¼ cup Kraft fat-free mayonnaise
> ¼ cup Land O Lakes no-fat sour cream
> 1 tablespoon dried onion flakes
> ¼ cup shredded Kraft reduced-fat Cheddar cheese
> ⅓ cup crushed Ruffles Light fat-free potato chips

Preheat oven to 350 degrees. Spray 2 (12-ounce) ovenproof custard cups with butter-flavored cooking spray. In a medium bowl, combine turkey, celery, and almonds. Add mayonnaise, sour cream, and onion flakes. Mix well to combine. Stir in Cheddar cheese. Evenly spoon mixture into prepared custard cups. Sprinkle potato chips evenly over top of each. Place filled custard cups on a baking sheet. Bake for 30 to 35 minutes. Place cups on a wire rack and let set for 5 minutes.

Each serving equals:

HE: 3¼ Protein • 1 Vegetable • ½ Bread • ½ Fat • ½ Slider • 10 Optional Calories

276 Calories • 8 gm Fat • 30 gm Protein • 21 gm Carbohydrate • 571 mg Sodium • 202 mg Calcium • 3 gm Fiber

DIABETIC EXCHANGES: 3 Meat • 1 Starch/Carbohydrate • ½ Fat • ½ Vegetable

CARB CHOICES: 1

Carrot and Beef Patties

We all talk about trying to eat less meat and more veggies, but fig-
uring out how to do it without feeling deprived is a great trick to
learn. This recipe combines carrots and meat (plus some lively seasoning) into veggie-meat burgers that deliver hearty, satisfying taste!

◐ Serves 2

½ cup shredded carrots
8 ounces extra-lean ground sirloin beef or turkey breast
¼ cup reduced-sodium ketchup
1 teaspoon Worcestershire sauce
1 teaspoon dried parsley flakes
⅛ teaspoon black pepper

Plug in and generously spray both sides of double-sided electric contact grill with butter-flavored cooking spray and preheat for
5 minutes. Meanwhile, in a medium bowl, combine carrots, meat,
ketchup, Worcestershire sauce, parsley flakes, and black pepper.
Using a ½ cup measuring cup as a guide, form into 2 patties.
Evenly arrange patties on prepared grill. Close lid and grill for 5 to
6 minutes. Serve as is or between hamburger buns.

Each serving equals:

HE: 3 Protein • ½ Vegetable • ¼ Slider • 10 Optional Calories

181 Calories • 5 gm Fat • 23 gm Protein • 11 gm Carbohydrate •
118 mg Sodium • 20 mg Calcium • 1 gm Fiber

DIABETIC EXCHANGES: 3 Meat • ½ Vegetable • ½ Other Carbohydrate

CARB CHOICES: 1

Zach's Meat Loaf

My grandkids love to cook along with me, and Zach was visiting the day I tested this recipe. He's usually enthusiastic about my latest recipes, but he really went "wild" over this one. So, Zach, this one's for you! ☻ Serves 2

>8 ounces extra-lean ground sirloin beef or turkey breast
>¼ cup Quick Quaker Oats
>1 tablespoon fat-free milk
>¼ cup reduced-sodium ketchup ☆
>2 teaspoons dried onion flakes
>½ teaspoon Worcestershire sauce
>½ teaspoon prepared yellow mustard
>½ teaspoon dried parsley flakes

Preheat oven to 350 degrees. Spray a 5¾-by-3⅛-by-2⅛-inch petite loaf pan with butter-flavored cooking spray. In a medium bowl, combine meat, oats, milk, 1 tablespoon ketchup, onion flakes, and Worcestershire sauce. Evenly pat meat mixture into prepared loaf pan. In a small bowl, combine remaining 3 tablespoons ketchup, mustard, and parsley flakes. Spread ketchup mixture evenly over top. Bake for 40 to 45 minutes. Place loaf pan on a wire rack and let set for 5 minutes. Divide into 2 servings.

HINT: If you don't have a petite loaf pan, divide mixture between 2 (12-ounce) ovenproof custard cups sprayed with butter-flavored cooking spray and place them on a baking sheet before baking. If using, test for doneness at least 10 minutes before suggested baking time.

Each serving equals:

HE: 3 Protein • ½ Bread • ¼ Slider • 12 Optional Calories

214 Calories • 6 gm Fat • 24 gm Protein • 16 gm Carbohydrate • 103 mg Sodium • 26 mg Calcium • 1 gm Fiber

DIABETIC EXCHANGES: 3 Meat • 1 Starch/Carbohydrate

CARB CHOICES: 1

Tomato-Basil Meat Loaf

Even though growing fresh basil on your kitchen windowsill isn't difficult, most of us choose to cook with the dried version of this delectable spice. Basil "loves" tomatoes the way I love my family, and so I made this meat loaf with that kind of enduring love in mind! ☻   Serves 2

8 ounces extra-lean ground sirloin beef or turkey breast
3 tablespoons dry bread crumbs
¼ cup reduced-sodium ketchup
1 teaspoon dried basil
⅛ teaspoon black pepper
¼ cup finely chopped onion
½ cup peeled and chopped fresh tomato

Preheat oven to 350 degrees. Spray a 5¾-by-3⅛-by-2⅛-inch petite loaf pan with butter-flavored cooking spray. In a medium bowl, combine meat, bread crumbs, ketchup, basil, and black pepper. Add onion and tomato. Mix gently just to combine. Evenly pat mixture into prepared loaf pan. Bake for 40 to 45 minutes. Place pan on a wire rack and let set for 5 minutes.

HINT: If you don't have a petite loaf pan, divide mixture between 2 (12-ounce) ovenproof custard cups sprayed with butter-flavored cooking spray and place them on a baking sheet before baking. If using, test for doneness at least 10 minutes before suggested baking time.

Each serving equals:

HE: 3 Protein • ¾ Vegetable • ½ Bread • ¼ Slider • 11 Optional Calories

226 Calories • 6 gm Fat • 24 gm Protein • 19 gm Carbohydrate •
148 mg Sodium • 44 mg Calcium • 2 gm Fiber

DIABETIC EXCHANGES: 3 Meat • 1 Starch/Carbohydrate • ½ Vegetable

CARB CHOICES: 1

One Skillet Beef and Noodles

Recipes like this skillet supper do a great job of "stretching" a little meat into a satisfying meal. Even your meat 'n' potatoes men will think they're eating a lot more than a couple ounces of meat—but you'll know what's really on the plate!   ☻   Serves 2 (1 cup)

> 4 ounces extra-lean ground sirloin beef or turkey breast
> ½ cup finely chopped onion
> 1 (8-ounce) can stewed tomatoes, finely chopped and
>   undrained
> ½ cup water
> 1 teaspoon Wyler's Beef Granules Instant Bouillon
> 2 teaspoons Splenda Granular
> ½ teaspoon dried parsley flakes
> ⅛ teaspoon black pepper
> ¾ cup uncooked noodles

In a medium skillet sprayed with butter-flavored cooking spray, brown meat and onion. Stir in undrained stewed tomatoes, water, dry beef bouillon, Splenda, parsley flakes, and black pepper. Add uncooked noodles. Mix well to combine. Bring mixture to a boil. Lower heat, cover, and simmer for 12 to 15 minutes or until noodles are tender, stirring occasionally.

Each serving equals:

HE: 1½ Protein • 1½ Vegetable • 1 Bread • 7 Optional Calories

228 Calories • 4 gm Fat • 16 gm Protein • 32 gm Carbohydrate •
768 mg Sodium • 59 mg Calcium • 3 gm Fiber

DIABETIC EXCHANGES: 1½ Meat • 1½ Vegetable • 1½ Starch

CARB CHOICES: 2

Speedy Spaghetti Skillet

One of the apparent disadvantages of cooking just for one or two is that you don't serve some popular favorites because they seem like too much work. But everyone loves spaghetti, and so I've trimmed down the number of servings without sacrificing all the yummy flavors in this Italian-American classic!

 Serves 2 (1¼ cups)

> 4 ounces extra-lean ground sirloin beef or turkey breast
> ½ cup finely chopped onion
> 1 (15-ounce) can diced tomatoes, undrained
> 1 (2.5-ounce) jar sliced mushrooms, drained
> 1 cup water
> 1½ teaspoons Italian seasoning
> 1 tablespoon Splenda Granular
> ⅛ teaspoon black pepper
> ⅔ cup broken uncooked spaghetti
> ¼ cup Kraft Reduced Fat Parmesan Style Grated Topping

In a medium skillet sprayed with olive oil–flavored cooking spray, brown meat and onion. Stir in undrained tomatoes, mushrooms, water, Italian seasoning, Splenda, and black pepper. Add uncooked spaghetti. Mix well to combine. Bring mixture to a boil, stirring occasionally. Lower heat, cover, and simmer for 15 to 20 minutes or until spaghetti is tender, stirring occasionally. When serving, top each with 2 tablespoons Parmesan cheese.

Each serving equals:

HE: 3 Vegetable • 2 Protein • 1 Bread • 3 Optional Calories

282 Calories • 6 gm Fat • 19 gm Protein • 38 gm Carbohydrate •
682 mg Sodium • 44 mg Calcium • 6 gm Fiber

DIABETIC EXCHANGES: 3 Vegetable • 2 Meat • 1½ Starch

CARB CHOICES: 3

Grande Taco Strata

It may sound strange to talk about "strata" as a main dish bread pudding, but that's truly what it is! Remember that strata means layers, and so this dish stacks the ingredients in a tower of pleasurable taste. ◐ Serves 2

> 4 ounces extra-lean ground sirloin beef or turkey breast
> ½ teaspoon taco seasoning
> 1 cup chunky salsa (mild, medium, or hot)
> 2 tablespoons reduced-sodium ketchup
> 2 tablespoons sliced ripe olives
> 3 slices reduced-calorie white bread, torn into large pieces
> ¼ cup shredded Kraft reduced-fat Cheddar cheese
> ⅓ cup Carnation Nonfat Dry Milk Powder
> ⅔ cup water
> 2 tablespoons egg substitute
> ½ teaspoon dried parsley flakes
> 2 tablespoons Land O Lakes no-fat sour cream

Preheat oven to 350 degrees. Spray 2 (12-ounce) ovenproof custard cups with butter-flavored cooking spray. In a medium skillet sprayed with butter-flavored cooking spray, brown meat. Stir in taco seasoning, salsa, ketchup, and olives. Lower heat and simmer for 5 minutes. Remove from heat. Divide half of bread pieces between prepared custard cups. Sprinkle 1 tablespoon Cheddar cheese over each. Divide half of meat mixture between cups. Repeat layers. In a small bowl, combine dry milk powder and water. Add egg substitute and parsley flakes. Mix well to combine. Evenly pour milk mixture over top of each cup. Place filled custard cups on a baking sheet. Bake for 22 to 26 minutes or until edges are lightly browned and center is firm. Place cups on a wire rack and let set for 2 to 3 minutes. When serving, top each with 1 tablespoon sour cream.

Each serving equals:

HE: 2¼ Protein • 1 Vegetable • ¾ Bread • ½ Fat Free Milk • ¼ Fat • ¼ Slider • 10 Optional Calories

291 Calories • 7 gm Fat • 26 gm Protein • 31 gm Carbohydrate • 995 mg Sodium • 317 mg Calcium • 7 gm Fat

DIABETIC EXCHANGES: 2½ Meat • 1 Vegetable • 1 Starch • ½ Fat Free Milk

CARB CHOICES: 2

Taco-Stuffed Peppers

very good

Filling the inside cavity of fruits or vegetables is a handy cook's way to serve something "everyday" with the pizzazz that makes it seem "extraordinary"! This old-fashioned but still popular dish stirs up some extra fun and fire with a taco-flavored filling that is downright fun to eat. ☻ Serves 2

2 (medium-size) green bell peppers
4 ounces extra-lean ground sirloin beef or turkey breast
¼ cup chopped onion
1 (8-ounce) can stewed tomatoes, chopped and undrained
¼ cup reduced-sodium ketchup
1½ teaspoons taco seasoning
½ cup coarsely crushed Dorito's Baked Corn Chips
½ cup shredded Kraft reduced-fat Cheddar cheese
2 tablespoons Land O Lakes no-fat sour cream

Cut a thin slice from stem end of each green pepper. Remove seeds and membrane. Rinse peppers. Preheat oven to 350 degrees. Place each green pepper in a (12-ounce) ovenproof custard cup. Place custard cups on a baking sheet. In a medium skillet sprayed with butter-flavored cooking spray, brown meat and onion. Stir in undrained stewed tomatoes, ketchup, and taco seasoning. Add corn chips and Cheddar cheese. Mix well to combine. Remove from heat. Evenly spoon a full ½ cup meat mixture into center of each green pepper. Bake for 18 to 20 minutes or just until green peppers are tender. When serving, top each with 1 tablespoon sour cream.

HINT: If you have more filling than the green peppers can hold, evenly spoon filling around the bottom of each pepper before baking.

Each serving equals:

HE: 2½ Protein • 2 Vegetable • ½ Bread • ½ Slider • 5 Optional Calories

297 Calories • 9 gm Fat • 20 gm Protein • 34 gm Carbohydrate •
753 mg Sodium • 304 mg Calcium • 4 gm Fiber

DIABETIC EXCHANGES: 2½ Meat • 2 Vegetable • 1 Optional Calories

CARB CHOICES: 2

Bistro Burgers

Not sure how to make a basic burger meal into a memorable evening? Here's one of my cleverest ideas for jazzing things up and giving them extra sparkle! It's the combination that makes this special, as these ingredients are probably on your shelf right now.

◉ Serves 2

4 ounces extra-lean ground
   sirloin beef or turkey
   breast
3 tablespoons dry bread crumbs
2 tablespoons reduced-sodium
   ketchup
2 tablespoons Worcestershire
   sauce ☆
1 cup sliced fresh mushrooms

½ cup coarsely chopped onion
2 tablespoons Kraft fat-free
   mayonnaise
1 teaspoon Grey Poupon
   Country Style Dijon
   Mustard
2 small hamburger buns
2 (¾-ounce) slices Kraft
   reduced-fat Cheddar cheese

Plug in and generously spray both sides of double-sided electric contact grill with butter-flavored cooking spray and preheat for 5 minutes. Meanwhile, in a medium bowl, combine meat, bread crumbs, ketchup, and 1 tablespoon Worcestershire sauce. Form into 2 patties. In another medium bowl, combine mushrooms, onion, and remaining 1 tablespoon Worcestershire sauce. Evenly arrange patties and mushroom mixture on prepared grill. Close lid and grill for 8 to 10 minutes or until patties are cooked through and vegetables are tender. In a small bowl, combine mayonnaise and mustard. For each sandwich, spread 1 tablespoon mayonnaise mixture on bottom half of each bun, arrange a patty over mayonnaise mixture, place 1 slice Cheddar cheese over patty, spoon about ½ cup vegetable mixture over cheese, and finish with top half of bun. Serve at once.

Each serving equals:

HE: 2½ Protein • 1½ Bread • 1 Vegetable • 10 Optional Calories

286 Calories • 6 gm Fat • 22 gm Protein • 36 gm Carbohydrate •
708 mg Sodium • 141 mg Calcium • 3 gm Fiber

DIABETIC EXCHANGES: 2½ Meat • 1½ Starch • 1 Vegetable

CARB CHOICES: 2

Supper Zucchini Skillet

What an easy, tasty way to serve pasta, veggies, and meat for two without breaking the bank or the chef's back! Pour the ingredients into your pan, and then let the cook blend 'til ready! You won't have to ring the dinner bell—everyone will find their way to the kitchen.

◐ Serves 2

> 4 ounces extra-lean ground sirloin beef or turkey breast
> ½ cup chopped onion
> 1 cup thinly sliced unpeeled zucchini
> 1 (8-ounce) can stewed tomatoes, chopped and undrained
> 2 tablespoons reduced-sodium ketchup
> ½ cup water
> ½ teaspoon Italian seasoning
> ⅔ cup uncooked elbow macaroni
> 2 tablespoons shredded Kraft reduced-fat mozzarella cheese

In a medium skillet sprayed with olive oil–flavored cooking spray, brown meat and onion. Stir in zucchini, undrained stewed tomatoes, ketchup, water, and Italian seasoning. Add uncooked macaroni. Mix well to combine. Bring mixture to a boil. Lower heat, cover, and simmer for 6 to 8 minutes or until macaroni is tender, stirring occasionally. For each serving, place 1½ cups macaroni mixture on a plate and sprinkle 1 tablespoon mozzarella cheese over top.

Each serving equals:

HE: 1¾ Protein • 2½ Vegetable • 1 Bread • 15 Optional Calories

256 Calories • 4 gm Fat • 19 gm Protein • 36 gm Carbohydrate •
346 mg Sodium • 116 mg Calcium • 3 gm Fiber

DIABETIC EXCHANGES: 2 Meat • 2 Vegetable • 1½ Starch

CARB CHOICES: 2

Grande Cabbage Supper Skillet ❄

Don't you just love a one-pot meal that's full of flavor—and good nutrition? To save time, you can pick up a package of pre-shredded cabbage at the supermarket if you like.

◐ Serves 2 (1 full cup)

>4 ounces extra-lean ground sirloin beef or turkey breast
>½ cup chopped onion
>¼ cup chopped green bell pepper
>1 cup peeled and chopped fresh tomatoes
>1 tablespoon Splenda Granular
>½ teaspoon chili seasoning
>¾ cup water
>1½ cups shredded cabbage
>⅓ cup uncooked Minute Rice
>½ cup cubed Velveeta Light processed cheese

In a medium skillet sprayed with butter-flavored cooking spray, brown meat, onion, and green pepper. Stir in tomatoes, Splenda, chili seasoning, and water. Add cabbage and uncooked instant rice. Mix well to combine. Lower heat, cover, and simmer for 15 minutes or until rice is tender, stirring occasionally. Stir in Velveeta cheese. Continue to simmer, uncovered, for 3 to 4 minutes or until cheese melts, stirring often.

Each serving equals:

HE: 2½ Protein • 2½ Vegetable • ½ Bread • 3 Optional Calories

246 Calories • 6 gm Fat • 20 gm Protein • 28 gm Carbohydrate • 508 mg Sodium • 220 mg Calcium • 4 gm Fiber

DIABETIC EXCHANGES: 2½ Meat • 2½ Vegetable • 1 Starch

CARB CHOICES: 2

German Supper Skillet

Too many people think sauerkraut has one role in life—to be piled on top of hot dogs. But if you love the taste of that tangy canned cabbage, this recipe will make you smile—and make you *hungry!*

● Serves 2 (1 cup)

> 4 ounces extra-lean ground sirloin beef or turkey breast
> ¼ cup chopped onion
> 1 (8-ounce) can sauerkraut, well drained
> ¼ cup reduced-sodium ketchup
> ¼ cup reduced-sodium tomato juice
> ⅓ cup uncooked Minute Rice
> ⅛ teaspoon black pepper

In a medium skillet sprayed with butter-flavored cooking spray, brown meat and onion. Stir in sauerkraut. Add ketchup, tomato juice, uncooked instant rice, and black pepper. Mix well to combine. Lower heat, cover, and simmer for 6 to 8 minutes or until rice is tender, stirring occasionally.

HINT: If you like your sauerkraut "sweeter," stir in 2 teaspoons Splenda with the tomato juice.

Each serving equals:

HE: 1½ Protein • 1½ Vegetable • ½ Bread • ¼ Slider • 10 Optional Calories

183 Calories • 3 gm Fat • 13 gm Protein • 26 gm Carbohydrate •
427 mg Sodium • 41 mg Calcium • 3 gm Fiber

DIABETIC EXCHANGES: 1½ Meat • 1½ Vegetable • 1 Starch/Carbohydrate

CARB CHOICES: 2

Mini Porcupine Bake

No, I'm not suggesting you hike into the forest and try to catch one of those spiny creatures. A clever cook decided that rice-studded meat resembled porcupines, and I've got to agree—it does!

Serves 2

> 8 ounces extra-lean ground sirloin beef or turkey breast
> 3 tablespoons uncooked Minute Rice
> ½ cup chopped onion
> 6 tablespoons reduced-sodium ketchup ☆
> 2 tablespoons Land O Lakes Fat Free Half & Half
> 1 teaspoon Worcestershire sauce
> 1 tablespoon Splenda Granular
> ½ teaspoon dried parsley flakes
> ⅛ teaspoon black pepper

Preheat oven to 350 degrees. Spray 2 (12-ounce) ovenproof custard cups with butter-flavored cooking spray. In a medium bowl, combine meat, uncooked instant rice, onion, ¼ cup ketchup, half & half, Worcestershire sauce, Splenda, parsley flakes, and black pepper. Mix well to combine. Evenly pat mixture into prepared custard cups. Place filled custard cups on a baking sheet. Bake for 30 to 40 minutes. Place cups on a wire rack and let set for 5 minutes.

Each serving equals:

HE: 3 Protein • ½ Vegetable • ¼ Bread • ½ Slider • 16 Optional Calories

241 Calories • 5 gm Fat • 24 gm Protein • 25 gm Carbohydrate • 125 mg Sodium • 38 mg Calcium • 1 gm Fiber

DIABETIC EXCHANGES: 3 Meat • 1 Starch/Carbohydrate • ½ Vegetable

CARB CHOICES: 1½

Beef and Broccoli Stir-Fry

Instead of spending a fortune at your local Chinese restaurant, why not stir up an Asian-inspired supper at home? With what you save, you could shop for some new kitchen equipment on eBay!

◑ Serves 2

> 4 ounces extra-lean ground sirloin beef or turkey breast
> ½ cup sliced onion
> 1½ cups frozen chopped broccoli, thawed
> ½ cup coarsely chopped red bell pepper
> 2 tablespoons reduced-sodium soy sauce
> ¼ cup reduced-sodium ketchup
> 1 cup hot cooked rice

In a medium skillet sprayed with butter-flavored cooking spray, brown meat and onion for 5 minutes. Add broccoli, red pepper, soy sauce, and ketchup. Mix well to combine. Cover and continue cooking for 4 to 6 minutes or just until vegetables are tender, stirring occasionally. When serving, place ½ cup rice on a plate and spoon about 1 cup meat mixture over top.

HINTS: 1. Thaw broccoli by rinsing in a colander under hot water for 1 minute.
2. Usually ⅔ cup uncooked instant or ½ cup regular rice cooks to about 1 cup.

Each serving equals:

HE: 2½ Vegetable • 1½ Protein • 1 Bread • ¼ Slider • 10 Optional Calories

234 Calories • 2 gm Fat • 16 gm Protein • 38 gm Carbohydrate •
583 mg Sodium • 72 mg Calcium • 5 gm Fiber

DIABETIC EXCHANGES: 2½ Vegetable • 1½ Meat • 1½ Starch/Carbohydrate

CARB CHOICES: 2

Easy Lasagna Bake

I love lasagna—and I think most people do, but it seems like a lot of work to fix a pan of it, which means you usually only make it for company. Here's a version designed just for two, so you can treat yourself like company more often!   ☻   Serves 2

> 4 ounces extra-lean ground sirloin beef or turkey breast
> 1 (8-ounce) can Hunt's Tomato Sauce
> 1 teaspoon Italian seasoning
> 2 teaspoons Splenda Granular
> 1 cup cooked mini lasagna noodles, rinsed and drained
> ½ cup fat-free cottage cheese
> ¼ cup shredded Kraft reduced-fat mozzarella cheese ☆
> 2 tablespoons Kraft Reduced Fat Parmesan Style Grated
>   Topping

Preheat oven to 350 degrees. Spray 2 (12-ounce) ovenproof custard cups with olive oil–flavored cooking spray. In a medium skillet sprayed with olive oil–flavored cooking spray, brown meat. Stir in tomato sauce, Italian seasoning, and Splenda. Add noodles. Mix well to combine. Continue cooking for 3 to 4 minutes, stirring occasionally. In a small bowl, combine cottage cheese, 2 tablespoons mozzarella cheese, and Parmesan cheese. Evenly spoon ½ cup noodle mixture into each prepared custard cup. Spoon ¼ cup cottage cheese mixture over top of each. Arrange about another ½ cup noodle mixture over cottage cheese. Top each with 1 tablespoon mozzarella cheese. Bake for 20 to 25 minutes. Place baking dish on a wire rack and let set for 5 minutes.

HINT: Usually a scant 1 cup uncooked mini lasagna cooks to about 1 cup.

Each serving equals:

HE: 2¾ Protein • 2 Vegetable • 1 Bread • 2 Optional Calories

332 Calories • 8 gm Fat • 29 gm Protein • 36 gm Carbohydrate •
989 mg Sodium • 258 mg Calcium • 2 gm Fiber

DIABETIC EXCHANGES: 3 Meat • 1½ Vegetable • 1½ Starch

CARB CHOICES: 2

Biscuit Beef Pot Pies

I had such fun stirring these up, creating miniaturized pot pies that look as irresistible as they taste! If you haven't used your baking mix for a while, buy a fresh box—you'll know the difference after just one bite.   ☻   Serves 2

> 4 ounces extra-lean ground sirloin beef or turkey breast
> ½ cup chopped onion
> 1 cup frozen mixed vegetables
> ¼ cup reduced-sodium ketchup
> 2 tablespoons chili sauce
> 1 teaspoon Worcestershire sauce
> 6 tablespoons Bisquick Heart Smart Baking Mix
> ½ teaspoon baking powder
> 2 tablespoons Land O Lakes no-fat sour cream
> 2 tablespoons Land O Lakes Fat Free Half & Half
> 1 teaspoon dried parsley flakes

Preheat oven to 375 degrees. Spray 2 (12-ounce) ovenproof custard cups with butter-flavored cooking spray. In a medium skillet sprayed with butter-flavored cooking spray, brown meat and onion. Stir in mixed vegetables. Add ketchup, chili sauce, and Worcestershire sauce. Mix well to combine. Continue cooking for 2 to 3 minutes, stirring occasionally. Evenly spoon mixture into prepared custard cups. In a small bowl, combine baking mix, baking powder, sour cream, half & half, and parsley flakes. Evenly spoon batter over top of each. Place filled custard cups on a baking sheet. Bake for 25 to 30 minutes or until biscuits are golden brown. Place cups on a wire rack and let set for 2 to 3 minutes.

Each serving equals:

HE: 1½ Protein • 1¼ Bread • 1¼ Vegetable • ½ Slider • 14 Optional Calories

252 Calories • 4 gm Fat • 16 gm Protein • 38 gm Carbohydrate •
833 mg Sodium • 152 mg Calcium • 3 gm Fiber

DIABETIC EXCHANGES: 2 Starch/Carbohydrate • 1½ Meat • 1 Vegetable

CARB CHOICES: 2½

Minute Steak Stroganoff

There are various stories about the origin of the Russian dish beef stroganoff, but the one I like the best is the one about the chef who created it for his master who'd lost his teeth and could no longer chew a regular steak! Even if you've got all your teeth (and I hope you do!), this is a dish to treasure.　　**☺**　Serves 2

> *3 tablespoons all-purpose flour*
> *1 teaspoon dried parsley flakes*
> *⅛ teaspoon black pepper*
> *2 (4-ounce) lean tenderized minute or cube steaks*
> *½ cup chopped onion*
> *1 (2.5-ounce) jar sliced mushrooms, undrained*
> *¼ cup Land O Lakes no-fat sour cream*
> *1 tablespoon Land O Lakes Fat Free Half & Half*

In a shallow saucer, combine flour, parsley flakes, and black pepper. Coat steaks on both sides in flour mixture. Place coated steaks in a large skillet sprayed with butter-flavored cooking spray. Brown for 4 to 5 minutes on each side. Meanwhile, in a small saucepan sprayed with butter-flavored cooking spray, sauté onion for 5 minutes. Stir in undrained mushrooms, sour cream, half & half, and any remaining flour mixture. Lower heat and simmer until steaks are browned, stirring occasionally. When serving, place 1 piece of steak on a plate and spoon about 6 tablespoons mushroom mixture over top.

Each serving equals:

HE: 3 Protein • 1 Vegetable • ½ Bread • ¼ Slider • 17 Optional Calories

232 Calories • 4 gm Fat • 29 gm Protein • 20 gm Carbohydrate •
250 mg Sodium • 67 mg Calcium • 2 gm Fiber

DIABETIC EXCHANGES: 3 Meat • 1 Vegetable • 1 Starch

CARB CHOICES: 1

Baked Steaks with Vegetables in Gravy

This dish starts on top of the stove and finishes in the oven, but the flavor is so special, the two-step process is worth the bit of extra fuss. If you've got fresh mushrooms on hand, feel free to use those instead.   ☻   Serves 2

2 (4-ounce) lean tenderized minute or cube steaks
½ cup chopped onion
½ cup grated carrots
1 (2.5-ounce) jar sliced mushrooms, drained
⅓ cup Carnation Nonfat Dry Milk Powder

1½ tablespoons all-purpose flour
¾ cup water
1 teaspoon dried parsley flakes
⅛ teaspoon black pepper
½ teaspoon Worcestershire sauce

Preheat oven to 350 degrees. Spray an 8-by-8-inch baking dish with butter-flavored cooking spray. In a medium skillet sprayed with butter-flavored cooking spray, brown steaks for 3 to 4 minutes on each side. Evenly arrange browned steaks in prepared baking dish. In same skillet, sauté onion for 3 minutes. Stir in carrots and mushrooms. Spoon vegetable mixture evenly over steaks. In a covered jar, combine dry milk powder, flour, and water. Shake well to blend. Pour milk mixture into same skillet. Add parsley flakes and black pepper. Mix well to combine. Cook over medium heat until mixture thickens, stirring often. Stir in Worcestershire sauce. Spoon gravy mixture evenly over vegetables. Cover and bake for 30 minutes. Uncover and continue baking for 10 minutes. Place baking dish on a wire rack and let set for 5 minutes. When serving, evenly spoon vegetables and gravy over meat.

Each serving equals:

HE: 3 Protein • 1½ Vegetable • ½ Fat Free Milk • ¼ Bread

248 Calories • 4 gm Fat • 33 gm Protein • 20 gm Carbohydrate • 318 mg Sodium • 183 mg Calcium • 2 gm Fiber

DIABETIC EXCHANGES: 3 Meat • 1 Vegetable • ½ Fat Free Milk • ½ Starch

CARB CHOICES: 1

Minute Steaks in Mushroom-Tomato Sauce

These little steaks are a great choice for a small household, so consider keeping these on hand. This sauce is easy yet elegant, and also tastes great on a grilled chicken breast if you've got leftovers.

● Serves 2

> 2 (4-ounce) lean tenderized minute or cube steaks
> 1½ cups chopped fresh mushrooms
> ½ cup chopped onion
> ½ cup tomato juice
> 1 tablespoon all-purpose flour
> 1 teaspoon Worcestershire sauce
> 2 teaspoons I Can't Believe It's Not Butter! Light Margarine

In a medium skillet sprayed with butter-flavored cooking spray, brown steaks for 3 to 4 minutes on each side. Remove steaks and keep warm. In same skillet, sauté mushrooms and onion for 5 to 6 minutes. In a covered jar, combine tomato juice and flour. Shake well to blend. Stir tomato juice mixture into vegetable mixture. Add Worcestershire sauce and margarine. Mix well to combine. Place steaks back into skillet and spoon vegetable mixture over top. Lower heat, cover, and simmer for 10 minutes or until meat is tender and sauce thickens, stirring occasionally. When serving, evenly spoon sauce over steaks.

Each serving equals:

HE: 3 Protein • 1¾ Vegetable • ½ Fat • 15 Optional Calories

242 Calories • 6 gm Fat • 33 gm Protein • 14 gm Carbohydrate • 479 mg Sodium • 35 mg Calcium • 3 gm Fiber

DIABETIC EXCHANGES: 3 Meat • 1½ Vegetable • ½ Fat

CARB CHOICES: 1

Grande Swiss Steak

I called this "grande" for the big, big flavor you'll taste in every mouthful! Make it spicy, make it mild, but definitely—make it!

◐ Serves 2

> 2 (4-ounce) lean tenderized minute or cube steaks
> ½ cup chunky salsa (mild, medium, or hot)
> 2 tablespoons reduced-sodium ketchup
> 1 teaspoon taco seasoning
> ½ cup coarsely chopped onion
> ½ cup coarsely chopped celery

Spray a 2 or 2½ quart slow cooker container with butter-flavored cooking spray. In a medium skillet sprayed with butter-flavored cooking spray, brown steaks for 4 to 5 minutes on each side. In a medium bowl, combine salsa, ketchup, and taco seasoning. Stir in onion and celery. Place 1 piece of browned steak in prepared slow cooker container and spoon half of salsa mixture over top. Repeat layers. Cover and cook for 6 to 8 hours. When serving, evenly spoon mixture over steak pieces.

HINT: If your small slow cooker has a temperature setting, choose LOW.

Each serving equals:

HE: 3 Protein • 1½ Vegetable • 15 Optional Calories

212 Calories • 4 gm Fat • 31 gm Protein • 13 gm Carbohydrate • 509 mg Sodium • 30 mg Calcium • 1 gm Fiber

DIABETIC EXCHANGES: 3 Meat • 2 Vegetable

CARB CHOICES: 1

Minute Steaks in Mushroom Sauce

Mushrooms have almost no calories, so they're a great splurge in any dish. Make sure you choose fresh mushrooms that don't have mushy or dark spots on them. Don't soak them to clean them, just brush the dirt off and give a fast rinse and dry.   ☻   Serves 2

2 (4-ounce) lean tenderized minute or cube steaks
2 cups sliced fresh mushrooms
¼ cup finely chopped onion
1 cup reduced-sodium tomato juice
1½ tablespoons all-purpose flour
1½ teaspoons Worcestershire sauce
1 teaspoon dried parsley flakes
⅛ teaspoon black pepper

In a medium skillet sprayed with butter-flavored cooking spray, brown steaks for 4 to 5 minutes on each side. Meanwhile, in a medium saucepan sprayed with butter-flavored cooking spray, sauté mushrooms and onion for 5 minutes. In a covered jar, combine tomato juice, flour, and Worcestershire sauce. Shake well to blend. Pour juice mixture into saucepan with mushrooms. Add parsley flakes and black pepper. Mix well to combine. Continue cooking for 3 to 4 minutes or until mixture starts to thicken, stirring often. Evenly spoon mushroom sauce over steaks. Lower heat, cover, and simmer for 10 minutes. When serving, evenly spoon mushroom sauce over steaks.

Each serving equals:

HE: 3 Protein • 2¼ Vegetable • ¼ Bread

217 Calories • 5 gm Fat • 30 gm Protein • 13 gm Carbohydrate •
166 mg Sodium • 36 mg Calcium • 1 gm Fiber

DIABETIC EXCHANGES: 3 Meat • 2 Vegetable

CARB CHOICES: 1

Steak Stir-Fry

If you always order veggie or chicken stir-fry at your favorite Chinese restaurant, go for the gusto—and slice up some steak! Combined with fresh, colorful vegetables, the steak is the star, and the prize goes to you. ☉ Serves 2

> 8 ounces lean sirloin steak, cut into 1-inch strips
> ½ cup chopped broccoli
> ½ cup chopped carrots
> ½ cup red or green bell pepper
> ¼ cup chopped green onion
> 2 tablespoons reduced-sodium soy sauce
> 2 tablespoons reduced-sodium ketchup
> 1 teaspoon Splenda Granular
> 2 tablespoons water
> 1 cup diced cabbage
> 1 cup hot cooked rice

In a large skillet sprayed with butter-flavored cooking spray, sauté steak for 3 minutes. Stir in broccoli, carrots, red pepper, green onion, soy sauce, ketchup, Splenda, and water. Continue sautéing for 5 minutes or just until meat and vegetables are tender. Add cabbage. Mix well to combine. Continue sautéing for 3 to 5 minutes. For each serving, place ½ cup hot rice on a plate and spoon about 1½ cups steak mixture over top.

HINT: Usually ⅔ cup uncooked instant or ½ cup regular rice cooks to about 1 cup.

Each serving equals:

HE: 3 Protein • 2¼ Vegetable • 1 Bread • 16 Optional Calories

309 Calories • 5 gm Fat • 32 gm Protein • 34 gm Carbohydrate •
629 mg Sodium • 68 mg Calcium • 5 gm Fiber

DIABETIC EXCHANGES: 3 Meat • 2 Vegetable • 1½ Starch

CARB CHOICES: 2

Pacific Rim Pepper Steak

Peppers are part of many cuisines around the world, but they've always seemed to me to be the perfect partners for beef. Here, I've used green pepper but you could also use red and/or yellow pepper, too. ○ Serves 2 (1½ cups)

8 ounces lean sirloin steak, cut into 1-inch strips
½ cup coarsely chopped onion
1 cup coarsely chopped green bell pepper
1 (14½-ounce) can stewed tomatoes, undrained
2 tablespoons reduced-sodium soy sauce
2 tablespoons reduced-sodium ketchup

In a large skillet sprayed with butter-flavored cooking spray, sauté steak, onion, and green pepper for 6 to 8 minutes. Add undrained stewed tomatoes, soy sauce, and ketchup. Mix well to combine. Lower heat and simmer for 6 to 8 minutes, stirring occasionally.

HINT: Good as is or served over rice or pasta.

Each serving equals:

HE: 3 Protein • 3 Vegetable • 15 Optional Calories

281 Calories • 5 gm Fat • 34 gm Protein • 25 gm Carbohydrate • 982 mg Sodium • 95 mg Calcium • 4 gm Fiber

DIABETIC EXCHANGES: 3 Meat • 3 Vegetable

CARB CHOICES: 1½

Beef Stroganoff

When a dish is a classic, why fiddle with what has worked for decades? This creamy dish tastes of luxury and rich ingredients, but you and I know the truth—that you can eat like a queen without destroying your waistline! ☻ Serves 2

> *8 ounces lean sirloin steak, cut into bite-size pieces*
> *1½ cups sliced fresh mushrooms*
> *½ cup chopped onion*
> *¼ cup water*
> *¼ cup Land O Lakes Fat Free Half & Half*
> *½ teaspoon dried minced garlic*
> *1 tablespoon chili sauce*
> *¼ cup Land O Lakes no-fat sour cream*
> *2 tablespoons chopped fresh parsley or 1 teaspoon dried parsley flakes*
> *1 cup hot cooked noodles, rinsed and drained*

In a large skillet sprayed with butter-flavored cooking spray, sauté steak pieces for 5 minutes. Stir in mushrooms and onion. Continue to sauté for 5 minutes. Add water, half & half, garlic, and chili sauce. Mix well to combine. Lower heat and simmer for 5 minutes or until most of liquid is absorbed. Stir in sour cream and parsley. Continue to simmer for 2 to 3 minutes or until mixture is heated through, stirring often. For each serving, place ½ cup noodles on a plate and spoon about ¾ cup meat mixture over top.

HINT: Usually ¾ cup uncooked noodles cook to about 1 cup.

Each serving equals:

HE: 3 Protein • 1¼ Vegetable • 1 Bread • ½ Slider • 18 Optional Calories

293 Calories • 5 gm Fat • 26 gm Protein • 36 gm Carbohydrate • 604 mg Sodium • 106 mg Calcium • 3 gm Fiber

DIABETIC EXCHANGES: 2 Meat • 1½ Starch/Carbohydrate • 1 Vegetable

CARB CHOICES: 2½

Southwestern Beef Skillet

If you've never cooked with chilies, you may be nervous about adding them to this tasty entrée—will they be too spicy, too intense for your taste buds? I'm happy to clear up the confusion. The canned kind are not tongue-testing hot, just flavorful.

○ Serves 2 (1½ cups)

> 4 ounces lean round steak, cut into bite-size pieces
> ½ cup coarsely chopped onion
> ½ cup water
> 1 teaspoon Wyler's Beef Granules Instant Bouillon
> ½ teaspoon chili seasoning mix
> 1 (8-ounce) can stewed tomatoes, undrained
> 1 (8-ounce) can whole-kernel corn, rinsed and drained
> 1 (4-ounce) can diced green chilies, drained

In a large skillet sprayed with butter-flavored cooking spray, sauté steak pieces and onion for 5 minutes. In a small bowl, combine water and dry beef bouillon. Stir bouillon mixture and chili seasoning into meat mixture. Add undrained stewed tomatoes, corn, and green chilies. Mix well to combine. Bring mixture to a boil. Lower heat, cover, and simmer for 20 to 30 minutes or until meat is tender, stirring occasionally.

Each serving equals:

HE: 3 Protein • 2½ Vegetable • 1½ Protein • 1 Bread • 5 Optional Calories

191 Calories • 3 gm Fat • 12 gm Protein • 29 gm Carbohydrate •
881 mg Sodium • 132 mg Calcium • 6 gm Fiber

DIABETIC EXCHANGES: 2½ Vegetable • 1½ Meat • 1 Starch

CARB CHOICES: 1½

Stove Top BBQ Steak and Mushrooms

Stirring up savory homemade sauces on top of the stove is easier than you might imagine, especially if you understand the power of heat to make ingredients "break down" and combine to form a great new taste. ❂ Serves 2 (¾ cup)

> 8 ounces lean round steak, cut into bite-size pieces
> ½ cup chopped onion
> ¼ cup reduced-sodium ketchup
> 2 tablespoons water
> 1 tablespoon Worcestershire sauce
> 2 tablespoons Splenda Granular
> ⅛ teaspoon black pepper
> 1 cup sliced fresh mushrooms

In a large skillet sprayed with butter-flavored cooking spray, sauté steak pieces and onion for 5 minutes. Stir in ketchup, water, Worcestershire sauce, Splenda, and black pepper. Add mushrooms. Mix well to combine. Lower heat, cover, and simmer for 20 minutes or until meat is tender, stirring occasionally.

HINT: Great as a sandwich filling or spooned over pasta, rice, or baked potato.

Each serving equals:

HE: 3 Protein • 1 Vegetable • ¼ Slider • 6 Optional Calories

228 Calories • 4 gm Fat • 32 gm Protein • 16 gm Carbohydrate • 130 mg Sodium • 28 mg Calcium • 1 gm Fiber

DIABETIC EXCHANGES: 3 Meat • 1 Vegetable • ½ Other Carbohydrate

CARB CHOICES: 1

Sauerbraten Beef and Cabbage

This German-inspired skillet entrée weaves together some unusual flavors—vinegar, ginger, graham cracker crumbs—to produce an astonishingly hearty and satisfying supper dish. Be brave, take a risk—and give it a try.   ☻   Serves 2 (2 cups)

8 ounces lean sirloin steak, cut into bite-size pieces
1½ cups water
2 tablespoons white distilled vinegar
1 teaspoon Wyler's Beef Granules Instant Bouillon
¼ cup finely chopped onion
1 teaspoon dried parsley flakes
⅛ teaspoon black pepper
2 cups coarsely chopped cabbage
1 cup unpeeled diced raw potatoes
3 tablespoons graham cracker crumbs
½ teaspoon ground ginger

In a medium skillet sprayed with butter-flavored cooking spray, brown steak pieces. In a small bowl, combine water, vinegar, dry beef bouillon, onion, parsley flakes, and black pepper. Pour mixture over meat. Bring mixture to a boil. Lower heat, cover, and simmer for 30 minutes. Add cabbage and potatoes. Mix well to combine. Re-cover and continue to simmer for 30 minutes or until meat and potatoes are tender. Remove mixture with a slotted spoon. Evenly spoon onto 2 serving plates, and cover. Add the graham cracker crumbs and ginger to remaining pan juice. Mix well to combine. Continue cooking until mixture thickens, stirring often. Evenly drizzle mixture over top of each plate. Serve at once.

Each serving equals:

HE: 3 Protein • 1 Bread • 1 Vegetable • 8 Optional Calories

298 Calories • 6 gm Fat • 36 gm Protein • 25 gm Carbohydrate • 125 mg Sodium • 58 mg Calcium • 3 gm Fiber

DIABETIC EXCHANGES: 3 Meat • 1½ Starch • 1 Vegetable

CARB CHOICES: 1½

Steak Parmesan

By coating the steak pieces in the flour mixture—a procedure known as dredging—you make it easier for the sauce to "stick" to your meat. And if there was ever a time you wanted your sauce to coat a piece of steak, this is it! ☻ Serves 2

> 3 tablespoons all-purpose flour
> 1 teaspoon dried parsley flakes
> ⅛ teaspoon black pepper
> 2 (4-ounce) lean tenderized minute or cube steaks
> 2 (¾-ounce) slices Kraft reduced-fat mozzarella cheese
> 1 (8-ounce) can Hunt's Tomato Sauce
> 1 (2.5-ounce) jar sliced mushrooms, drained
> 1 teaspoon Italian seasoning
> 1 tablespoon Splenda Granular
> 2 teaspoons Kraft Reduced Fat Parmesan Style Grated
>   Topping

Preheat oven to 350 degrees. Spray an 8-by-8-inch baking dish with olive oil–flavored cooking spray. In a shallow bowl, combine flour, parsley flakes, and black pepper. Coat steak pieces on each side in flour mixture. Place coated steaks in a large skillet sprayed with olive oil–flavored cooking spray. Brown steaks for 5 minutes on each side. Place browned steaks in prepared baking dish. Evenly arrange 1 slice of mozzarella cheese over top of each. In same skillet, combine tomato sauce, mushrooms, Italian seasoning, and Splenda. Cook over medium heat for 2 to 3 minutes. Drizzle sauce mixture over top of each steak. Evenly sprinkle 1 tablespoon Parmesan cheese over top of each. Bake for 20 to 25 minutes. Place baking dish on a wire rack and let set for 2 to 3 minutes.

Each serving equals:

HE: 4 Protein • 2½ Vegetable • ½ Bread • 12 Optional Calories

321 Calories • 9 gm Fat • 39 gm Protein • 21 gm Carbohydrate • 896 mg Sodium • 165 mg Calcium • 3 gm Fiber

DIABETIC EXCHANGES: 4 Meat • 2 Vegetable • ½ Starch

CARB CHOICES: 1½

Drunken Pork Tenders

Cooking with beer is an old American tradition, made popular by camp cooks on cattle drives, but it's also a classic preparation brought here by German immigrants. You get all of the flavor but none of the alcohol, so everyone can enjoy it ☺ Serves 2

2 (4-ounce) lean tenderized pork tenderloins or cutlets
¼ cup non-alcoholic beer
¼ cup reduced-sodium ketchup
1 tablespoon Splenda Granular
2 teaspoons dried onion flakes

In a medium skillet sprayed with butter-flavored cooking spray, brown pork tenderloins for 3 to 4 minutes on each side. In a small bowl, combine beer, ketchup, Splenda, and onion flakes. Evenly spoon mixture over browned tenderloins. Lower heat, cover, and simmer for 20 minutes or until pork is cooked through.

Each serving equals:

HE: 3 Protein • ¼ Slider • 19 Optional Calories

172 Calories • 4 gm Fat • 23 gm Protein • 11 gm Carbohydrate •
51 mg Sodium • 15 mg Calcium • 0 gm Fiber

DIABETIC EXCHANGES: 3 Meat • ½ Other Carbohydrate

CARB CHOICES: 1

Pork Tenders with Corn Salsa

If your local market doesn't keep pork cutlets in stock, don't accept it—*ask*! This lean meat is an excellent choice for anyone concerned about good health, and prepared this way, it's juicy and flavorful.

◐ Serves 2

> 2 (4-ounce) lean tenderized pork tenderloins or cutlets
> 1 cup chunky salsa (mild, medium, or hot)
> 1 tablespoon reduced-sodium ketchup
> ½ teaspoon taco seasoning
> 1 tablespoon Splenda Granular
> 1 teaspoon dried parsley flakes
> ½ cup frozen whole-kernel corn, thawed

In a medium skillet sprayed with butter-flavored cooking spray, brown pork tenderloins for 3 to 4 minutes on each side. In a medium bowl, combine salsa, ketchup, taco seasoning, Splenda, and parsley flakes. Stir in corn. Evenly spoon salsa mixture over browned tenderloins. Lower heat, cover, and simmer for 20 minutes or until pork is cooked through. When serving, evenly spoon salsa mixture over browned tenderloins.

HINT: Thaw corn by rinsing in a colander under hot water for 1 minute.

Each serving equals:

HE: 3 Protein • 1 Vegetable • ½ Bread • 11 Optional Calories

244 Calories • 4 gm Fat • 28 gm Protein • 24 gm Carbohydrate • 806 mg Sodium • 9 mg Calcium • 4 gm Fiber

DIABETIC EXCHANGES: 3 Meat • 1 Vegetable • ½ Starch

CARB CHOICES: 2

Baked Breaded Pork Tenders

Isn't it great that you don't have to give up delectable breaded meats? Baking is a fantastic cooking method and can give you a crisp crust when you cook it low and slow.   ☻   Serves 2

> ¼ cup barbecue sauce
> 6 tablespoons dry bread crumbs
> ½ teaspoon Italian seasoning
> ⅛ teaspoon black pepper
> 2 (4-ounce) lean tenderized pork tenderloins or cutlets

Preheat oven to 325 degrees. Spray an 8-by-8-inch baking dish with butter-flavored cooking spray. Place barbecue sauce in a shallow saucer. In another shallow saucer, combine bread crumbs, Italian seasoning, and black pepper. Dip tenderloins first in barbecue sauce, then in crumb mixture, being sure to coat both sides. Evenly arrange tenderloins in prepared baking dish. Drizzle any remaining barbecue sauce or crumb mixture evenly over top. Bake for 45 to 50 minutes. Place baking dish on a wire rack and let set for 5 minutes.

Each serving equals:

HE: 3 Protein • 1 Bread • ¼ Slider • 4 Optional Calories

234 Calories • 6 gm Fat • 27 gm Protein • 18 gm Carbohydrate • 237 mg Sodium • 48 mg Calcium • 2 gm Fiber

DIABETIC EXCHANGES: 3 Meat • 1 Starch

CARB CHOICES: 1

Barbecue Ham Sandwiches

Most barbecue cooks keep their sauces a deep, dark secret, but I won't leave you to figure out the magic blend in this dish. Sharing what works is how we healthy folk stick together!

◐ Serves 2

¼ cup finely chopped celery
¼ cup finely chopped onion
½ cup reduced-sodium tomato juice
2 tablespoons reduced-sodium ketchup
1 tablespoon Splenda Granular
1 teaspoon Worcestershire sauce
1 teaspoon prepared yellow mustard
1 teaspoon dried parsley flakes
1 (6-ounce) package lean ham slices, shredded
2 small hamburger buns

In a medium skillet sprayed with butter-flavored cooking spray, sauté celery and onion for 5 minutes. Add tomato juice, ketchup, Splenda, Worcestershire, mustard, and parsley flakes. Mix well to combine. Bring mixture to a boil, stirring occasionally. Stir in shredded ham. Lower heat and simmer for 6 to 8 minutes, stirring occasionally. For each sandwich, spoon a full ½ cup ham mixture between a hamburger bun.

Each serving equals:

HE: 2 Protein • 1 Bread • 1 Vegetable • 18 Optional Calories

199 Calories • 3 gm Fat • 17 gm Protein • 26 gm Carbohydrate • 956 mg Sodium • 32 mg Calcium • 2 gm Fiber

DIABETIC EXCHANGES: 2 Meat • 1 Starch • 1 Vegetable

CARB CHOICES: 1½

Ham Supper Skillet

I've been buying peas by the bag instead of the box while working on this cookbook. It's just easier to measure out the amount I need and then clip the bag closed. Of course, if you love this dish as much as my tasters did, you'll use those peas up fast!

☻ Serves 2 (1 cup)

> 2 cups purchased coleslaw mix
> 1 full cup diced Dubuque 97% fat-free ham or any extra-
>   lean ham
> ¾ cup frozen peas, thawed
> 1 cup fat-free milk
> 2 tablespoons Land O Lakes Fat Free Half & Half
> 1½ tablespoons all-purpose flour
> 1 teaspoon dried parsley flakes
> ⅛ teaspoon black pepper

In a medium skillet sprayed with butter-flavored cooking spray, sauté coleslaw mix and ham for 8 to 10 minutes or just until cabbage is tender. Stir in peas. In a covered jar, combine milk, half & half, and flour. Shake well to blend. Stir milk mixture into ham mixture. Add parsley flakes and black pepper. Mix well to combine. Lower heat and simmer for 5 minutes or until mixture thickens, stirring often.

HINTS: 1. 1¾ cups shredded cabbage and ¼ cup shredded car-
    rots may be used in place of purchased coleslaw mix.
2. Thaw peas by rinsing in a colander under hot water for
    1 minute.

Each serving equals:

HE: 2 Protein • 1 Bread • 1 Vegetable • ½ Fat Free Milk • 9 Optional Calories

227 Calories • 3 gm Fat • 23 gm Protein • 27 gm Carbohydrate •
809 mg Sodium • 223 mg Calcium • 5 gm Fiber

DIABETIC EXCHANGES: 2 Meat • 1 Starch • 1 Vegetable • ½ Fat Free Milk

CARB CHOICES: 1½

Ham and Peach Skillet

This makes a wonderful brunch entrée, especially if you're dining a bit after noon. It's sweet and tangy, which brings out the best in the ham and in the peaches.   ☻   Serves 2

> 2 (3-ounce) slices Dubuque 97% fat-free ham or any extra-
>   lean ham
> 1 (8-ounce) can sliced peaches, packed in fruit juice,
>   drained, coarsely chopped, and 2 tablespoons liquid
>   reserved
> 2 tablespoons Splenda Granular
> ⅛ teaspoon ground cinnamon

In a medium skillet sprayed with butter-flavored cooking spray, brown ham for 3 to 4 minutes on each side. Evenly spoon peach slices over ham slices. In a small bowl, combine reserved fruit juice, Splenda, and cinnamon. Drizzle mixture evenly over top of sliced peaches. Cover and continue cooking for 3 to 4 minutes or until ham is browned and peaches are heated through. Serve at once.

HINT: A 3-ounce slice of ham is about ⅓ inch thick.

Each serving equals:

HE: 2 Protein • 1 Fruit • 6 Optional Calories

138 Calories • 2 gm Fat • 14 gm Protein • 16 gm Carbohydrate •
673 mg Sodium • 8 mg Calcium • 1 gm Fiber

DIABETIC EXCHANGES: 2 Meat • 1 Fruit

CARB CHOICES: 1

Ham and Potatoes au Gratin

Does your heart beat faster when you read a recipe that ends in "au gratin"? You know it means there'll be *cheese* involved, and that's got to be good! This blend of ham, potatoes, and beans is a definite man-pleaser, but every woman who tried it loved it just as much.

◑ Serves 2 (1 cup)

2¼ cups frozen loose-packed shredded hash brown potatoes
1 cup diced Dubuque 97% fat-free ham or any extra-lean
    ham
1 cup frozen cut green beans, thawed
½ cup diced onion
2 tablespoons water
¼ cup Land O Lakes Fat Free Half & Half
1 teaspoon dried parsley flakes
¾ cup diced Velveeta Light processed cheese

Spray a 2 or 2½ quart slow cooker container with butter-flavored cooking spray. In prepared container, combine potatoes, ham, green beans, and onion. Add water, half & half, and parsley flakes. Mix well to combine. Stir in Velveeta cheese. Cover and cook for 4 hours.

HINTS: 1. Mr. Dell's frozen shredded potatoes are a good choice or raw shredded potatoes, rinsed and patted dry, may be used in place of frozen potatoes.
2. Thaw green beans by rinsing in a colander under hot water for 1 minute.
3. If your small slow cooker has a temperature control, choose LOW.

Each serving equals:

HE: 3½ Protein • 1½ Vegetable • ¾ Bread • 18 Optional Calories

295 Calories • 7 gm Fat • 27 gm Protein • 31 gm Carbohydrate •
994 mg Sodium • 325 mg Calcium • 4 gm Fiber

DIABETIC EXCHANGES: 3½ Meat • 1½ Vegetable • 1 Starch

CARB CHOICES: 2

Spanish Sausage Supper

Stupendous! Spectacular! And downright swell! I went looking for s-words to tell you how satisfying (another one) and sensational (another) this dish is. Don't wait for Cinco de Mayo to try it—it's good anytime. ● Serves 2 (1¼ cups)

> 4 ounces Healthy Choice 97% lean kielbasa or polish
>   sausage, cut into bite-size pieces
> ¼ cup chopped green bell pepper
> ¼ cup chopped onion
> ½ cup chopped celery
> 1 (8-ounce) can tomatoes, finely chopped and undrained
> ¾ cup reduced-sodium tomato juice
> 2 teaspoons Splenda Granular
> ¼ teaspoon chili seasoning
> ⅛ teaspoon black pepper
> ⅔ cup uncooked Minute Rice

In a medium skillet sprayed with butter-flavored cooking spray, sauté sausage pieces, green pepper, onion, and celery for 6 to 8 minutes. Stir in undrained tomatoes, tomato juice, Splenda, chili seasoning, and black pepper. Add uncooked instant rice. Mix well to combine. Bring mixture to a boil. Lower heat and simmer for 6 to 8 minutes or until rice is tender and most of liquid is absorbed, stirring often.

HINT: If you can't find lean kielbasa, use either lean sausage or frankfurters.

Each serving equals:

HE: 2¾ Vegetable • 1½ Protein • 1 Bread • 2 Optional Calories

222 Calories • 2 gm Fat • 12 gm Protein • 39 gm Carbohydrate •
724 mg Sodium • 83 mg Calcium • 4 gm Fiber

DIABETIC EXCHANGES: 2½ Vegetable • 1½ Meat • 1½ Starch

CARB CHOICES: 3

Bavarian Kielbasa Supper

Here's a great choice for a chilly fall night watching Monday Night Football with your family! It's easy to fix, completely filling, and leaves just enough room for dessert. ☾ Serves 2 (1 cup)

> 6 ounces Healthy Choice 97% lean kielbasa or polish
>   sausage, cut into bite-size pieces
> 1 (8-ounce) can sauerkraut, well drained
> 1 cup (1 medium) cored, peeled, and diced cooking apple
> ¼ cup finely chopped onion
> ½ cup non-alcoholic beer
> 1 tablespoon Splenda Granular
> ¼ teaspoon caraway seeds
> 1 tablespoon cornstarch
> 2 tablespoons water

In a medium skillet sprayed with butter-flavored cooking spray, combine sausage pieces, sauerkraut, apple, and onion. Stir in beer, Splenda, and caraway seeds. Cook over medium heat for 10 minutes, stirring often. In a small bowl, combine cornstarch and water using a wire whisk. Add cornstarch mixture to sausage mixture. Mix well to combine. Continue cooking for 3 to 4 minutes or until mixture thickens, stirring often.

HINT: If you can't find lean kielbasa, use either lean sausage or frankfurters.

Each serving equals:

HE: 2¼ Protein • 1¼ Vegetable • ½ Fruit • ¼ Slider • 10 Optional Calories

174 Calories • 2 gm Fat • 11 gm Protein • 28 gm Carbohydrate • 975 mg Sodium • 59 mg Calcium • 3 gm Fiber

DIABETIC EXCHANGES: 2 Meat • 1 Vegetable • ½ Fruit • ½ Starch/Carbohydrate

CARB CHOICES: 2

Creamed Corned Beef Casserole

I know this may not be to everyone's taste, but if you've ever eaten and loved a creamy corned beef dish on St. Patrick's Day, you might just be thrilled! Put on a green scarf, play the *Clancy Brothers' Greatest Hits*, and enjoy.   ☺   Serves 2

1 cup fat-free milk
1½ tablespoons all-purpose flour
1 (2.5-ounce) package Carl Buddig lean corned beef, shredded
¼ cup (2 ounces) Philadelphia fat-free cream cheese
1 (2.5-ounce) jar sliced mushrooms, drained and chopped
¾ cup cooked noodles, rinsed and drained
2 tablespoons Land O Lakes no-fat sour cream
1 teaspoon dried onion flakes
1 teaspoon dried parsley flakes
2 tablespoons shredded Kraft reduced-fat Cheddar cheese

Preheat oven to 350 degrees. Spray 2 (12-ounce) ovenproof custard cups with butter-flavored cooking spray. In a covered jar, combine milk and flour. Shake well to blend. Pour milk mixture into a medium skillet sprayed with butter-flavored cooking spray. Stir in corned beef and cream cheese. Cook over medium heat until mixture thickens and cream cheese melts, stirring often. Add mushrooms, noodles, sour cream, onion flakes, and parsley flakes. Mix well to combine. Evenly spoon mixture into prepared custard cups. Sprinkle 1 tablespoon Cheddar cheese over top of each. Place filled custard cups on a baking sheet. Bake for 15 to 18 minutes. Place cups on a wire rack and let set for 2 to 3 minutes.

HINT: Usually ½ cup uncooked noodles cook to about ¾ cup.

Each serving equals:

HE: 2 Protein • 1 Bread • ½ Fat Free Milk • ½ Vegetable • 15 Optional Calories

257 Calories • 5 gm Fat • 21 gm Protein • 32 gm Carbohydrate •
854 mg Sodium • 323 mg Calcium • 2 gm Fiber

DIABETIC EXCHANGES: 2 Meat • 1½ Starch/Carbohydrate • ½ Fat Free Milk

CARB CHOICES: 2

Franks and Corn Scallop

This is fun food, and my grandkids gobbled it down when I served it not long ago. All those bits of corn and chunks of frankfurter coupled with cheesy-creamy sauce and crunchy Doritos—doesn't that just sound like heaven on a plate? ◑ Serves 2

> 1 (8-ounce) can cream-style corn
> 1 egg, or equivalent in egg substitute
> 2 tablespoons Land O Lakes no-fat sour cream
> 4 ounces Oscar Mayer or Healthy Choice reduced-fat
>   frankfurters, cut into ¼-inch pieces
> ¼ cup shredded Kraft reduced-fat Cheddar cheese
> ¼ cup finely chopped onion
> ¼ cup coarsely crushed Dorito's Baked Corn Chips

Preheat oven to 350 degrees. Spray 2 (12-ounce) ovenproof custard cups with butter-flavored cooking spray. In a medium bowl, combine corn, egg, and sour cream. Stir in frankfurter pieces and Cheddar cheese. Add onion. Mix gently to combine. Evenly spoon mixture into prepared custard cups. Sprinkle crushed corn chips evenly over top of each. Place filled custard cups on a baking sheet. Bake for 30 minutes. Place cups on a wire rack and let set for 2 to 3 minutes.

Each serving equals:

HE: 2½ Protein • 1½ Bread • ¼ Vegetable • 15 Optional Calories

295 Calories • 7 gm Fat • 20 gm Protein • 38 gm Carbohydrate •
989 mg Sodium • 157 mg Calcium • 2 gm Fiber

DIABETIC EXCHANGES: 2½ Meat • 2 Starch/Carbohydrate

CARB CHOICES: 2½

Doubly Good

Desserts

Most of my dessert recipes over the year have served eight, especially my cheesecakes. That's great if you've got a big family or a huge freezer, but what about those of you who live alone or as a couple, and those apartment dwellers who must make do with smaller appliances? It's one thing to enjoy a piece of healthy pie on Monday, but having to eat the same pie for the next few days takes away a little of the fun.

I had to put on my "common sense" chef's hat to figure out how to handle this particular challenge while not depriving readers of a variety of different kinds of dessert delights. Could I still serve pie, and cake, and cheesecake, when my maximum number of servings had to stop at two? I bet you can guess the answer!

This chapter brims over with dazzling desserts of every kind, all of them healthy and low in sugar and fat. It's been my pleasure to try and make dozens of dessert dreams come true in these pages, so let me entice you with a little preview of the temptations that follow. If pudding is your passion, surrender to Velvety Chocolate Walnut Pudding *or* Hawaiian Rhubarb Banana Cream Treats. *If sweet fruit spins your wheels, I'm offering* Fresh Peach Crisp, Cran-Apple Cobbler, *and* Orange Marmalade Bread Pudding. *If cake, cake, and nothing but cake is your choice, try* Cliff's Chocolate Mocha Sour Cream Cake *or* Vanilla Custard Pudding Cake. *Charmed by cheesecake? Opt for* Almond Cheesecake with Sour Cream Topping. *And if Pie Power is your theme, I hope you'll try* Coconut Orange Meringue Pies!

Rice Pudding with Raisins

For an old-fashioned taste of truly homemade, here's a dessert that will bring you memories of Grandma's just-for-you treats! This is a good recipe to stir up if you've got some leftover rice from a takeout meal. ☻ Serves 2

⅓ cup Carnation Nonfat Dry Milk Powder
1 cup water
1 tablespoon cornstarch
1 cup cooked rice
¼ cup Splenda Granular
¾ teaspoon vanilla extract
2 tablespoons seedless raisins
¼ teaspoon ground cinnamon
2 tablespoons Cool Whip Lite

In a medium saucepan, combine dry milk powder, water, and cornstarch using a wire whisk. Add rice and Splenda. Mix well to combine. Cook over medium heat until mixture just comes to a boil, stirring often. Continue cooking for 1 minute, stirring constantly. Remove from heat. Stir in vanilla extract and raisins. Evenly spoon mixture into 2 dessert dishes. Sprinkle ⅛ teaspoon cinnamon evenly over top of each. Garnish each with 1 tablespoon Cool Whip Lite. Refrigerate for at least 30 minutes.

HINTS: 1. Usually ⅔ cup uncooked instant or ½ cup regular rice cooks to about 1 cup.
2. To plump up raisins without "cooking," place in a glass measuring cup and microwave on HIGH for 20 seconds.

Each serving equals:

HE: 1 Bread • ½ Fat Free Milk • ½ Fruit • ¼ Slider • 17 Optional Calories

177 Calories • 1 gm Fat • 6 gm Protein • 36 gm Carbohydrate • 66 mg Sodium • 164 mg Calcium • 1 gm Fiber

DIABETIC EXCHANGES: 1½ Starch • ½ Fat Free Milk • ½ Fruit

CARB CHOICES: 2

Apricot Walnut Rice Pudding

I love to combine tastes and textures in search of a scrumptious combination, and I think I've found a terrific pair in apricots and walnuts. Crunchy and sweet, rough and smooth, and a great contrast to the cooled pudding.   ❂   Serves 2

¾ cup water
⅔ cup uncooked Minute Rice
¼ cup chopped dried apricots
2 tablespoons Splenda Granular
¼ cup Land O Lakes Fat Free Half & Half
2 tablespoons chopped walnuts
½ teaspoon vanilla extract
¼ cup Cool Whip Free

In a medium saucepan, combine water, uncooked instant rice, dried apricots, and Splenda. Cover and cook over medium heat for 6 to 8 minutes, stirring occasionally. Remove from heat and let set for 5 minutes or until all water is absorbed, stirring occasionally. Stir in half & half, walnuts, and vanilla extract. Spoon rice mixture into a small bowl and refrigerate for at least 15 minutes. Add Cool Whip Free. Mix gently just to combine. Evenly spoon mixture into 2 dessert dishes. Refrigerate for at least 15 minutes.

Each serving equals:

HE: 1 Bread • 1 Fruit • ½ Fat • ¼ Protein • ¼ Slider • 18 Optional Calories

217 Calories • 5 gm Fat • 5 gm Protein • 38 gm Carbohydrate • 53 mg Sodium • 52 mg Calcium • 3 gm Fiber

DIABETIC EXCHANGES: 1½ Starch • 1 Fruit • 1 Fat

CARB CHOICES: 2½

Rhubarb-Pineapple Swirl Dessert

You might just be "bowled over" when you spoon this fruited marvel into your mouth—it's that good! Each bite brings a little gift of flavor that will make you smile.   ☻   Serves 2

> 1 cup finely chopped fresh or frozen rhubarb, thawed
> 1 (8-ounce) can crushed pineapple, packed in fruit juice,
>   drained and 2 tablespoons liquid reserved
> ¼ cup Splenda Granular
> ½ cup Cool Whip Free
> 2 tablespoons miniature marshmallows
> ¼ cup graham cracker crumbs ☆
> 1 tablespoon chopped pecans

In a small saucepan, combine rhubarb and reserved pineapple juice. Cover and cook over medium heat for 6 to 8 minutes or until rhubarb is tender, stirring occasionally. Remove from heat. Add pineapple and Splenda. Mix well to combine. Place uncovered saucepan on a wire rack and allow to cool for 30 minutes, stirring occasionally. Stir in Cool Whip Free and marshmallows. Place 1½ tablespoons graham cracker crumbs in 2 (12-ounce) custard cups. Evenly spoon rhubarb mixture into each custard cup. In a small bowl, combine remaining 1 tablespoon graham cracker crumbs and pecans. Sprinkle crumb mixture evenly over top of each.

HINT: For those who like their desserts sweeter, add an extra tablespoon or two of Splenda.

Each serving equals:

HE: 1 Fruit • ⅔ Bread • ½ Vegetable • ¼ Fat • ½ Slider • 12 Optional Calories

188 Calories • 4 gm Fat • 2 gm Protein • 36 gm Carbohydrate • 84 mg Sodium • 138 mg Calcium • 2 gm Fiber

DIABETIC EXCHANGES: 1 Fruit • 1 Starch/Carbohydrate • ½ Fat

CARB CHOICES: 2

Sweet Cherry Dessert

Cherries are sweet and mysterious, a dark and rich fruit that ripens only a few weeks a year. Lucky us, we get to enjoy them all year long through the miracle of flash-frozen harvests!

◐ Serves 2

> 2 slices reduced-calorie white bread, cut into 1-inch cubes
> ½ cup Diet Mountain Dew
> 1 tablespoon cornstarch
> 2 tablespoons Splenda Granular
> 1½ cups frozen unsweetened dark sweet or Bing cherries
> 2 tablespoons Cool Whip Lite
> 2 teaspoons slivered almonds

In a large skillet sprayed with butter-flavored cooking spray, sauté bread cubes for 5 minutes or until browned. Evenly spoon browned bread cubes into 2 (12-ounce) custard cups. In same skillet, combine Diet Mountain Dew, cornstarch, and Splenda using a wire whisk. Add cherries. Mix well to combine. Cook over medium heat until mixture thickens and starts to boil, stirring often and being careful not to crush the cherries. Evenly spoon cherry mixture over bread cubes. Top each with 1 tablespoon Cool Whip Lite and 1 teaspoon almonds. Serve at once.

Each serving equals:

HE: 1½ Fruit • ½ Bread • ½ Slider • 8 Optional Calories

154 Calories • 2 gm Fat • 4 gm Protein • 30 gm Carbohydrate •
121 mg Sodium • 39 mg Calcium • 3 gm Fiber

DIABETIC EXCHANGES: 1½ Fruit • ½ Starch

CARB CHOICES: 2

Hawaiian Rhubarb Banana Cream Treats

Aloha! Feel the island breezes, and feel yourself relax when you dig your spoon into this sweet delight! ☻ Serves 2

> 2 cups finely chopped fresh or frozen rhubarb, thawed
> 2 tablespoons water
> ½ cup Splenda
> ½ teaspoon coconut extract
> 3–4 drops red food coloring
> ¼ cup Land O Lakes no-fat sour cream
> ¼ cup Cool Whip Lite ☆
> 1 cup (1 medium) sliced banana
> 2 teaspoons flaked coconut

In a medium saucepan, combine rhubarb and water. Cover and cook over medium heat for 8 minutes or until rhubarb is soft. Remove from heat. Stir in Splenda, coconut extract, and red food coloring. Place saucepan on a wire rack and let set for 15 minutes, stirring occasionally. Gently fold in sour cream and 2 tablespoons Cool Whip Lite. Divide banana slices between 2 dessert dishes. Evenly spoon rhubarb mixture over banana. Top each with 1 tablespoon Cool Whip Lite and 1 teaspoon coconut. Refrigerate for at least 30 minutes.

HINT: To prevent banana from turning brown, mix with 1 teaspoon lemon juice or sprinkle with Fruit Fresh.

Each serving equals:

HE: 1 Fruit • 1 Vegetable • ¾ Slider • 14 Optional Calories

174 Calories • 2 gm Fat • 3 gm Protein • 36 gm Carbohydrate • 49 mg Sodium • 148 mg Calcium • 3 gm Fiber

DIABETIC EXCHANGES: 1½ Fruit • 1 Starch/Carbohydrate

CARB CHOICES: 2

Velvety Chocolate-Walnut Pudding

Never made pudding from scratch before? Welcome to your latest culinary adventure, and I promise you will be surprised by how easy it is to make your own! ☕ Serves 2

> 4 tablespoons + 1½ teaspoons Bisquick Heart Smart Baking Mix
> 2 tablespoons unsweetened cocoa powder
> ½ cup Splenda Granular
> 1½ cups fat-free milk
> ½ teaspoon vanilla extract
> 2 tablespoons chopped walnuts

In a medium saucepan sprayed with butter-flavored cooking spray, combine baking mix, cocoa, and Splenda. Add milk. Mix well to combine using a wire whisk. Cook over medium heat until mixture thickens and starts to boil, stirring constantly. Remove from heat. Stir in vanilla extract and walnuts. Evenly spoon mixture into 2 dessert dishes. Cover each and refrigerate for at least 1 hour.

HINT: Good topped with Cool Whip Lite, but don't forget to count the additional calories.

Each serving equals:

HE: ¾ Fat Free Milk • ¾ Bread • ½ Fat • ¼ Protein • ¼ Slider • 16 Optional Calories

192 Calories • 4 gm Fat • 9 gm Protein • 30 gm Carbohydrate • 274 mg Sodium • 257 mg Calcium • 2 gm Fiber

DIABETIC EXCHANGES: 1 Fat Free Milk • 1 Fat • 1 Starch

CARB CHOICES: 2

Chocolate Cappuccino Pudding

If ever there was a beautiful friendship (besides Bogart and Claude Rains in *Casablanca*), I think it has to be chocolate and coffee. Add a bit of vanilla and cinnamon, and you've got a touch of heaven.

◐ Serves 2

> ⅓ cup Carnation Nonfat Dry Milk Powder
> 2 tablespoons unsweetened cocoa powder
> ½ cup Splenda Granular
> 2 tablespoons cornstarch
> 1 cup cold coffee
> 2 teaspoons I Can't Believe It's Not Butter! Light Margarine
> ¼ teaspoon vanilla extract
> ¼ teaspoon ground cinnamon
> 2 tablespoons Cool Whip Lite

In a small saucepan, combine dry milk powder, cocoa, Splenda, and cornstarch. Stir in coffee. Cook over medium heat for 3 minutes or until mixture thickens and starts to boil, stirring constantly with a wire whisk. Remove from heat. Add margarine, vanilla extract, and cinnamon. Mix well to combine. Evenly spoon mixture into 2 dessert dishes. Refrigerate for at least 1 hour. When serving, top each with 1 tablespoon Cool Whip Lite.

Each serving equals:

HE: ½ Fat Free Milk • ½ Fat • ¾ Slider • 16 Optional Calories

144 Calories • 4 gm Fat • 5 gm Protein • 22 gm Carbohydrate •
110 mg Sodium • 161 mg Calcium • 2 gm Fiber

DIABETIC EXCHANGES: 1 Starch/Carbohydrate • ½ Fat Free Milk • ½ Fat

CARB CHOICES: 1½

Dreamy Banana Dessert

When life is going a little crazy, close your eyes and imagine a dessert that will take you away from all that! This pretty finale is a tasty dream come true.   ☺   Serves 2

> 6 tablespoons Dannon plain fat-free yogurt
> ¼ cup Cool Whip Free
> 2 tablespoons Splenda Granular
> ½ teaspoon vanilla extract
> 2 tablespoons miniature marshmallows
> 1 cup (1 medium) diced banana
> 3 (2½-inch) graham cracker squares made into coarse
>   crumbs
> 1 tablespoon chopped walnuts

In a medium bowl, combine yogurt, Cool Whip Free, Splenda, and vanilla extract. Fold in marshmallows and banana. Evenly spoon mixture into 2 dessert dishes. In a small bowl, combine graham cracker crumbs and walnuts. Sprinkle mixture evenly over top of each dessert. Refrigerate for at least 15 minutes.

HINT: To prevent banana from turning brown, mix with 1 teaspoon lemon juice or sprinkle with Fruit Fresh.

Each serving equals:

HE: 1 Fruit • ½ Bread • ¼ Fat Free Milk • ¼ Fat • ½ Slider •
6 Optional Calories

200 Calories • 4 gm Fat • 5 gm Protein • 36 gm Carbohydrate •
107 mg Sodium • 101 mg Calcium • 2 gm Fiber

DIABETIC EXCHANGES: 1½ Starch • 1 Fruit • ½ Fat

CARB CHOICES: 2½

Orange Pudding Delight

Luscious in color and in flavor, this delectable dessert will win you a round of applause from the lucky guest who shares your meal. And if you're enjoying a bit of solitude, you're bound to cheer that you can have it again tomorrow. ☕ Serves 2

> ⅓ cup Carnation Nonfat Dry Milk Powder
> 2 tablespoons cornstarch
> ⅓ cup Splenda Granular
> 1 cup water
> ½ teaspoon coconut extract
> 3 to 4 drops yellow food coloring
> 1 (11-ounce) can mandarin oranges, rinsed and drained
> 1 (2½-inch) chocolate graham cracker square made into fine crumbs
> 2 teaspoons flaked coconut
> 2 tablespoons Cool Whip Lite

In a medium saucepan, combine dry milk powder, cornstarch, Splenda, and water. Cook over medium heat for 6 to 8 minutes or until mixture thickens and starts to boil, stirring often with a wire whisk. Remove from heat. Stir in coconut extract, yellow food coloring, and mandarin oranges. Mix well to combine. Evenly spoon mixture into 2 dessert dishes. Refrigerate for at least 1 hour. In a small bowl, combine chocolate graham cracker crumbs and coconut. Sprinkle crumb mixture evenly over top of each. Top each with 1 tablespoon Cool Whip Lite.

Each serving equals:

HE: 1 Fruit • ½ Fat Free Milk • ⅓ Bread • ¾ Slider • 10 Optional Calories

145 Calories • 1 gm Fat • 5 gm Protein • 29 gm Carbohydrate • 83 mg Sodium • 162 mg Calcium • 1 gm Fiber

DIABETIC EXCHANGES: 1 Fruit • ½ Fat Free Milk • ½ Starch

CARB CHOICES: 2

Tropical Fruit Pudding

This taste of the tropics is just right for those times when you're ready for a holiday from everyday, or as singer Alan Jackson reminds us, when it's "five o'clock somewhere!"

◐ Serves 2

⅓ cup Carnation Nonfat Dry Milk Powder
2 tablespoons cornstarch
¼ cup Splenda Granular
¾ cup water
1 (8-ounce) can fruit cocktail, packed in fruit juice, drained
    and ¼ cup liquid reserved
½ teaspoon rum extract
3 to 4 drops yellow food coloring
2 tablespoons Cool Whip Lite
1 maraschino cherry, halved

In a medium saucepan, combine dry milk powder, cornstarch, Splenda, water, and reserved fruit cocktail liquid. Cook over medium heat for 6 to 8 minutes or until mixture thickens and starts to boil, stirring constantly with a wire whisk. Remove from heat. Stir in rum extract, yellow food coloring, and fruit cocktail. Evenly spoon mixture into 2 dessert dishes. Refrigerate for at least 1 hour. Just before serving, top each with 1 tablespoon Cool Whip Lite and garnish with a cherry half.

Each serving equals:

HE: 1 Fruit • ½ Fat Free Milk • ½ Slider • 17 Optional Calories

152 Calories • 0 gm Fat • 5 gm Protein • 33 gm Carbohydrate • 68 mg Sodium • 159 mg Calcium • 1 gm Fiber

DIABETIC EXCHANGES: 1 Fruit • ½ Fat Free Milk • ½ Starch

CARB CHOICES: 2

Creamy Chocolate Pudding Treats

I thought it might seem like too much work to make pudding from individual ingredients instead of using the packaged kind, but it took only a little more time, and it made me feel as if I was putting even more of myself into the dishes I prepared. For any chocolate lover, this recipe is a true palate pleaser! ☻ Serves 2

> 3 tablespoons graham cracker crumbs
> ½ cup Splenda Granular
> ⅓ cup Carnation Nonfat Dry Milk Powder
> 1 cup water
> 1½ tablespoons cornstarch
> 2 tablespoons unsweetened cocoa powder
> ½ cup (4 ounces) Philadelphia fat-free cream cheese
> ½ teaspoon vanilla extract

In a small bowl, combine graham cracker crumbs and 2 tablespoons Splenda. Reserve 1 tablespoon crumb mixture. Evenly divide remaining crumb mixture between 2 dessert dishes. In a small saucepan sprayed with butter-flavored cooking spray, combine dry milk powder and water. Stir in cornstarch, cocoa, and remaining 6 tablespoons Splenda. Cook over medium heat for 2 to 3 minutes or until mixture thickens, stirring constantly using a wire whisk. Remove from heat. Blend in cream cheese. Add vanilla extract. Mix well to combine. Evenly spoon pudding mixture into each dessert dish. Top each with 1½ teaspoons reserved graham cracker crumb mixture. Refrigerate for at least 30 minutes.

Each serving equals:

HE: 1½ Protein • ½ Fat Free Milk • ½ Bread • ½ Slider • 18 Optional Calories

197 Calories • 1 gm Fat • 14 gm Protein • 33 gm Carbohydrate • 799 mg Sodium • 674 mg Calcium • 2 gm Fiber

DIABETIC EXCHANGES: 1½ Starch/Carbohydrate • 1 Meat • ½ Fat Free Milk

CARB CHOICES: 2

Spiced Baked Apple Slices

Whether you've got your own apple trees or do your "picking" at the farmers' market, you'll love having another great way to bring out their best! This is wonderful on its own or spooned over oatmeal. ☻ Serves 2

> 1½ cups (3 small) cored, peeled, and sliced cooking apples
> 2 tablespoons seedless raisins
> ¼ cup Splenda Granular
> ½ teaspoon apple pie spice
> 2 tablespoons chopped walnuts
> 2 tablespoons water
> 2 teaspoons I Can't Believe It's Not Butter! Light Margarine

Preheat oven to 350 degrees. Spray 2 (12-ounce) ovenproof custard cups with butter-flavored cooking spray. In a medium bowl, combine apple slices, raisins, Splenda, apple pie spice, and walnuts. Add water. Mix gently to combine. Evenly spoon mixture into prepared custard cups. Drop 1 teaspoon margarine over top of each. Place filled custard cups on a baking sheet. Bake for 25 to 30 minutes or until apples are soft. Place cups on a wire rack and let set for 2 to 3 minutes.

Each serving equals:

HE: 1½ Fruit • 1 Fat • ¼ Protein • 12 Optional Calories

159 Calories • 7 gm Fat • 1 gm Protein • 23 gm Carbohydrate • 47 mg Sodium • 23 mg Calcium • 3 gm Fiber

DIABETIC EXCHANGES: 1½ Fruit • 1 Fat

CARB CHOICES: 1½

Apple Walnut Betty

Once you start making these pairs of individual desserts, you'll love looking into your refrigerator and having such a variety to choose from. This traditional recipe makes a lovely end to dinner on a brisk fall evening. ● Serves 2

> 1½ cups (3 small) cored, peeled, and chopped cooking apples
> ¼ cup Splenda Granular ☆
> ½ teaspoon apple pie spice
> ¼ cup graham cracker crumbs
> 2 teaspoons I Can't Believe It's Not Butter! Light Margarine, melted
> 2 tablespoons chopped walnuts
> ½ cup unsweetened apple juice

Preheat oven to 350 degrees. Spray 2 (12-ounce) ovenproof custard cups with butter-flavored cooking spray. Evenly divide apples between prepared custard cups. Sprinkle 1 tablespoon Splenda and ¼ teaspoon apple pie spice over top of each. In a small bowl, combine graham cracker crumbs, remaining 2 tablespoons Splenda, and melted margarine. Stir in walnuts. Evenly sprinkle crumb mixture over top of each. Pour ¼ cup apple juice over top of each. Cover with aluminum foil. Place filled custard cups on a baking sheet. Bake for 30 minutes. Uncover and continue baking for 10 minutes or until apples are tender. Place cups on a wire rack and let set for 2 to 3 minutes. Serve warm.

HINT: Good topped with Cool Whip Lite, but don't forget to count the additional calories.

Each serving equals:

HE: 1½ Fruit • 1 Bread • 1 Fat • ¼ Protein • 12 Optional Calories

204 Calories • 8 gm Fat • 2 gm Protein • 31 gm Carbohydrate •
111 mg Sodium • 25 mg Calcium • 3 gm Fiber

DIABETIC EXCHANGES: 1½ Fruit • 1 Fat • ½ Starch

CARB CHOICES: 2

Fresh Peach Crisp

There is just something heavenly about fresh ripe peaches, and whenever I have them on hand, I want to bake! This easy dessert is a summer festival in a bowl.　❍　Serves 2

>1½ cups sliced fresh peaches
>¼ cup Splenda Granular ☆
>2 tablespoons Quaker Quick Oats
>1½ tablespoons all-purpose flour
>⅛ teaspoon ground cinnamon
>2 teaspoons I Can't Believe It's Not Butter! Light Margarine
>1 tablespoon chopped pecans

Preheat oven to 350 degrees. Spray 2 (12-ounce) ovenproof custard cups with butter-flavored cooking spray. Evenly divide peaches between prepared custard cups. Sprinkle 1 tablespoon Splenda over each. In a small bowl, combine oats, flour, remaining 2 tablespoons Splenda, and cinnamon. Add margarine. Mix well using a pastry blender or 2 forks until mixture becomes crumbly. Stir in pecans. Evenly sprinkle crumb mixture over top of peaches. Place filled custard cups on a baking sheet. Bake for 30 minutes or until peaches are tender. Place cups on a wire rack and let set for at least 5 minutes.

HINT: Good served warm with sugar- and fat-free vanilla ice cream or cold with Cool Whip Lite. If using, don't forget to count the additional calories.

Each serving equals:

HE: 1½ Fruit • 1 Fat • ½ Bread • 12 Optional Calories

149 Calories • 5 gm Fat • 3 gm protein • 23 gm Carbohydrate • 46 mg Sodium • 15 mg Calcium • 3 gm Fiber

DIABETIC EXCHANGES: 1½ Fruit • 1 Fat • ½ Starch

CARB CHOICES: 2

Cran-Apple Cobbler

Talk about a happy couple! Cranberry juice brings out both sweetness and tartness in whatever fresh apples you choose for this dish. I like it with Macintosh or Golden Delicious, but there are lots of choices.　　●　Serves 2

> 2 cups (2 medium) cored, peeled, and sliced cooking apples
> ½ cup Ocean Spray Cranberry Juice Cocktail
> ¼ cup Splenda Granular ☆
> 1 tablespoon all-purpose flour
> ⅛ teaspoon apple pie spice
> 6 tablespoons Bisquick Heart Smart Baking Mix
> 2 tablespoons Land O Lakes Fat Free Half & Half
> 1 tablespoon Land O Lakes no-fat sour cream

Preheat oven to 375 degrees. Spray 2 (12-ounce) ovenproof custard cups with butter-flavored cooking spray. In a medium saucepan, combine apple slices and cranberry juice cocktail. Cover and cook over medium heat for 5 to 6 minutes or until apples are tender, stirring occasionally. Add 3 tablespoons Splenda, flour, and apple pie spice. Mix well to combine. Continue cooking for 3 to 4 minutes or until mixture thickens, stirring often. Evenly spoon apple mixture into prepared custard cups. In a small bowl, combine baking mix, remaining 1 tablespoon Splenda, half & half, and sour cream. Evenly spoon batter over apple mixture. Place filled custard cups on a baking sheet. Bake for 20 to 25 minutes or until top is browned. Place custard cups on a wire rack and let set for at least 10 minutes.

Each serving equals:

HE: 1¼ Fruit • 1 Bread • ½ Slider • 2 Optional Calories

186 Calories • 2 gm Fat • 4 gm Protein • 38 gm Carbohydrate • 295 mg Sodium • 61 mg Calcium • 3 gm Fiber

DIABETIC EXCHANGES: 1½ Fruit • 1 Starch

CARB CHOICES: 2

Rhubarb Walnut Cobbler

When it comes to cooking with rhubarb, you need plenty of sweetening for such a tart fruit. Luckily, Splenda makes a wonderful partner in pleasure!   ☺   Serves 2

> 1 cup diced fresh or frozen rhubarb, thawed
> ½ cup + 2 tablespoons Splenda Granular ☆
> 6 tablespoons Bisquick Heart Smart Baking Mix
> 2 tablespoons Land O Lakes no-fat sour cream
> 3 tablespoons Land O Lakes Fat Free Half & Half
> ¼ teaspoon vanilla extract
> 1 tablespoon chopped walnuts

Preheat oven to 350 degrees. Spray 2 (12-ounce) ovenproof custard cups with butter-flavored cooking spray. Place ½ cup rhubarb in each prepared custard cup. Sprinkle ¼ cup Splenda over top of each. In a small bowl, combine baking mix, sour cream, half & half, and vanilla extract. Evenly spoon batter over rhubarb mixture. Sprinkle 1½ teaspoons walnuts over top of each. Place filled custard cups on a baking sheet. Bake for 35 to 40 minutes. Place cups on a wire rack and let set for at least 10 minutes.

Each serving equals:

HE: 1 Bread • 1 Vegetable • ¼ Fat • ½ Slider • 18 Optional Calories

176 Calories • 4 gm Fat • 5 gm Protein • 30 gm Carbohydrate •
316 mg Sodium • 120 mg Calcium • 1 gm Fiber

DIABETIC EXCHANGES: 2 Starch

CARB CHOICES: 2

Skillet Strawberry-Almond Cobbler

This top-of-the-stove sensation is a great choice for a gray summer day when you need cheering up! Its rosy color and sweet 'n' crunchy taste will bring a smile to your face. ☻ Serves 2

1 cup water
1 tablespoon cornstarch
½ cup + 2 tablespoons Splenda Granular ☆
½ teaspoon almond extract
3–5 drops red food coloring
2 cups chopped fresh strawberries
3 tablespoons Bisquick Heart Smart Baking Mix
2 tablespoons Land O Lakes Fat Free Half & Half
1½ teaspoons Land O Lakes no-fat sour cream
2 teaspoons slivered almonds

In a medium skillet sprayed with butter-flavored cooking spray, combine water and cornstarch using a wire whisk. Stir in ½ cup Splenda, almond extract, and red food coloring. Add strawberries. Mix gently to combine. Cook over medium heat for 5 to 6 minutes or until mixture thickens and strawberries start to soften, stirring occasionally. In a small bowl, combine baking mix, remaining 2 tablespoons Splenda, half & half, and sour cream. Drop batter by spoonful over strawberry mixture to form 2 mounds. Sprinkle ½ teaspoon almonds over top of each mound. Cover and cook for 5 minutes. Uncover and continue cooking for 2 to 3 minutes. Remove from heat. Evenly spoon into 2 dessert dishes.

HINT: Good served warm or cold.

Each serving equals:

HE: 1 Fruit • ½ Bread • ¾ Slider • 15 Optional Calories

175 Calories • 3 gm Fat • 3 gm Protein • 34 Carbohydrate • 159 mg Sodium • 64 mg Calcium • 3 gm Fiber

DIABETIC EXCHANGES: 1 Fruit • 1 Starch

CARB CHOICES: 2

Blueberry Orange Cobbler

This is one of my favorite combinations—both the colors blue and orange, and the flavors blueberry and orange, too! If you're trying to add more fruit servings to your menu, this dessert delivers.

◖ Serves 2

 ½ cup unsweetened orange juice
 1 tablespoon cornstarch
 6 tablespoons Splenda Granular ☆
 1 cup fresh or frozen blueberries, thawed
 6 tablespoons Bisquick Heart Smart Baking Mix
 2 tablespoons Land O Lakes Fat Free Half & Half
 1 tablespoon Land O Lakes fat-free sour cream

Preheat oven to 375 degrees. Spray 2 (12-ounce) ovenproof custard cups with butter-flavored cooking spray. In a medium saucepan, combine orange juice, cornstarch, and ¼ cup Splenda. Cook over medium heat until mixture starts to thicken, stirring often. Add blueberries. Mix gently to combine. Evenly spoon blueberry mixture into prepared custard cups. In a small bowl, combine baking mix, remaining 2 tablespoons Splenda, half & half, and sour cream. Spoon batter evenly over blueberries. Place custard cups on a baking sheet. Bake for 28 to 32 minutes or until topping is lightly browned. Place cups on a wire rack and let set for at least 5 minutes.

HINT: Good as is or served warm with sugar- and fat-free vanilla ice cream or cold with Cool Whip Lite. If using, don't forget to count the additional calories.

Each serving equals:

HE: 1 Bread • 1 Fruit • ½ Slider • 9 Optional Calories

194 Calories • 2 gm Fat • 4 gm Protein • 40 gm Carbohydrate •
295 mg Sodium • 58 mg Calcium • 3 gm Fiber

DIABETIC EXCHANGES: 1½ Starch/Carbohydrate • 1 Fruit

CARB CHOICES: 3

Southern Peach Shortcake

It's the state fruit of Georgia, the sweet flavor of the summer sun—and it makes a wonderful choice for shortcake. Even though I've always said I prefer strawberry shortcake, I sometimes just feel in the mood for peach. ☉ Serves 2

> 1 cup peeled and finely chopped fresh peaches ☆
> 6 tablespoons Splenda Granular ☆
> 2 tablespoons unsweetened orange juice
> 1 tablespoon + 2 teaspoons water ☆
> 6 tablespoons Bisquick Heart Smart Baking Mix
> 3 tablespoons Land O Lakes Fat Free Half & Half
> 1 tablespoon Land O Lakes no-fat sour cream
> 1 tablespoon chopped pecans
> 2 tablespoons Cool Whip Lite

Spray a baking sheet with butter-flavored cooking spray. Place ½ cup peaches, ¼ cup Splenda, orange juice, and 1 tablespoon water in a blender container. Cover and process on BLEND for 30 seconds or until mixture is smooth. In a small bowl, combine remaining ½ cup chopped peaches and blended peach mixture. Cover and refrigerate until ready to serve. Preheat oven to 425 degrees. In a medium bowl, combine baking mix, remaining 2 tablespoons Splenda, half & half, remaining 2 teaspoons water, and sour cream. Stir in pecans. Drop batter by tablespoonful onto prepared baking sheet to form 2 shortcakes. Bake for 7 to 9 minutes or until golden brown. Place shortcakes on a wire rack and let cool for at least 5 minutes. For each serving, place 1 shortcake in a dessert dish, spoon 1 full ⅓ cup peach mixture over shortcake, and top with 1 tablespoon Cool Whip Lite.

Each serving equals:

HE: 1 Bread • 1 Fruit • ¼ Fat • ½ Slider • 8 Optional Calories

197 Calories • 5 gm Fat • 4 gm Protein • 34 gm Carbohydrate •
304 mg Sodium • 63 mg Calcium • 2 gm Fiber

DIABETIC EXCHANGES: 1 Starch/Carbohydrate • 1 Fruit • 1 Fat

CARB CHOICES: 2

Orange Marmalade Bread Pudding

It's a splendid dessert no matter the flavor, and think of all the possibilities when you create with spreadable fruit! I liked this one best, but if you're a raspberry fan or just adore strawberry, give it a try! ☻ Serves 2

⅓ cup Carnation Nonfat Dry Milk Powder
1 tablespoon cornstarch
¼ cup Splenda Granular
1 cup water
3 tablespoons orange marmalade spreadable fruit
½ teaspoon vanilla extract
3 slices reduced-calorie white bread, torn into small pieces
2 tablespoons chopped walnuts

Preheat oven to 350 degrees. Spray 2 (12-ounce) ovenproof custard cups with butter-flavored cooking spray. In a medium saucepan, combine dry milk powder, cornstarch, Splenda, and water. Cook over medium heat for 3 minutes or until mixture thickens and starts to boil, stirring constantly. Remove from heat. Stir in orange marmalade and vanilla extract. Add bread pieces and walnuts. Mix gently just to combine. Evenly spoon mixture into prepared custard cups. Place filled custard cups on a baking sheet. Bake for 25 to 30 minutes. Place cups on a wire rack and let set for at least 10 minutes.

Each serving equals:

HE: 1 Fruit • ¾ Bread • ½ Fat Free Milk • ½ Fat • ¼ Protein • ¼ Slider •
7 Optional Calories

226 Calories • 6 gm Fat • 9 gm Protein • 34 gm Carbohydrate •
235 mg Sodium • 183 mg Calcium • 1 gm Fiber

DIABETIC EXCHANGES: 1 Fruit • 1 Starch • ½ Fat Free Milk

CARB CHOICES: 2

Hot Chocolate Peanut Butter Sundaes

This is my friend Barbara's idea of happiness in the dessert department—she just l-o-v-e-s chocolate and peanut butter! She can't get Blue Bunny in New York just yet, but she finds other sugar-free and fat-free ice creams there.   ☻   Serves 2

> 2 tablespoons Peter Pan or Skippy reduced-fat peanut butter
> ¼ cup Hershey's Sugar-Free Chocolate Syrup
> 1 cup Wells' Blue Bunny sugar- and fat-free vanilla ice cream
> 2 tablespoons Cool Whip Lite

In a small microwave-safe mixing bowl, combine peanut butter and chocolate syrup. Microwave on HIGH (100% power) for 30 seconds or until peanut butter is melted, stirring every 15 seconds. For each serving, place ½ cup ice cream in a dessert dish, drizzle a full 2 tablespoons hot sauce over ice cream, and top with 1 tablespoon Cool Whip Lite.

Each serving equals:

HE: 1 Protein • 1 Fat • ½ Fat Free Milk • 1 Slider • 20 Optional Calories

234 Calories • 6 gm Fat • 8 gm Protein • 37 gm Carbohydrate • 210 mg Sodium • 123 mg Calcium • 1 gm Fiber

DIABETIC EXCHANGES: 2 Starch/Carbohydrate • ½ Meat • ½ Fat

CARB CHOICES: 2

Almond Cheesecake with Sour Cream Topping

Almond is one of the most popular choices when it comes to store-bought cheesecakes. This version is rich and creamy, smooth and luscious—and very hard to resist. So don't! ○ Serves 2

3 tablespoons graham cracker crumbs

½ cup Splenda Granular

½ cup (4 ounces) Philadelphia fat-free cream cheese

2 teaspoons cornstarch

2 tablespoons Land O Lakes Fat Free Half & Half

1 egg, or equivalent in egg substitute

⅛ teaspoon almond extract

¼ cup Land O Lakes no-fat sour cream

1 tablespoon sliced almonds

Preheat oven to 350 degrees. Spray 2 (12-ounce) ovenproof custard cups with butter-flavored cooking spray. In a small bowl, combine graham cracker crumbs and 2 tablespoons Splenda. Evenly divide crumb mixture between prepared custard cups. In a medium bowl, stir cream cheese with a sturdy spoon until soft. Add ¼ cup Splenda, cornstarch, half & half, egg, and almond extract. Mix well to combine. Evenly spoon cream cheese mixture into prepared custard cups. Place custard cups on a baking sheet. Bake for 15 minutes. Meanwhile, in a small bowl, combine sour cream and remaining 2 tablespoons Splenda. Spread mixture evenly over top of partially baked cheesecakes. Sprinkle 1½ teaspoons almonds over top of each. Continue baking for 10 to 12 minutes or until filling is set. Place cups on a wire rack and let set for 30 minutes. Refrigerate for at least 1 hour.

Each serving equals:

HE: 2 Protein • ½ Bread • ¼ Fat • ¾ Slider • 12 Optional Calories

214 Calories • 6 gm Fat • 14 gm Protein • 26 gm Carbohydrate • 424 mg Sodium • 240 mg Calcium • 1 gm Fiber

DIABETIC EXCHANGES: 2 Meat • 1½ Starch/Carbohydrate

CARB CHOICES: 1½

Holiday Cheesecake

Instead of cookies and milk, why not leave this for Santa this year? I bet you'll see an increase in the number of gifts you find under the tree! ❤ Serves 2

> 3 tablespoons graham cracker crumbs ☆
> ½ cup (4 ounces) Philadelphia fat-free cream cheese
> 1 egg, or equivalent in egg substitute
> 2 tablespoons Land O Lakes no-fat sour cream
> 1 tablespoon Land O Lakes Fat Free Half & Half
> ¼ cup Splenda Granular
> ¼ teaspoon rum extract
> ⅛ teaspoon ground nutmeg
> 2 tablespoons Cool Whip Lite

Preheat oven to 350 degrees. Spray 2 (12-ounce) ovenproof custard cups with butter-flavored cooking spray. Evenly sprinkle 1 tablespoon graham cracker crumbs into each prepared custard cup. In a medium bowl, stir cream cheese with a sturdy spoon until soft. Add egg, sour cream, half & half, and Splenda. Mix well to combine. Stir in rum extract and nutmeg. Evenly spoon mixture into custard cups. Sprinkle 1½ teaspoons graham cracker crumbs over top of each. Place filled custard cups on a baking sheet. Bake for 20 to 25 minutes or until filling is set. Place cups on a wire rack and let set for 15 minutes. Refrigerate for at least 1 hour. When serving, top each with 1 tablespoon Cool Whip Lite.

Each serving equals:

HE: 2 Protein • ½ Bread • ½ Slider • 1 Optional Calorie

160 Calories • 4 gm Fat • 13 gm Protein • 18 gm Carbohydrate • 393 mg Sodium • 202 mg Calcium • 0 gm Fiber

DIABETIC EXCHANGES: 2 Meat • 1 Starch/Carbohydrate

CARB CHOICES: 1

Mini Apple Raisin Crumb Pies

Oh, are these delicious! The crumbs at the bottom of the custard cup are a delightful surprise, and the apples and raisins just get better and better inside a cozy-hot oven. ☺ Serves 2

> 3 tablespoons all-purpose flour
> 3 tablespoons graham cracker crumbs
> 6 tablespoons Splenda Granular ☆
> 1 tablespoon + 1 teaspoon I Can't Believe It's Not Butter!
>   Light Margarine
> 1 cup (1 medium) cored, peeled, and sliced cooking apples
> ½ teaspoon apple pie spice
> 2 tablespoons seedless raisins
> 2 tablespoons Land O Lakes Fat Free Half & Half

Preheat oven to 375 degrees. Spray 2 (12-ounce) ovenproof custard cups with butter-flavored cooking spray. In a small bowl, combine flour, graham cracker crumbs, and ¼ cup Splenda. Evenly sprinkle 1 tablespoon crumb mixture into each prepared custard cup. Add margarine to remaining crumb mixture. Mix well using a pastry blender or 2 forks until mixture becomes crumbly. Set aside. In a medium bowl, combine apple slices, apple pie spice, and raisins. Evenly spoon apple mixture into custard cups. Drizzle 1 tablespoon half & half and sprinkle 1 tablespoon Splenda over each. Sprinkle crumb mixture evenly over tops. Place filled custard cups on a baking sheet. Bake for 35 to 45 minutes or until apples are tender and topping is browned. Place cups on a wire rack and let set for at least 10 minutes.

Each serving equals:

HE: 1 Bread • 1 Fruit • 1 Fat • ¼ Slider • 7 Optional Calories

197 Calories • 5 gm Fat • 2 gm Protein • 36 gm Carbohydrate •
162 mg Sodium • 32 mg Calcium • 2 gm Fiber

DIABETIC EXCHANGES: 1 Starch • 1 Fruit • 1 Fat

CARB CHOICES: 2

Peach-Pecan Custard Pies

With all the baking you're going to be doing after getting this book, you may want to stock up on custard cups! There are lots available online, at various auction sites, or you can hunt through local thrift stores for kitchen treasures.　　◐　Serves 2

¼ cup Land O Lakes Fat Free Half & Half
2 tablespoons Land O Lakes no-fat sour cream
2 tablespoons egg substitute
⅓ cup Splenda Granular
⅛ teaspoon vanilla extract
3 tablespoons Bisquick Heart Smart Baking Mix
1 cup peeled and finely chopped fresh peaches
1 tablespoon chopped pecans

Preheat oven to 375 degrees. Spray 2 (12-ounce) ovenproof custard cups with butter-flavored cooking spray. In a medium bowl, combine half & half, sour cream, and egg substitute using a wire whisk. Stir in Splenda and vanilla extract. Add baking mix. Mix gently just to combine. Fold in chopped peaches. Evenly spoon mixture into prepared custard cups. Sprinkle 1½ teaspoons pecans over top of each. Place filled custard cups on a baking sheet. Bake for 22 to 26 minutes or until peaches are tender. Place cups on a wire rack and let set for at least 10 minutes.

Each serving equals:

HE: 1 Fruit • ½ Bread • ½ Fat • ¼ Protein • ½ Slider • 9 Optional Calories

160 Calories • 4 gm Fat • 5 gm Protein • 26 gm Carbohydrate •
221 mg Sodium • 76 mg Calcium • 2 gm Fiber

DIABETIC EXCHANGES: 1 Fruit • 1 Starch • ½ Fat

CARB CHOICES: 2

Coconut Orange Meringue Pies

I don't think I've ever tasted this pair of flavors in a meringue pie at a diner or a potluck, but it just seemed to me that orange and coconut "made sense!" One is citrus-y, the other tropical, and together a seductive invitation to eat and enjoy. ☻ Serves 2

> 3 tablespoons graham cracker crumbs
> 1 tablespoon cornstarch
> 6 tablespoons Splenda Granular ☆
> ⅓ cup Carnation Nonfat Dry Milk Powder
> ⅔ cup water
> ¾ teaspoon coconut extract ☆
> 2–3 drops yellow food coloring
> 1 (11-ounce) can mandarin oranges, rinsed and drained
> 2 egg whites
> 2 teaspoons flaked coconut

Preheat oven to 375 degrees. Spray 2 (12-ounce) ovenproof custard cups with butter-flavored cooking spray. Sprinkle 1½ tablespoons graham cracker crumbs into each prepared custard cup. In a small saucepan, combine cornstarch, ¼ cup Splenda, dry milk powder, and water. Cook over medium heat until mixture thickens and starts to boil, stirring often using a wire whisk. Remove from heat. Stir in ½ teaspoon coconut extract and yellow food coloring. Add mandarin oranges. Mix gently just to combine. Evenly spoon mixture into custard cups. In a small glass bowl, beat egg whites with an electric mixer on HIGH until soft peaks form. Add remaining 2 tablespoons Splenda and remaining ¼ teaspoon coconut extract. Continue beating on HIGH until stiff peaks form. Spread meringue mixture evenly over filling mixture, being sure to seal to edges of cup. Sprinkle 1 teaspoon coconut over top of each. Place filled custard cups on a baking sheet. Bake for 10 to 15 minutes or until meringue starts to turn golden brown. Place cups on a wire rack and let set for 30 minutes. Refrigerate for at least 1 hour.

HINT: Egg whites beat best at room temperature.

Each serving equals:

HE: 1 Fruit • ½ Fat Free Milk • ½ Bread • ⅓ Protein • ¼ Slider • 19 Optional Calories

177 Calories • 1 gm Fat • 9 gm Protein • 33 gm Carbohydrate • 176 mg Sodium • 168 mg Calcium • 1 gm Fiber

DIABETIC EXCHANGES: 1 Fruit • 1 Starch • ½ Fat Free Milk

CARB CHOICES: 2

Banana Cream Meringue Pies

These little pies look so good, you'll want to invite friends over to sample them! Choose a ripe banana, but not as soft as one you'd use for banana bread. ● Serves 2

⅓ cup Carnation Nonfat Dry
  Milk Powder
1½ tablespoons cornstarch
½ cup Splenda Granular ☆
1 cup water
½ teaspoon vanilla extract ☆

3–4 drops yellow food coloring
3 tablespoons graham cracker
  crumbs
1 cup sliced banana
2 egg whites

Preheat oven to 375 degrees. Spray 2 (12-ounce) ovenproof custard cups with butter-flavored cooking spray. In a medium saucepan, combine dry milk powder, cornstarch, ¼ cup Splenda, and water. Cook over medium heat until mixture thickens and starts to boil, stirring constantly using a wire whisk. Remove from heat. Stir in ¼ teaspoon vanilla extract and yellow food coloring. Place saucepan on a wire rack. Meanwhile, evenly sprinkle 1½ table-spoons graham cracker crumbs into each prepared custard cup. Divide bananas evenly between custard cups. Evenly spoon pudding mixture over banana slices. In a medium glass bowl, beat egg whites with an electric mixer on HIGH until soft peaks form. Add remaining ¼ cup Splenda and remaining ¼ teaspoon vanilla extract. Continue beating on HIGH until stiff peaks form. Spread meringue mixture evenly over filling mixture, being sure to seal to edges of cup. Place filled custard cups on a baking sheet. Bake for 15 minutes or until meringue starts to turn golden brown. Place cups on a wire rack and let set for 30 minutes. Refrigerate for at least 30 minutes.

HINT: Egg whites beat best at room temperature.

Each serving equals:

HE: 1 Fruit • ½ Fat Free Milk • ½ Bread • ⅓ Protein • ½ Slider • 6 Optional Calories

201 Calories • 1 gm Fat • 10 gm Protein • 38 gm Carbohydrate •
167 mg Sodium • 158 mg Calcium • 2 gm Fiber

DIABETIC EXCHANGES: 1 Fruit • 1 Starch/Carbohydrate • ½ Fat Free Milk

CARB CHOICES: 2½

Mini Mincemeat Tarts

Here's a fun idea for the holidays—instead of making full-size pies to bring to a family meal, why not make a few pairs of desserts like this one and arrive with a little tray of treats? You're sure to win hearts and cheers from the crowd! ☻ Serves 2

1 tablespoon cornstarch
¼ cup Splenda Granular
½ cup unsweetened apple juice
2 tablespoons seedless raisins
1 cup (1 medium) cored, peeled, and finely chopped cooking
apples
½ teaspoon apple pie spice
¼ teaspoon rum extract
2 single-serve Keebler graham cracker crusts
2 tablespoons Cool Whip Lite

In a medium saucepan, combine cornstarch, Splenda, and apple juice. Stir in raisins and apples. Cook over medium heat for 6 to 8 minutes or until mixture thickens and apples soften. Remove from heat. Add apple pie spice and rum extract. Mix well to combine. Evenly spoon filling mixture into graham cracker crusts. Refrigerate for at least 30 minutes. When serving, top each with 1 tablespoon Cool Whip Lite.

Each serving equals:

HE: 1½ Fruit • 1 Bread • ½ Fat • ¼ Slider • 17 Optional Calories

230 Calories • 6 gm Fat • 2 gm Protein • 42 gm Carbohydrate •
154 mg Sodium • 18 mg Calcium • 2 gm Fiber

DIABETIC EXCHANGES: 1½ Fruit • 1 Starch • 1 Fat

CARB CHOICES: 3

Jam Cake Gems

Here's a new jewel for you to add to your "crown" of reliable recipes for special occasions. Planning a dinner for two and want to impress your guest? Serve these and feel confident you've chosen well.   ☺   Serves 2

> 1 tablespoon + 1 teaspoon I Can't Believe It's Not Butter!
>   Light Margarine
> ¼ cup Splenda Granular
> 2 tablespoons Land O Lakes Fat Free Half & Half
> 2 tablespoons water
> 1 egg, or equivalent in egg substitute
> 6 tablespoons Bisquick Heart Smart Baking Mix
> ¼ teaspoon baking powder
> ¼ teaspoon vanilla extract
> 3 tablespoons spreadable fruit, any flavor

Preheat oven to 350 degrees. Spray 2 (12-ounce) ovenproof custard cups with butter-flavored cooking spray. In a small bowl, combine margarine and Splenda. Stir in half & half and water. Add egg, baking mix, baking powder, and vanilla extract. Mix gently just to combine. Evenly spoon ¼ cup batter into each prepared custard cup. Top each with 1½ tablespoons spreadable fruit. Spoon remaining batter evenly over top of each. Place filled custard cups on a baking sheet. Bake for 30 to 34 minutes or until a toothpick inserted in center comes out clean. Place cups on a wire rack and let set for at least 10 minutes.

Each serving equals:

HE: 1 Bread • 1 Fruit • 1 Fat • ½ Protein • ¼ Slider • 1 Optional Calorie

232 Calories • 8 gm Fat • 5 gm Protein • 35 gm Carbohydrate •
458 mg Sodium • 82 mg Calcium • 1 gm Fiber

DIABETIC EXCHANGES: 1 Starch • 1 Fruit • 1 Fat • ½ Meat

CARB CHOICES: 2

Mini Pound Cake

This is such a classic dessert, you may wonder if this version will really resemble the "real" kind. My taste testers were tough on every recipe, helping me perfect each one with their comments. This one got great reviews! ◐ Serves 2

> 1 tablespoon + 1 teaspoon I Can't Believe It's Not Butter!
>   Light Margarine
> 1 tablespoon + 2 teaspoons Land O Lakes no-fat sour cream
> 6 tablespoons Splenda Granular
> 1 egg, or equivalent in egg substitute
> 2 tablespoons unsweetened orange juice
> ¼ teaspoon vanilla extract
> 6 tablespoons Bisquick Heart Smart Baking Mix
> ⅛ teaspoon baking soda

Preheat oven to 350 degrees. Spray a 5¾-by-3⅛-by-2⅛-inch petite loaf pan with butter-flavored cooking spray. In a medium bowl, combine margarine, sour cream, and Splenda. Stir in egg. Add orange juice and vanilla extract. Mix well to combine. Stir in baking mix and baking soda. Evenly spoon batter into prepared pan. Bake for 30 to 34 minutes. Place pan on a wire rack and let set for 10 minutes. Remove cake from pan and place on wire rack to cool completely. Cut into 2 servings.

HINT: If you don't have a petite loaf pan, use 2 (12-ounce) oven-proof custard cups instead and place them on a baking sheet before baking. If using, test for doneness at least 10 minutes before suggested baking time.

Each serving equals:

HE: 1 Bread • 1 Fat • ½ Protein • ¼ Slider • 16 Optional Calories

179 Calories • 7 gm Fat • 5 gm Protein • 24 gm Carbohydrate •
482 mg Sodium • 55 mg Calcium • 1 gm Fiber

DIABETIC EXCHANGES: 1½ Starch/Carbohydrate • ½ Meat • ½ Fat

CARB CHOICES: 1½

White Cake with Chocolate Frosting

Whether you're celebrating a birthday or a graduation, an A on your paper or a kiss from a new love, this is *the* dessert to choose! The cake is fluffy, the frosting is light and rich, and the overall effect is WOW! ☻ Serves 2

> 1 tablespoon + 1 teaspoon I Can't Believe It's Not Butter! Light Margarine ☆
> 2 tablespoons Land O Lakes no-fat sour cream ☆
> ⅓ cup + 2 tablespoons Splenda Granular ☆
> 2 tablespoons egg substitute
> 3 tablespoons fat-free milk
> ¾ teaspoon vanilla extract ☆
> 6 tablespoons Bisquick Heart Smart Baking Mix
> ¼ teaspoon baking powder
> 2 tablespoons mini chocolate chips

Preheat oven to 350 degrees. Spray a 5¾-by-3⅛-by-2⅛-inch petite loaf pan with butter-flavored cooking spray. In a medium bowl, combine 2 teaspoons margarine, 1 tablespoon sour cream, 2 tablespoons Splenda, and egg substitute. Stir in milk and ½ teaspoon vanilla extract. Add baking mix and baking powder. Mix gently just to combine. Evenly spread batter into prepared pan. Bake for 16 to 20 minutes or until a toothpick inserted in center comes out clean. Place pan on a wire rack and let set for 10 minutes. Run a table knife around the sides of pan to loosen cake. Remove cake and place on serving dish and allow to cool completely. Meanwhile, in a small microwave-safe bowl, melt chocolate chips in microwave on HIGH (100% power) for 1½ minutes. Stir in remaining 1 tablespoon sour cream, remaining 2 teaspoons margarine, and remaining ¼ teaspoon vanilla extract. Add remaining ⅓ cup Splenda. Mix well to combine. Drizzle chocolate frosting evenly over cooled cake. Cut into 2 servings.

HINT: If you don't have a petite loaf pan, use 2 (12-ounce) oven-proof custard cups instead and place them on a baking sheet before baking. If using, test for doneness at least 10 minutes before suggested baking time.

Each serving equals:

HE: 1 Bread • 1 Fat • ¼ Protein • 1 Slider • 15 Optional Calories

220 Calories • 8 gm Fat • 5 gm Protein • 32 gm Carbohydrate • 460 mg Sodium • 115 mg Calcium • 1 gm Fiber

DIABETIC EXCHANGES: 2 Starch/Carbohydrate • 1 Fat

CARB CHOICES: 2

Vanilla Custard Pudding Cakes

If a moist cake is your desire, pudding cake is the place to start. But if you want an even more luscious dessert, stir up a custard pudding cake like this one! There's lot of vanilla in this recipe, and it's important to use the real thing, not artificial flavoring.

◐ Serves 2

> 1 tablespoon + 1 teaspoon I Can't Believe It's Not Butter!
>   Light Margarine
> ½ cup Splenda Granular ☆
> 3 tablespoons Land O Lakes Fat Free Half & Half
> 6 tablespoons cake flour
> ½ teaspoon baking powder
> ⅛ teaspoon table salt
> ⅓ cup Carnation Nonfat Dry Milk Powder
> 1 tablespoon cornstarch
> ⅔ cup hot water
> 1½ teaspoons vanilla extract

Preheat oven to 350 degrees. Spray 2 (10-ounce) custard cups with butter-flavored cooking spray. In a medium bowl, combine margarine, 2 tablespoons Splenda, and half & half. Add flour, baking powder, and salt. Mix gently just to combine. Evenly spoon batter into prepared custard cups. In a small bowl, combine dry milk powder, remaining 6 tablespoons Splenda, and cornstarch. Add hot water and vanilla extract. Mix well to combine using a wire whisk. Drizzle about ¼ cup milk mixture over top of each. Place filled custard cups on a baking sheet. Bake for 22 to 26 minutes or until set around the sides and the top is soft and slightly bubbly. Place cups on a wire rack and let set for at least 10 minutes.

Each serving equals:

HE: 1 Bread • 1 Fat • ½ Fat Free Milk • ½ Slider • 12 Optional Calories

196 Calories • 4 gm Fat • 6 gm Protein • 34 gm Carbohydrate •
431 mg Sodium • 235 mg Calcium • 1 gm Fiber

DIABETIC EXCHANGES: 1½ Starch • 1 Fat • ½ Fat Free Milk

CARB CHOICES: 2

Hawaiian Pleasure Dessert Cakes

When the sun rises in Hawaii, the landscape comes alive with color, and it's pretty impossible to stay in bed! That's the feeling I wanted to get in this dessert delight—that irresistible call to live fully and with joy. ☻ Serves 2

> 6 tablespoons Bisquick Heart Smart Baking Mix
> 3 tablespoons Splenda Granular
> 1 (8-ounce) can crushed pineapple, packed in fruit juice,
>   drained and 1 tablespoon liquid reserved
> 2 tablespoons egg substitute
> 2 teaspoons I Can't Believe It's Not Butter! Light Margarine
> ¼ teaspoon coconut extract
> 1 tablespoon chopped pecans
> 2 maraschino cherries, quartered
> 2 teaspoons flaked coconut

Preheat oven to 350 degrees. Spray 2 (12-ounce) ovenproof custard cups with butter-flavored cooking spray. In a medium bowl, combine baking mix and Splenda. Add pineapple, reserved pineapple liquid, egg substitute, and margarine. Mix gently just to combine. Fold in coconut extract, pecans, and cherry pieces. Evenly spoon batter into prepared custard cups. Sprinkle 1 teaspoon coconut evenly over top of each. Place filled custard cups on a baking sheet. Bake for 30 to 34 minutes. Place cups on a wire rack and let set for 10 minutes.

Each serving equals:

HE: 1 Bread • 1 Fruit • 1 Fat • ¼ Protein • ¼ Slider • 6 Optional Calories

211 Calories • 7 gm Fat • 4 gm Protein • 33 gm Carbohydrate •
339 mg Sodium • 46 mg Calcium • 2 gm Fiber

DIABETIC EXCHANGES: 1 Starch • 1 Fruit • 1 Fat

CARB CHOICES: 2

Snickerdoodle Mini Cake

Some desserts remind us of happy childhood days, especially treats like snickerdoodles—so I decided to create a cake recipe that delivered the same pleasure and fun. Act like a kid again, and gobble this one down! ○ Serves 2

2 tablespoons Land O Lakes
   Fat Free Half & Half
1 tablespoon + 1 teaspoon I
   Can't Believe It's Not
   Butter! Light Margarine
1 tablespoon Land O Lakes
   no-fat sour cream
¼ teaspoon vanilla extract

½ cup + 1 teaspoon Splenda
   Granular ☆
2 tablespoons egg substitute
6 tablespoons Bisquick Heart
   Smart Baking Mix
¼ teaspoon baking powder
⅛ teaspoon ground cinnamon

Preheat oven to 350 degrees. Spray a 5¾-by-3⅛-by-2⅛-inch petite loaf pan with butter-flavored cooking spray. In a medium bowl, combine half & half, margarine, sour cream, and vanilla extract using a wire whisk. Stir in ½ cup Splenda and egg substitute. Add baking mix and baking powder. Mix gently just to combine using a sturdy spoon. Evenly spoon batter into prepared pan. In a small bowl, combine remaining 1 teaspoon Splenda and cinnamon. Sprinkle mixture evenly over top. Bake for 20 to 25 minutes or until a toothpick inserted in center comes out clean. Place pan on a wire rack and let set for 10 minutes. Run a table knife around the sides of pan to loosen cake. Remove cake and place on wire rack and allow to cool completely. Cut into 2 servings.

HINT: If you don't have a petite loaf pan, use 2 (12-ounce) oven-proof custard cups instead and place them on a baking sheet before baking. If using, test for doneness at least 10 minutes before suggested baking time.

Each serving equals:

HE: 1 Bread • 1 Fat • ¼ Protein • ½ Slider • 1 Optional Calorie

170 Calories • 6 gm Fat • 4 gm Protein • 25 gm Carbohydrate • 461 mg Sodium • 88 mg Calcium • 1 gm Fiber

DIABETIC EXCHANGES: 1½ Starch/Carbohydrate • 1 Fat

CARB CHOICES: 1½

Mini Apple Spice Cake

This cake layers flavors to great advantage, as I mixed in apple pie spice, applesauce, *and* finely chopped apples. It's a triple threat and a double delight! ☉ Serves 2

> 6 tablespoons Bisquick Heart Smart Baking Mix
> 2 tablespoons Splenda Granular
> ¼ teaspoon baking powder
> ½ teaspoon apple pie spice
> ¼ cup unsweetened applesauce
> 2 teaspoons I Can't Believe It's Not Butter! Light Margarine
> 2 tablespoons egg substitute
> 1 tablespoon Land O Lakes Fat Free Half & Half
> ½ cup cored, peeled, and finely chopped cooking apple
> 2 tablespoons chopped walnuts

Preheat oven to 350 degrees. Spray a 5¾-by-3⅛-by-2⅛-inch petite loaf pan with butter-flavored cooking spray. In a medium bowl, combine baking mix, Splenda, baking powder, and apple pie spice. Add applesauce, margarine, egg substitute, and half & half. Mix well just to combine. Fold in apple and walnuts. Evenly spread batter into prepared pan. Bake for 30 to 34 minutes or until a toothpick inserted in center comes out clean. Place pan on a wire rack and let set for 10 minutes. Remove cake from pan and place on wire rack and allow to cool completely. Cut into 2 servings.

HINT: If you don't have a petite loaf pan, use 2 (12-ounce) ovenproof custard cups instead and place them on a baking sheet before baking. If using, test for doneness at least 10 minutes before suggested baking time.

Each serving equals:

HE: 1 Bread • 1 Fat • ¾ Fruit • ½ Protein • 10 Optional Calories

193 Calories • 9 gm Fat • 5 gm Protein • 23 gm Carbohydrate •
396 mg Sodium • 83 mg Calcium • 2 gm Fiber

DIABETIC EXCHANGES: 1 Starch • 1 Fruit • 1 Fat

CARB CHOICES: 1½

Chocolate Cake with Apricot-Pecan Glaze

Sometimes you don't need thick frosting to top off a cake. On those occasions, a nutty, fruity glaze is your best bet—and this is one of my best ever!   ☻   Serves 2

6 tablespoons Bisquick Heart
  Smart Baking Mix
2 tablespoons Splenda
  Granular
1½ tablespoons unsweetened
  cocoa powder
¼ teaspoon baking soda

2 tablespoons Kraft fat-free
  mayonnaise
2 tablespoons fat-free milk
½ teaspoon vanilla extract
3 tablespoons apricot
  spreadable fruit
1 tablespoon chopped pecans

Preheat oven to 350 degrees. Spray a 5¾-by-3⅛-by-2⅛-inch petite loaf pan with butter-flavored cooking spray. In a small bowl, combine baking mix, Splenda, cocoa, and baking soda. Add mayonnaise, milk, and vanilla extract. Mix well just to combine. Evenly spread batter in prepared pan. Bake for 14 to 16 minutes or until a toothpick inserted in center comes out clean. Place pan on a wire rack for 5 minutes. Run a table knife around the sides of pan to loosen cake. Remove cake and place on serving plate. In a small bowl, stir spreadable fruit until soft. Stir in pecans. Evenly spread mixture over top of warm cake. Continue cooling for at least 15 minutes. Cut into 2 servings.

HINT: If you don't have a petite loaf pan, use 2 (12-ounce) oven-proof custard cups instead and place them on a baking sheet before baking. If using, test for doneness at least 10 minutes before suggested baking time.

Each serving equals:

HE: 1 Bread • 1 Fruit • ¼ Fat • ¼ Slider • 11 Optional Calories

205 Calories • 5 gm Fat • 3 gm Protein • 37 gm Carbohydrate •
545 mg Sodium • 50 mg Calcium • 2 gm Fiber

DIABETIC EXCHANGES: 1½ Starch/Carbohydrate • 1 Fruit • ½ Fat

CARB CHOICES: 2½

Cliff's Chocolate Mocha Sour Cream Cake

I love cooking for the man I love, especially since Cliff has gone out on the road as a long-distance trucker again. When he comes home, I want him to enjoy every minute, and this cake won his heart after a recent long trip!   ☻   Serves 2

> 3 tablespoons Land O Lakes no-fat sour cream
> 2 teaspoons I Can't Believe It's Not Butter! Light Margarine
> 3 tablespoons Splenda Granular
> 2 tablespoons egg substitute
> 2 tablespoons Land O Lakes Fat Free Half & Half
> ½ teaspoon vanilla extract
> 6 tablespoons Bisquick Heart Smart Baking Mix
> 2 tablespoons unsweetened cocoa powder
> 1 tablespoon mini chocolate chips

Preheat oven to 350 degrees. Spray a 5¾-by-3⅛-by-2⅛-inch petite loaf pan with butter-flavored cooking spray. In a medium bowl, combine sour cream, margarine, and Splenda. Stir in egg substitute, half & half, and vanilla extract. Add baking mix and cocoa powder. Mix gently just to combine. Fold in chocolate chips. Evenly spoon batter into prepared pan. Bake for 18 to 22 minutes or until a toothpick inserted in center comes out clean. Place pan on a wire rack and let set for 10 minutes. Remove cake from pan and place on wire rack and allow to cool completely. Cut into 2 servings.

Each serving equals:

HE: 1 Bread • ½ Fat • ¼ Protein • ¾ Slider • 17 Optional Calories

198 Calories • 6 gm Fat • 6 gm Protein • 30 gm Carbohydrate • 387 mg Sodium • 85 mg Calcium • 2 gm Fiber

DIABETIC EXCHANGES: 2 Starch/Carbohydrate • ½ Fat

CARB CHOICES: 2

S'More Mini Cake

As a grandma—and as a cook—I love hearing my grandkids say, "May I please have some more?" (They're polite kids, even when it comes to food.) To hear that at your house, stir up this appealing treat tonight!　●　Serves 2

>   ¼ cup Bisquick Heart Smart Baking Mix
>   3 tablespoons graham cracker crumbs ☆
>   ¼ cup Splenda Granular
>   1 tablespoon + 1 teaspoon unsweetened cocoa powder
>   ¼ teaspoon baking powder
>   3 tablespoons Land O Lakes Fat Free Half & Half
>   2 tablespoons egg substitute
>   1 tablespoon + 1 teaspoon I Can't Believe It's Not Butter!
>   Light Margarine
>   ½ teaspoon vanilla extract
>   16 miniature marshmallows
>   1 tablespoon mini chocolate chips

Preheat oven to 350 degrees. Spray a 5¾-by-3⅛-by 2⅛-inch petite loaf pan with butter-flavored cooking spray. In a medium bowl, combine baking mix, 2 tablespoons graham cracker crumbs, Splenda, cocoa, and baking powder. Add half & half, egg substitute, margarine, and vanilla extract. Mix gently just to combine. Spread batter evenly into prepared pan. Evenly sprinkle marshmallows over top. In a small bowl, combine remaining 1 tablespoon graham cracker crumbs and chocolate chips. Sprinkle crumb mixture evenly over top. Bake for 22 to 26 minutes or until a toothpick inserted in center comes out clean. Place pan on a wire rack and let set for 10 minutes. Remove cake from pan and place on wire rack and allow to cool completely. Cut into 2 servings.

HINT: If you don't have a petite loaf pan, use 2 (12-ounce) oven-proof custard cups instead and place them on a baking sheet before baking. If using, test for doneness at least 10 minutes before suggested baking time.

Each serving equals:

HE: 1 Bread • 1 Fat • ¼ Protein • ¾ Slider • 17 Optional Calories

211 Calories • 7 gm Fat • 5 gm Protein • 32 gm Carbohydrate •
428 mg Sodium • 85 mg Calcium • 2 gm Fiber

DIABETIC EXCHANGES: 2 Starch/Carbohydrate • 1 Fat

CARB CHOICES: 2

Raisin-Walnut Sour Cream Cake

I've had a really good time baking with sour cream recently, and every time I stir it into a cake batter, I marvel yet again how manufacturers figured out a way to take out the fat but leave the creamy texture and perfect flavor. Thanks, guys! ☻ Serves 2

2 tablespoons Land O Lakes
    no-fat sour cream
2 teaspoons I Can't Believe
    It's Not Butter! Light
    Margarine
2 tablespoons egg substitute
1 tablespoon Land O Lakes
    Half & Half
2 tablespoons Splenda Granular

¼ teaspoon vanilla extract
6 tablespoons cake flour
¼ teaspoon baking powder
⅛ teaspoon baking soda
¼ teaspoon ground cinnamon
3 tablespoons seedless raisins
2 tablespoons chopped walnuts

Preheat oven to 350 degrees. Spray a 5¾-by-3⅛-by-2⅛-inch petite loaf pan with butter-flavored cooking spray. In a medium bowl, combine sour cream, margarine, egg substitute, and half & half. Stir in Splenda and vanilla extract. Add flour, baking powder, baking soda, cinnamon, raisins, and walnuts. Mix gently just to combine. Evenly spoon batter into prepared pan. Bake for 20 to 24 minutes or until a toothpick inserted in center comes out clean. Place pan on a wire rack and let set for 10 minutes. Remove cake from pan and place on wire rack and allow to cool completely. Cut into 2 servings.

HINT: If you don't have a petite loaf pan, use 2 (12-ounce) oven-proof custard cups instead and place them on a baking sheet before baking. If using, test for doneness at least 10 minutes before suggested baking time.

Each serving equals:

HE: 1 Bread • 1 Fat • ¾ Fruit • ½ Protein • ¼ Slider • 5 Optional Calories

220 Calories • 8 gm Fat • 5 gm Protein • 32 gm Carbohydrate •
232 mg Sodium • 88 mg Calcium • 1 gm Fiber

DIABETIC EXCHANGES: 1 Starch • 1 Fat • 1 Fruit • ½ Meat

CARB CHOICES: 2

Mini Angel Food Loaf Cake

Mini loaf pans are a big help when it comes to portion control, and I've seen it even more clearly while working on this book. It also saves room in the fridge, which many of us need!

◐ Serves 2

> 3 tablespoons cake flour
> ¼ cup Splenda Granular ☆
> 2 egg whites
> ½ teaspoon vanilla extract
> ⅛ teaspoon table salt

Preheat oven to 350 degrees. In a small bowl, combine flour and 2 tablespoons Splenda using a wire whisk. In a medium glass bowl, beat egg whites with an electric mixer on HIGH until foamy. Add vanilla extract and salt. Continue beating until stiff enough to form soft peaks. Add remaining 2 tablespoons Splenda while continuing to beat egg whites until stiff peaks form. Fold in flour mixture using a spatula or wire whisk. Evenly spoon batter into an ungreased 5¾-by-3⅛-by-2⅛-inch metal petite loaf pan. Bake for 14 to 16 minutes or until cake springs back when lightly touched. Do not overbake. Place pan on a wire rack and let set for 5 minutes. Run a table knife around the sides of pan to loosen cake. Remove from pan and continue to cool on wire rack. Cut into 2 servings.

HINTS: 1. Egg whites beat best at room temperature.

2. If you don't have a petite loaf pan, use 2 (12-ounce) ovenproof custard cups instead and place them on a baking sheet before baking. If using, test for doneness at least 5 minutes before suggested baking time.

Each serving equals:

HE: ½ Bread • ⅓ Protein • 12 Optional Calories

64 Calories • 0 gm Fat • 5 gm Protein • 11 gm Carbohydrate • 201 mg Sodium • 4 mg Calcium • 0 gm Fiber

DIABETIC EXCHANGES: 1 Starch

CARB CHOICES: 1

This and That

(A Dynamic Duo)

Breakfast for two, or brunch on your own? Drinks *à deux*, or inviting a friend to watch the Academy Awards? Here's a lively selection of just what you'll need to serve splendidly on any occasion, day or evening, spring or fall, soothingly solitary or perfectly paired.

Anything is possible, even when the crowd is smaller, especially when you treat yourself to the right cooking tools. Those ovenproof custard cups are like a basic black dress—ideal for all kinds of occasions. And oh, my, what you can do with a mini loaf pan that never demands that you sacrifice flavor for size.

Wake up with ease and appetite when you're minutes from enjoying Baked Hash Brown Egg Cups *or a savory* Mushroom Frittata. *Serve with* Eye-Opener Muffins *or* Banana Coffee Cakes with Strawberry Glaze *for a spectacular start to the day! And how refreshing it will be on a summer afternoon to sip a* Piña Colada Frappe *or* Cranberry Spritzers . . . *or when you can serve your special guest your favorite chips with* Salsa Paradise Dip. *I've even stirred up some* Peach "Ice Cream" *to make every day delicious in every way I could!*

Baked Hash Brown Egg Cups

This is one of my favorite new ways to serve breakfast—and it's all because I'm cooking in custard cups! These are so simple to serve, and they look terrific. In fact, these are "worth getting up for!"

◐ Serves 2

½ cup shredded Kraft reduced-fat Cheddar cheese ☆
2¼ cups frozen loose-packed shredded hash brown potatoes
¼ cup finely chopped green onion
2 eggs, or equivalent in egg substitute
1 tablespoon Land O Lakes Fat Free Half & Half
½ teaspoon lemon pepper

Preheat oven to 375 degrees. Spray two (12-ounce) ovenproof custard cups with butter-flavored cooking spray. Reserve 2 tablespoons Cheddar cheese. In a medium bowl, combine potatoes, remaining 6 tablespoons Cheddar cheese, and onion. Press mixture in bottom and up sides of prepared custard cups, leaving an indentation in center. Place custard cups on a baking sheet and bake for 25 minutes. In a small bowl, combine eggs, half & half, and lemon pepper. Evenly spoon egg mixture in center of hash brown crusts. Sprinkle 1 tablespoon reserved Cheddar cheese evenly over top. Continue baking for 8 to 12 minutes or until eggs are set and cooked to desired doneness.

HINT: Mr. Dell's frozen shredded potatoes are a good choice or raw shredded potatoes, rinsed and patted dry, may be used in place of frozen potatoes.

Each serving equals:

HE: 2 Protein • ¾ Bread • ¼ Vegetable • 4 Optional Calories

226 Calories • 10 gm Fat • 17 gm Protein • 17 gm Carbohydrate • 450 mg Sodium • 245 mg Calcium • 2 gm Fiber

DIABETIC EXCHANGES: 2 Meat • 1 Starch

CARB CHOICES: 1

Mushroom Frittata

Downright delicious, this skillet entrée is spectacular for brunch! Instead of preparing several dishes, blend them all together: the potatoes, the eggs, the veggies—yum, yum!   ☻   Serves 2

> ½ cup sliced fresh mushrooms
> 1½ cups frozen loose-packed shredded hash brown potatoes
> ¼ cup chopped green onion
> 3 eggs, beaten
> ¼ cup Land O Lakes Fat Free Half & Half
> ½ teaspoon dried basil
> ⅛ teaspoon black pepper
> ¼ cup shredded Kraft reduced-fat Cheddar cheese

In a medium skillet sprayed with butter-flavored cooking spray, sauté mushrooms, potatoes, and green onion for 5 minutes. In a small bowl, combine eggs, half & half, basil, and black pepper. Mix well using a wire whisk. Pour egg mixture into skillet with mushroom mixture. Cook for 3 minutes or until egg mixture is set, running a spatula around the edge of the skillet and lifting mixture so uncooked portion can run underneath. Sprinkle Cheddar cheese evenly over top. Remove from heat. Evenly divide into 2 servings.

HINT: Mr. Dell's frozen shredded potatoes are a good choice or raw shredded potatoes, rinsed and patted dry, may be used in place of frozen potatoes.

Each serving equals:

HE: 2 Protein • ½ Bread • ½ Vegetable • 18 Optional Calories

210 Calories • 10 gm Fat • 16 gm Protein • 14 gm Carbohydrate • 281 mg Sodium • 183 mg Calcium • 1 gm Fiber

DIABETIC EXCHANGES: 2 Meat • 1 Starch • ½ Vegetable

CARB CHOICES: 1

Dilly Deviled Eggs

Have you eaten more than your share of deviled eggs over the years? Most of us have, so I figured it was time for a new take on this popular classic. A little dill goes a long way, so measure carefully. ◑ Serves 2 (2 halves each)

> 2 hard-boiled eggs, rinsed and cooled
> 2 tablespoons Kraft fat-free mayonnaise
> 1 teaspoon Land O Lakes no-fat sour cream
> ¼ teaspoon dried dill weed
> ½ teaspoon dried onion flakes
> ⅛ teaspoon black pepper

Cut eggs in half lengthwise and remove yolks. Place yolks in a small bowl and mash well using a fork. Add mayonnaise and sour cream. Mix gently to combine. Stir in dill, onion flakes, and black pepper. Evenly spoon yolk mixture into center of white halves. Cover and refrigerate for at least 15 minutes.

Each serving equals:

HE: 1 Protein • 12 Optional Calories

90 Calories • 6 gm Fat • 6 gm Protein • 3 gm Carbohydrate • 185 mg Sodium • 33 mg Calcium • 0 gm Fiber

DIABETIC EXCHANGES: 1 Meat

CARB CHOICES: 0

Refrigerator Relish

I'm a fan of relish from a jar, which is where I got mine for most of my life. But when I first stirred up fresh relish at home, I was astounded at how good it was! This one asks only that you let the flavors tango together in your refrigerator before you spoon it onto burgers or other dishes. ☯ Serves 2 (½ cup)

1 teaspoon vegetable oil
1½ teaspoons white distilled vinegar
1 tablespoon Splenda Granular
⅛ teaspoon dried dill weed
⅛ teaspoon table salt
⅛ teaspoon black pepper
½ cup shredded cabbage
¼ cup shredded unpeeled cucumber
1 tablespoon chopped onion
1 tablespoon chopped red bell pepper

In a medium bowl, combine vegetable oil, vinegar, and Splenda. Stir in dill weed, salt, and black pepper. Add cabbage, cucumber, onion, and red pepper. Mix well to combine. Cover and refrigerate for at least 24 hours. Mix well before using. Will keep for 1 week.

Each serving equals:

HE: ½ Fat • ½ Vegetable • 3 Optional Calories

30 Calories • 2 gm Fat • 0 gm Protein • 3 gm Carbohydrate • 150 mg Sodium • 15 mg Calcium • 1 gm Fiber

DIABETIC EXCHANGES: ½ Fat • ½ Vegetable

CARB CHOICES: 0

"Homemade" Spaghetti Sauce

Why bother making sauce when there are so many good ones that come in a jar or can? Good question, and here's my response: Sauce made with fresh tomatoes tastes fantastic, and it's not all that much extra work for you. Also, you can make it from food on hand some night when you want pasta and don't have a jar on your shelf.

⭘ Serves 2 (½ cup)

> ½ cup finely chopped fresh mushrooms
> ¼ cup finely chopped onion
> 1 (8-ounce) can Hunt's Tomato Sauce
> 1 cup peeled and chopped fresh tomatoes
> ¼ cup water
> 1 tablespoon Splenda Granular
> ¾ teaspoon Italian seasoning
> 1 teaspoon olive oil

In a medium saucepan sprayed with olive oil–flavored cooking spray, sauté mushrooms and onion for 5 minutes. Stir in tomato sauce, tomatoes, and water. Add Splenda, Italian seasoning, and olive oil. Mix well to combine. Lower heat and simmer for 15 minutes, stirring occasionally.

Each serving equals:

HE: 3½ Vegetable • ½ Fat • 3 Optional Calories

103 Calories • 3 gm Fat • 3 gm Protein • 16 gm Carbohydrate • 647 mg Sodium • 30 mg Calcium • 3 gm Fiber

DIABETIC EXCHANGES: 3 Vegetable • ½ Fat

CARB CHOICES: 1

Salsa Paradise Dip

Just as the beat inspires us to dance a salsa rhythm, this dip will enliven any dinner for two! Make it hot or not, I always say—then eat to your heart's content.   ○   Serves 2 (½ cup)

>   ½ cup chunky salsa (mild, medium, or hot)
>   1 tablespoon Splenda Granular
>   ½ teaspoon dried parsley flakes
>   ¼ cup Land O Lakes no-fat sour cream

In a small bowl, combine salsa, Splenda, and parsley flakes. Add sour cream. Mix gently just to combine. Cover and refrigerate for a least 30 minutes.

HINT: Great with vegetables and crackers. Also wonderful spooned over a hot baked potato.

Each serving equals:

HE: ½ Vegetable • ¼ Slider • 13 Optional Calories

44 Calories • 0 gm Fat • 1 gm Protein • 10 gm Carbohydrate • 500 mg Sodium • 40 mg Calcium • 0 gm Fiber

DIABETIC EXCHANGES: ½ Vegetable • ½ Other Carbohydrate

CARB CHOICES: ½

Quick Cocktail Sauce

Here's a great recipe to have on hand, just in case you need cocktail sauce in a hurry and don't want to race to the store! It's so good, you may not bother with the store-bought kind ever again.

🌀 Serves 2 (2 tablespoons)

¼ cup reduced-sodium ketchup
2 teaspoons prepared horseradish sauce
2 teaspoons lemon juice
½ teaspoon dried onion flakes

In a small bowl, combine ketchup, horseradish sauce, lemon juice, and onion flakes. Cover and refrigerate for at least 10 minutes.

Each serving equals:

HE: ¼ Slider • 12 Optional Calories

32 Calories • 0 gm Fat • 0 gm Protein • 8 gm Carbohydrate • 56 mg Sodium • 6 mg Calcium • 0 gm Fiber

DIABETIC EXCHANGES: ½ Other Carbohydrate

CARB CHOICES: ½

Munchy Trail Mix

Sure, you can buy all kinds of snack mixes, but they bring with them lots of extra fat or sugar—and nobody needs that! This version is crunchy and fresh, with lots of lively flavors, so take a bag on your car trip or hike in the woods.

Serves 2 (¾ cup)

6 tablespoons Wheat Chex
½ cup Corn Chex
¼ cup dried mixed fruit
2 tablespoons coarsely chopped walnuts
2 tablespoons Splenda Granular
⅛ teaspoon ground cinnamon

In a medium bowl, combine Wheat Chex, Corn Chex, mixed fruit, and walnuts. Add Splenda and cinnamon. Mix well to combine. Store each serving in a resealable sandwich bag.

Each serving equals:

HE: 1 Bread • 1 Fruit • ½ Fat • ¼ Protein • 3 Optional Calories

157 Calories • 5 gm Fat • 2 gm Protein • 26 gm Carbohydrate • 152 mg Sodium • 55 mg Calcium • 3 gm Fiber

DIABETIC EXCHANGES: 1 Starch • 1 Fruit • 1 Fat

CARB CHOICES: 1½

Peach "Ice Cream"

So you forgot to put the ice-cream maker container in your tiny freezer, but you're still longing for a dish of ice cream tonight. Here's a c-o-o-l way to enjoy what you love without doing so much work!   ◐   Serves 2 (¾ cup)

> 2 tablespoons Land O Lakes Fat Free Half & Half
> ¼ cup cold Diet Mountain Dew
> ⅓ cup Carnation Nonfat Dry Milk Powder
> ¼ cup Splenda Granular
> 1½ cups frozen peach slices, slightly thawed

In a blender container, combine half & half and Diet Mountain Dew. Cover and process on BLEND for 10 seconds. Add dry milk powder and Splenda. Re-cover and process on BLEND for 10 seconds. Add peach slices. Re-cover and process on CHOP for 30 seconds or until mixture is smooth. Evenly spoon into 2 dessert dishes. Serve at once.

Each serving equals:

HE: 1 Fruit • ½ Fat Free Milk • ¼ Slider • 1 Optional Calorie

108 Calories • 0 gm Fat • 5 gm Protein • 22 gm Carbohydrate • 87 mg Sodium • 172 mg Calcium • 2 gm Fiber

DIABETIC EXCHANGES: 1 Fruit • ½ Fat Free Milk

CARB CHOICES: 2

Spiced Banana Shake

Make your blender earn its place on your crowded kitchen counter by making recipes that let it shine! This one is wildly satisfying and sure to add a "shot" of pleasure to a busy day.

☻ Serves 2 (1 full cup)

> 1 cup fat-free milk
> 1 cup (1 medium) sliced banana
> ½ cup Wells' Blue Bunny sugar- and fat-free vanilla ice
>   cream or any sugar- and fat-free ice cream
> ⅛ teaspoon ground cinnamon

In a blender container, combine milk and banana. Cover and process on BLEND for 15 seconds. Add ice cream and cinnamon. Re-cover and process on BLEND for 30 seconds or until mixture is smooth. Serve at once.

Each serving equals:

HE: 1 Fruit • ½ Fat Free Milk • ½ Slider

152 Calories • 0 gm Fat • 6 gm Protein • 32 gm Carbohydrate • 77 mg Sodium • 218 mg Calcium • 2 gm Fiber

DIABETIC EXCHANGES: 1 Fruit • ½ Fat Free Milk • ½ Other Carbohydrate

CARB CHOICES: 2

Chocolate-Banana Fizz

What a great day it is—you're getting good-for-you fruit in your diet, and you're also getting a treat that will reward you for all you've done today. And—it's got zero fat in it!

◐ Serves 2 (1 cup)

> 1 cup club soda
> 1 cup (1 medium) sliced ripe banana
> ¾ cup Wells' Blue Bunny sugar- and fat-free vanilla ice
>   cream or any sugar- and fat-free ice cream
> 1 tablespoon Hershey's Sugar-Free Chocolate Syrup
> 2 tablespoons Splenda Granular

In a blender container, combine club soda, banana, chocolate syrup, and Splenda. Cover and process on BLEND for 30 to 45 seconds or until mixture is smooth. Pour into 2 glasses. Serve at once.

Each serving equals:

HE: 1 Fruit • ¾ Slider • 16 Optional Calories

156 Calories • 0 gm Fat • 4 gm Protein • 35 gm Carbohydrate • 72 mg Sodium • 100 mg Calcium • 2 gm Fiber

DIABETIC EXCHANGES: 1 Fruit • 1 Other Carbohydrate

CARB CHOICES: 2

Piña Colada Frappe

A frappe is a northeastern version of a milkshake with juicy fruit mixed in, and this is a delightful combo with the flavor of a popular tropical cocktail. Lucky you—and it's good for you, too!

◐ Serves 2 (1 cup)

> ¼ cup Land O Lakes Fat Free Half & Half
> 1 (8-ounce) can crushed pineapple, packed in fruit juice, undrained
> 2 tablespoons Splenda Granular
> ½ teaspoon coconut extract
> ½ teaspoon rum extract
> ¾ cup Dannon plain fat-free yogurt
> 2 teaspoons flaked coconut
> 4 ice cubes

In a blender container, combine half & half, undrained pineapple, Splenda, coconut extract, and rum extract. Cover and process on BLEND for 15 seconds. Add yogurt, coconut, and ice cubes. Re-cover and process on BLEND for 30 seconds or until mixture is smooth. Serve at once.

Each serving equals:

HE: 1 Fruit • ½ Fat Free Milk • ¼ Slider • 11 Optional Calories

148 Calories • 0 gm Fat • 7 gm Protein • 30 gm Carbohydrate • 119 mg Sodium • 228 mg Calcium • 1 gm Fiber

DIABETIC EXCHANGES: 1 Fruit • ½ Fat Free Milk

CARB CHOICES: 2

Cranberry Spritzers

Here's a glamorous but easy way to serve a gorgeously colorful drink that has zero alcohol in it. It's pretty, it's practically calorie-free, and you can enjoy whenever you like!

◐ Serves 2 (1 cup)

> 1 cup cold Ocean Spray reduced-calorie cranberry juice
>   cocktail
> ¾ cup cold diet white grape soda pop
> ¼ cup cold club soda
> Ice

In a small pitcher, combine cranberry juice cocktail and diet white grape soda pop. Add club soda. Mix well to combine. Pour into tall glasses filled with ice. Serve at once.

Each serving equals:

HE: ½ Fruit

20 Calories • 0 gm Fat • 0 gm Protein • 5 gm Carbohydrate • 23 mg Sodium • 12 mg Calcium • 0 gm Fiber

DIABETIC EXCHANGES: Free Food

CARB CHOICES: 0

Cranberry Orange Cooler

We eat with our eyes as well as our taste buds, and this chilled beverage is one of the most colorful around! Sometimes, when you think you're hungry, you're really thirsty, and a drink like this one could fill the bill perfectly.   ☕   Serves 2 (1 full cup)

> 1 cup cold Ocean Spray reduced-calorie cranberry juice
>   cocktail
> 1 (11-ounce) can mandarin oranges, rinsed and drained
> ½ cup cold Diet Mountain Dew
> Ice

In a blender container, combine cranberry juice cocktail and mandarin oranges. Cover and process on BLEND for 15 seconds. Add Diet Mountain Dew. Re-cover and process on BLEND for 30 seconds or until mixture is smooth. Pour into tall glasses filled with ice. Serve at once.

Each serving equals:

HE: 1 Fruit

40 Calories • 0 gm Fat • 0 gm Protein • 10 gm Carbohydrate • 5 mg Sodium • 14 mg Calcium • 0 gm Fiber

DIABETIC EXCHANGES: 1 Fruit

CARB CHOICES: ½

Sunrise Muffins

These muffins make any morning extra-special, and they're so quick you can fix them on a workday if you plan ahead just a bit. Chop the nuts the night before, make sure you know where the dry milk powder is, and so on. ☻ Serves 2

⅓ cup Carnation Nonfat Dry Milk Powder
¼ cup unsweetened orange juice
2 teaspoons I Can't Believe It's Not Butter! Light Margarine
2 tablespoons egg substitute
2 tablespoons Splenda Granular
6 tablespoons Bisquick Heart Smart Baking Mix
2 tablespoons seedless raisins
1 tablespoon chopped walnuts

Preheat oven to 375 degrees. Spray 2 muffin wells with butter-flavored cooking spray or line with paper liners. In a medium bowl, combine dry milk powder and orange juice. Stir in margarine, egg substitute, and Splenda using a wire whisk. Add baking mix. Mix gently just to combine using a sturdy spoon. Fold in raisins and walnuts. Evenly spoon batter into prepared muffin wells. Bake for 16 to 20 minutes or until a toothpick inserted in center comes out clean. Place muffin pan on a wire rack and let set for 5 minutes. Remove muffins from pan and continue cooling on wire rack.

HINT: Fill unused muffin wells with water. It protects the muffin tin and ensures even baking.

Each serving equals:

HE: 1 Bread • 1 Fat • ¾ Fruit • ½ Fat Free Milk • ¼ Protein • ¼ Slider • 10 Optional Calories

222 Calories • 6 gm Fat • 8 gm Protein • 34 gm Carbohydrate • 398 mg Sodium • 192 mg Calcium • 1 gm Fiber

DIABETIC EXCHANGES: 1 Starch • 1 Fat • 1 Fruit • ½ Fat Free Milk

CARB CHOICES: 2

Eye-Opener Muffins

Need a good reason for climbing out of bed in the morning, especially on the weekend? You're not alone! These are fruity-good, bright, and sunny-tasting. ☻ Serves 2

2 teaspoons I Can't Believe It's Not Butter! Light Margarine
2 tablespoons egg substitute
1 tablespoon Splenda Granular
2 tablespoons Diet Mountain Dew
6 tablespoons Bisquick Heart Smart Baking Mix
1½ tablespoons orange marmalade spreadable fruit
1 tablespoon chopped pecans

Preheat oven to 375 degrees. Spray 2 muffin wells with butter-flavored cooking spray or line with paper liners. In a medium bowl, combine margarine, egg substitute, and Splenda. Stir in Diet Mountain Dew. Add baking mix, orange marmalade, and pecans. Mix gently just to combine. Evenly spoon batter into prepared muffin wells. Bake for 16 to 20 minutes or until a toothpick inserted in center comes out clean. Place muffin pan on a wire rack and let set for 5 minutes. Remove muffins from pan and continue cooling on wire rack.

HINT: Fill unused muffin wells with water. It protects the muffin tin and ensures even baking.

Each serving equals:

HE: 1 Bread • 1 Fat • ½ Fruit • ¼ Protein • 3 Optional Calories

170 Calories • 6 gm Fat • 4 gm Protein • 25 gm Carbohydrate •
336 mg Sodium • 35 mg Calcium • 1 gm Fiber

DIABETIC EXCHANGES: 1 Starch • 1 Fat • ½ Fruit • ½ Meat

CARB CHOICES: 1½

Majestic Muffins

Remember the lyrics of "America the Beautiful" that recall the "purple mountain majesties above the fruited plain"? These were so gloriously scrumptious that they inspired me to sing a few bars!

○ Serves 2

> 2 tablespoons Splenda Granular
> 2 teaspoons vegetable oil
> 1 egg, or equivalent in egg substitute
> 1 tablespoon Land O Lakes Fat Free Half & Half
> 6 tablespoons Bisquick Heart Smart Baking Mix
> ½ teaspoon baking powder

Preheat oven to 375 degrees. Spray 2 muffin wells with butter-flavored cooking spray or line with paper liners. In a small bowl, combine Splenda, vegetable oil, egg, and half & half. Add baking mix and baking powder. Mix gently just to combine. Evenly spoon batter into prepared muffin wells. Bake for 14 to 18 minutes or until a toothpick inserted in center comes out clean. Place muffin pan on a wire rack and let set for 5 minutes. Remove muffins from pan and continue cooling on wire rack.

HINT: Fill unused muffin wells with water. It protects the muffin tin and ensures even baking.

Each serving equals:

HE: 1 Bread • 1 Fat • ½ Protein • 10 Optional Calories

164 Calories • 8 gm Fat • 5 gm Protein • 18 gm Carbohydrate • 407 mg Sodium • 103 mg Calcium • 1 gm Fiber

DIABETIC EXCHANGES: 1 Starch • 1 Fat • ½ Meat

CARB CHOICES: 1

Savory Dill Cheese Muffins

Love and marriage, Scotch and soda, and dill and cheese—three duos that go together really well! I would serve these with a bowl of hearty soup for a satisfying supper, or take one to work for an afternoon snack. ☻ Serves 2

6 tablespoons Bisquick Heart Smart Baking Mix
¼ teaspoon baking powder
1 tablespoon Splenda Granular
¾ teaspoon dried dill weed
2 tablespoons shredded Kraft reduced-fat Cheddar cheese
2 tablespoons shredded Kraft reduced-fat mozzarella cheese
2 tablespoons Land O Lakes Fat Free Half & Half
1 tablespoon Land O Lakes no-fat sour cream
1 tablespoon I Can't Believe It's Not Butter! Light Margarine
2 tablespoons egg substitute
¾ teaspoon prepared yellow mustard

Preheat oven to 375 degrees. Spray 2 wells of a muffin pan with butter-flavored cooking spray or line with paper liners. In a medium bowl, combine baking mix, baking powder, Splenda, and dill weed. Stir in Cheddar and mozzarella cheeses. In a small bowl, combine half & half, sour cream, margarine, egg substitute, and mustard. Add liquid mixture to dry mixture. Mix gently just to combine using a sturdy spoon. Evenly spoon batter into prepared muffin wells. Bake for 16 to 20 minutes or until a toothpick inserted in center comes out clean. Place muffin pan on a wire rack and let set for 5 minutes. Remove muffins from pan and continue cooling on wire rack.

HINT: Fill unused muffin wells with water. It protects the muffin tin and ensures even baking.

Each serving equals:

HE: 1 Bread • ¾ Protein • ¾ Fat • 19 Optional Calories

179 Calories • 7 gm Fat • 9 gm Protein • 20 gm Carbohydrate •
581 mg Sodium • 196 mg Calcium • 1 gm Fiber

DIABETIC EXCHANGES: 1 Starch • 1 Meat • 1 Fat

CARB CHOICES: 1

Cranberry Chocolate Chip Muffins

Are you surprised that the recipe calls for the same amounts of cranberries and Splenda? (Well, have you ever tasted an unsweetened cranberry?!) These are tart and sweet and pretty as a picture, ideal for a mother-daughter brunch dessert. ☻ Serves 2

> 2 tablespoons chopped fresh cranberries
> 7 tablespoons all-purpose flour ☆
> 2 tablespoons Splenda Granular ☆
> 1 tablespoon I Can't Believe It's Not Butter! Light Margarine
> 2 tablespoons Land O Lakes Fat Free Half & Half
> 1 tablespoon egg substitute
> ⅛ teaspoon baking soda
> 1 tablespoon mini chocolate chips

Preheat oven to 375 degrees. Spray 2 muffin wells with butter-flavored cooking spray or line with paper liners. In a small bowl, combine cranberries, 1 tablespoon flour, and 1 tablespoon Splenda. Set aside. In a medium bowl, combine margarine, half & half, and egg substitute using a wire whisk. In a small bowl, combine remaining 6 tablespoons flour, remaining 1 tablespoon Splenda, and baking soda. Add flour mixture to margarine mixture. Mix gently just to combine using a sturdy spoon. Stir in cranberry mixture and chocolate chips. Evenly spoon batter into prepared muffin wells. Bake for 20 to 24 minutes or until a toothpick inserted in center comes out clean. Place muffin pan on a wire rack and let set for 5 minutes. Remove muffins from pan and continue cooling on wire rack.

HINT: Fill unused muffin wells with water. It protects the muffin tin and ensures even baking.

Each serving equals:

HE: 1 Bread • ¾ Fat • ½ Slider • 1 Optional Calorie

173 Calories • 5 gm Fat • 4 gm Protein • 28 gm Carbohydrate • 183 mg Sodium • 26 mg Calcium • 1 gm Fiber

DIABETIC EXCHANGES: 2 Starch/Carbohydrate • 1 Fat

CARB CHOICES: 2

Sweet Cornmeal Muffins

Some people like their cornbread savory, even with veggies like corn and peppers mixed in. Others, like me on the day I created this recipe, enjoy celebrating the natural sweetness of this grain. With a dab of spreadable fruit, these are just right to satisfy the urge for "a little something." ☻ Serves 2

> 3 tablespoons fat-free milk
> 1 egg, or equivalent in egg substitute
> 2 teaspoons vegetable oil
> 2 tablespoons Splenda Granular
> 2 tablespoons yellow cornmeal
> 3 tablespoons Bisquick Heart Smart Baking Mix
> ½ teaspoon baking powder

Preheat oven to 375 degrees. Spray 2 muffin wells with butter-flavored cooking spray or line with paper liners. In a medium bowl, combine milk, egg, vegetable oil, and Splenda. Add cornmeal, baking mix, and baking powder. Mix gently just to combine. Evenly spoon batter into prepared muffin wells. Bake for 14 to 18 minutes or until a toothpick inserted in center comes out clean. Place muffin pan on a wire rack and let set for 5 minutes. Remove muffins from pan and continue cooling on wire rack.

HINT: Fill unused muffin wells with water. It protects the muffin tin and ensures even baking.

Each serving equals:

HE: 1 Bread • 1 Fat • ½ Protein • 14 Optional Calories

160 Calories • 8 gm Fat • 5 gm Protein • 17 gm Carbohydrate • 275 mg Sodium • 113 mg Calcium • 1 gm Fiber

DIABETIC EXCHANGES: 1 Starch • 1 Fat • ½ Meat

CARB CHOICES: 1

Cornbread for Two

Want your cornbread to be really moist and marvelous? The mayonnaise is the secret ingredient here, and it works! (The milk helps, too.) What a great go-with this would make with chili or stew.

○ Serves 2

> ¼ cup yellow cornmeal
> 3 tablespoons all-purpose flour
> 1 tablespoon Splenda Granular
> 1 teaspoon baking powder
> ¼ teaspoon table salt
> ¼ cup fat-free milk
> 2 tablespoons Kraft fat-free mayonnaise

Preheat oven to 400 degrees. Spray two (12-ounce) ovenproof custard cups with butter-flavored cooking spray. In a small bowl, combine cornmeal, flour, Splenda, baking powder, and salt. Add milk and mayonnaise. Mix gently just to combine. Evenly spoon batter into prepared custard cups. Place cups on a baking sheet and bake for 13 minutes or until a toothpick inserted in center comes out clean. Place cups on a wire rack and let set for at least 5 minutes.

Each serving equals:

HE: 1½ Bread • ¼ Slider • 4 Optional Calories

120 Calories • 0 gm Fat • 4 gm Protein • 26 gm Carbohydrate • 478 mg Sodium • 162 mg Calcium • 2 gm Fiber

DIABETIC EXCHANGES: 1½ Starch

CARB CHOICES: 1½

Banana Coffee Cakes with Strawberry Glaze

These are as pretty as they are yummy—and a fun choice for entertaining a special friend! I've always loved creating banana-flavored desserts, and I think strawberry makes a dynamic dance partner!

◐ Serves 2

6 tablespoons Bisquick Heart Smart Baking Mix
3 tablespoons Splenda Granular
¼ teaspoon ground cinnamon
2 tablespoons chopped walnuts
⅓ cup (1 medium) mashed ripe banana
2 tablespoons Land O Lakes no-fat sour cream

1 tablespoon Land O Lakes Fat Free Half & Half
2 tablespoons egg substitute
1½ tablespoons strawberry spreadable fruit
¼ teaspoon coconut extract
2 teaspoons flaked coconut

Preheat oven to 375 degrees. Spray 2 (12-ounce) ovenproof custard cups with butter-flavored cooking spray. In a medium bowl, combine baking mix, Splenda, cinnamon, and walnuts. In a small bowl, combine mashed banana, sour cream, half & half, and egg substitute. Add liquid mixture to dry mixture. Mix gently just to combine. Evenly spoon batter into prepared custard cups. In another small bowl, combine spreadable fruit and coconut extract. Microwave on HIGH (100% power) for 20 seconds. Drizzle hot fruit spread evenly over top of each coffee cake. Evenly sprinkle 1 teaspoon coconut over top of each. Place filled custard cups on a baking sheet. Bake for 30 to 34 minutes or until a toothpick inserted in center comes out clean. Place custard cups on a wire rack and let set for at least 15 minutes.

Each serving equals:

HE: 1½ Fruit • 1 Bread • ½ Fat • ¼ Protein • ½ Slider • 2 Optional Calories

256 Calories • 8 gm Fat • 6 gm Protein • 40 gm Carbohydrate • 333 mg Sodium • 70 mg Calcium • 2 gm Fiber

DIABETIC EXCHANGES: 1½ Fruit • 1 Starch • 1 Fat

CARB CHOICES: 2½

Applesauce Quick Bread

Now that you've got your petite loaf pan, you're ready to bake the perfect size bread in about half the time it takes to bake the big one! The fruity-moist texture is as delectable as ever, and the aroma will attract the laziest slug-a-bed. ● Serves 2

6 tablespoons all-purpose
    flour
2 tablespoons Splenda
    Granular
¼ teaspoon baking powder
⅛ teaspoon baking soda

¼ teaspoon apple pie spice
¼ cup unsweetened applesauce
2 tablespoons egg substitute
2 teaspoons vegetable oil
1 tablespoon chopped walnuts

Preheat oven to 350 degrees. Spray a 5¾-by-3⅛-by-2⅛-inch petite loaf pan with butter-flavored cooking spray. In a medium bowl, combine flour, Splenda, baking powder, baking soda, and apple pie spice. Add applesauce, egg substitute, and vegetable oil. Mix gently just to combine. Fold in walnuts. Evenly spread batter into prepared loaf pan. Bake for 25 to 30 minutes or until a toothpick inserted in center comes out clean. Place loaf pan on a wire rack and let set for 5 minutes. Remove bread from pan and continue cooling on wire rack. Cut into 2 servings.

HINT: If you don't have a petite loaf pan, divide batter between 2 (12-ounce) ovenproof custard cups sprayed with butter-flavored cooking spray and place them on a baking sheet before baking. If using, test for doneness at least 10 minutes before suggested baking time.

Each serving equals:

HE: 1 Bread • 1 Fat • ¼ Protein • ¼ Fruit • ¼ Slider • 10 Optional Calories

184 Calories • 8 gm Fat • 5 gm Protein • 23 gm Carbohydrate • 157 mg Sodium • 49 mg Calcium • 1 gm Fiber

DIABETIC EXCHANGES: 1½ Starch • 1½ Fat

CARB CHOICES: 1½

Oatmeal Chocolate Chippers

For those cookie lovers who can't quite decide which they prefer, oatmeal cookies or chocolate chip, here's my culinary compromise: a cookie that combines the best of both! Does it seem silly to make just four cookies? I don't think so, especially when you're working on making healthier choices. ☺ Serves 2 (2 each)

1 tablespoon + 1 teaspoon I Can't Believe It's Not Butter!
    Light Margarine
¼ cup Splenda Granular
1 egg, or equivalent in egg substitute
½ teaspoon vanilla extract
3 tablespoons Bisquick Heart Smart Baking Mix
¼ cup quick oats
¼ teaspoon ground cinnamon
¼ teaspoon baking powder
1 tablespoon mini chocolate chips

Preheat oven to 375 degrees. Spray a baking sheet with butter-flavored cooking spray. In a large bowl, combine margarine, Splenda, and egg using a wire whisk. Stir in vanilla extract. In a small bowl, combine baking mix, quick oats, cinnamon, and baking powder. Add flour mixture to margarine mixture using a sturdy spoon. Fold in chocolate chips. Drop batter by rounded teaspoon onto prepared baking sheet to form 4 cookies. Lightly flatten cookies with the bottom of a glass sprayed with butter-flavored cooking spray. Bake for 14 to 16 minutes. Do not overbake. Place baking sheet on a wire rack and let set for 5 minutes. Remove cookies from pan and continue cooling on wire rack.

Each serving equals:

HE: 1 Bread • 1 Fat • ½ Protein • ¼ Slider • 18 Optional Calories

171 Calories • 7 gm Fat • 6 gm Protein • 21 gm Carbohydrate •
327 mg Sodium • 64 mg Calcium • 1 gm Fiber

DIABETIC EXCHANGES: 1 Starch/Carbohydrate • 1 Fat • ½ Meat

CARB CHOICES: 1

Peanut Butter Pleasure Cookies

You *could* stand at the kitchen sink and lick a tablespoon of peanut butter straight from the jar, but why not treat yourself to a home-baked delight served on a plate instead? You deserve to sit and relax with a cup of coffee and two great cookies, even if you're not in the habit of doing so.   ◑   Serves 2 (2 each)

> 2 tablespoons Peter Pan or Skippy reduced-fat creamy
>   peanut butter
> 1 tablespoon Land O Lakes no-fat sour cream
> 3 tablespoons Splenda Granular
> 3 tablespoons egg substitute
> ½ teaspoon vanilla extract
> 6 tablespoons Bisquick Heart Smart Baking Mix

Preheat oven to 375 degrees. Spray a baking sheet with butter-flavored cooking spray. In a small bowl, combine peanut butter, sour cream, and Splenda using a wire whisk. Stir in egg substitute and vanilla extract. Add baking mix to peanut butter mixture. Mix gently just to combine using a sturdy spoon. Drop batter by rounded teaspoonful onto prepared baking sheet to form 4 cookies. Flatten cookies with a fork dipped in water. Bake for 7 to 9 minutes. Do not overbake. Place baking sheet on a wire rack and let set for 5 minutes. Remove cookies from baking sheet and continue cooling on wire rack.

Each serving equals:

HE: 1¾ Protein • 1 Bread • 1 Fat • 16 Optional Calories

212 Calories • 8 gm Fat • 8 gm Protein • 27 gm Carbohydrate •
408 mg Sodium • 45 mg Calcium • 1 gm Fiber

DIABETIC EXCHANGES: 1½ Starch/Carbohydrate • 1 Meat • ½ Fat

CARB CHOICES: 2

Menus for Dining Delightfully When the Table's Set for Two

You don't need a crowd to make a meal an occasion, just a willingness to plan a menu and prepare a tasty meal. Here are some ideas for you to try in the upcoming months, as you develop a repertoire of dishes designed *à deux*.

"You and Me Always" Cozy Fireside Evening

(with Your Best Friend)

Golden Broccoli Bisque
Parmesan Noodles
Tomato-Basil Meat Loaf
Hot Chocolate Peanut Butter Sundaes

"Kiss the Cook" Romantic Rendezvous

Special Spinach Salad
Grande Vegetable Pilaf
Pacific Rim Pepper Steak
Almond Cheesecake with Sour Cream Topping

"Oh-So-Chic" Ladies' Spring Luncheon

Creamy Dilled Cucumbers
Easy Chicken Alfredo
Fresh Peach Crisp
Piña Colada Frappe

"Splashdown" Poolside Picnic

Dilly Deviled Eggs
Hawaii Chicken Pasta Salad
Chicken BLT Sandwich
Snickerdoodle Mini Cakes

"Leaf-Peeping" Autumn Brunch

Spiced Baked Apple Slices
Eye-Opener Muffins
Mushroom Frittata
Velvety Chocolate-Walnut Pudding

"Shop Til We Drop" Super Sale Supper

Tex-Mex Tomato Corn Sauté
Taco Stuffed Peppers
Cliff's Chocolate Mocha Sour Cream Cake
Cranberry Spritzers

Making Healthy Exchanges Work for You

You're ready now to begin a wonderful journey to better health. In the preceding pages, you've discovered the remarkable variety of good food available to you when you begin eating the Healthy Exchanges way. You've stocked your pantry and learned many of my food preparation "secrets" that will point you on the way to delicious success.

But before I let you go, I'd like to share a few tips that I've learned while traveling toward healthier eating habits. It took me a long time to learn how to eat *smarter*. In fact, I'm still working on it. But I am getting better. For years, I could *inhale* a five-course meal in five minutes flat—and still make room for a second helping of dessert!

Now I follow certain signposts on the road that help me stay on the right path. I hope these ideas will help point you in the right direction as well.

1. **Eat slowly** so your brain has time to catch up with your tummy. Cut and chew each bite slowly. Try putting your fork down between bites. Stop eating as soon as you feel full. Crumple your napkin and throw it on top of your plate so you don't continue to eat when you are no longer hungry.

2. **Smaller plates** may help you feel more satisfied by your food portions *and* limit the amount you can put on the plate.

3. **Watch portion size.** If you are *truly* hungry, you can always add more food to your plate once you've finished

your initial serving. But remember to count the additional food accordingly.

4. **Always eat at your dining-room or kitchen table.** You deserve better than nibbling from an open refrigerator or over the sink. Make an attractive place setting, even if you're eating alone. Feed your eyes as well as your stomach. By always eating at a table, you will become much more aware of your true food intake. For some reason, many of us conveniently "forget" the food we swallow while standing over the stove or munching in the car or on the run.

5. **Avoid doing anything else while you are eating.** If you read the paper or watch television while you eat, it's easy to consume too much food without realizing it, because you are concentrating on something else besides what you're eating. Then, when you look down at your plate and see that it's empty, you wonder where all the food went and why you still feel hungry.

Day by day, as you travel the path to good health, it will become easier to make the right choices, to eat *smarter*. But don't ever fool yourself into thinking that you'll be able to put your eating habits on cruise control and forget about them. Making a commitment to eat good, healthy food and sticking to it takes some effort. But with all the good-tasting recipes in this Healthy Exchanges cookbook, just think how well you're going to eat—and enjoy it— from now on!

Healthy Lean Bon Appétit!

Index

I want to hear from you . . .

Besides my family, the love of my life is creating "common folk" healthy recipes and solving everyday cooking questions in *The Healthy Exchanges Way*. Everyone who uses my recipes is considered part of the Healthy Exchanges Family, so please write to me if you have any questions, comments, or suggestions. I will do my best to answer. With your support, I'll continue to stir up even more recipes and cooking tips for the Family in the years to come.

Write to: JoAnna M. Lund
             c/o Healthy Exchanges, Inc.
             P.O. Box 80
             DeWitt, IA 52742-0080

If you prefer, you can fax me at 1-563-659-2126 or contact me via e-mail by writing to HealthyJo@aol.com. Or visit my Healthy Exchanges Internet web site at: http://www.healthyexchanges.com.

Now That You've Seen *Cooking for Two,* Why Not Order *The Healthy Exchanges Food Newsletter?*

If you enjoyed the recipes in this cookbook and would like to cook up even more of my "common folk" healthy dishes, you may want to subscribe to *The Healthy Exchanges Food Newsletter.*

This monthly 12-page newsletter contains 30-plus new recipes *every month* in such columns as:

- Reader Exchange
- Reader Requests
- Recipe Makeover
- Micro Corner
- Dinner for Two
- Crock Pot Luck
- Meatless Main Dishes
- Rise & Shine
- Our Small World
- Brown Bagging It
- Snack Attack
- Side Dishes
- Main Dishes
- Desserts

In addition to all the recipes, other regular features include:

- The Editor's Motivational Corner
- Dining Out Question & Answer
- Cooking Question & Answer
- New Product Alert
- Success Profiles of Winners in the Losing Game
- Exercise Advice from a Cardiac Rehab Specialist
- Nutrition Advice from a Registered Dietitian
- Positive Thought for the Month

The cost for a one-year (12-issue) subscription is $25. To order, call our toll-free number and pay with any major credit card—or send a check to the address on page 305 of this book.

1-800-766-8961 for Customer Orders
1-563-659-8234 for Customer Service

Thank you for your order, and for choosing to become a part of the Healthy Exchanges Family!